AS I WAS SAYING

AS I WAS SAYING

by Lynn Ashby

85035

TexasMonthlyPress

Texas Monthly Press, Inc.
P.O. Box 1569
Austin, Texas 78767

A B C D E F G H

Library of Congress Cataloging in Publication Data

Ashby, Lynn, 1938-
    As I was saying—.

    I. Title.
PN4874.A58A25   1984   814'.54   84-8436
ISBN 0-932012-29-9

To my wife

Contents

The State of the Family

THE DEN—"All right, little family," I say. "Quiet, please. And hold your applause until I'm finished."

"What's this all about, anyway?" says one of the underlings. "I got important engagements. *The Rockford Files* starts in a minute."

"Quiet, because I am now about to deliver the State of the Family address."

"The what?"

"Surely you jest."

"Daddy, I'm going to do homework."

"I've got to shampoo the dog."

"The driveway needs paving."

"Hold it!" I shout. "Everyone sit down. Look, we've had the State of the Nation and the State of the State as warm-ups. But now we get down to the important stuff. The State of the Family. I'll dispense with the doorkeeper's announcement and the standing ovations and get right to the address."

"Whoopee!"

"First, we must have a new deal, a great society, a new frontier, and an alliance for progress. We must go forward into a greater tomorrow, while preserving our cherished traditions."

"So much for the specifics, Daddy, what about the big picture?"

"I'm getting to that. First, the budget. We must cut the fat without cutting the bone."

"That reminds me," says my wife. "I think supper's burning."

"I've got to paint the front walk."

"The books need counting."

"Sit down! Where was I? Oh, yes, the budget. Now, just like a nation, a family must keep within its budget. Last year our expenditures overran our income and aggravated an inflationary trend, not to mention what it did to my ulcer. I have here a balanced budget, which will allow us to continue the necessary services but will prevent runaway overruns. We must hold the line on excess family spending."

"Do you know what a loaf of bread costs now?" my wife asks.

"We've got to run this family like a business," I say.

"Right," pipes up my youngest. "Let's fix prices, tap our neighbors' phones, and cheat on our taxes."

"Waiter, where are my three martinis?" asks the eldest.

"I plan to cut social services." I continue, above it all.

"Like what?"

"Allowances."

"To the barricades! Up against the wall! Power to the people!"

"But increase defense spending."

"What defense spending?"

"I'm going to get a new lock for the back door."

"That's dumb," says my daughter. "How will I get in when you go off and forget to leave the key with a neighbor?"

"I will not get bogged down in details in a State of the Family speech. This is just like the other State speeches, a smokescreen of high-sounding words carefully designed to get me maximum coverage with minimum effort. And like the others, being the center of attention is good for my ego."

"Daddy, it's almost time for *The Rockford Files.*"

"Now we come to the energy problem. Our utilities are ridiculous. Henceforth, we set the thermometer at 80 in the summer and 65 in the winter. Not the other way around."

"You got no class, Daddy."

"As for civil rights, I am a firm believer in them for adults. Anyone in this family who is not an adult has no civil rights. However, I am always ready for suggestions. My door is always open."

"I thought you were getting a new lock."

"Don't get smart. I meant I am easily approachable, an absolute cream puff."

"You?"

"Yes. Now sit down and shut up before I break your arms. The next item is worker productivity. Like mowing the lawn. Our back yard puts the American tradition of workmanship in dire jeopardy."

"How about competition from foreign markets, Daddy?"

"Huh?"

"Let's get a Mexican yardman."

"I don't think this group is on the same wavelength. Finally, in my State of the Family address, we must preserve our natural environment. Specifically, I want those rooms cleaned up. At least so I can see the rugs. Now, are there any questions?"

"Yeah. When can we have a recall election?"

Sometimes You Can't Get There From Here

RIVER OAKS BOULEVARD — Here I am, puttering along, awash in the pleasant knowledge that I am driving the only 1972 VW Beetle in the neighborhood. But, ambivalently, I am also thunderstruck with fear. Mortal, gnawing fear. Because *being* on River Oaks Boulevard does not bother me nearly as much as being *discovered* on River Oaks Boulevard.

The reason is, I have no business here or anywhere near here. It is not on my way to or from any spot on my agenda. I've got to get back to a place that makes sense before anyone sees me. Gad, what if I'm in a car wreck? What if I get a ticket? How will I ever explain it? Who will believe me?

I shall die here. That's what will happen. A cement truck late to a coffee break shall swat me flat. I will not be around to explain the questions that shall arise from my demise.

"Why was he there?"

"You got me."

"Maybe he lives there."

"Get serious."

Proper questions. Why am I here? Because bit by bit, street by street, I got nudged away from my prescribed route and am now literally miles from anyplace I want to be. No, I am not lost. I know every signpost and every street around here, which only adds to my frustration, not to mention my fear.

"We are gathered here today to mourn the loss of this victim of a late cement truck. If anyone knows why he was on River Oaks Boulevard at 5 p.m. on a rainy afternoon, speak up now or forever hold your peace."

Total silence.

My problem began just off Westheimer, over there several miles. I was picking up a TV set from a repair shop. I headed down the little side street toward Westheimer, but the village idiot, nay, even the Oiler management, could see that Westheimer was not moving. It was stopped dead in a rainy rush hour. So I did a U-turn and headed north, trying to go west. Through a neighborhood unto San Felipe, which was so choked with traffic that I could not turn left.

After waiting perhaps 10 minutes and realizing there was no hope, I turned right, with the traffic. No matter, I planned to go back the other way at the first chance. The first chance had a large sign,

"No Left Turn." So I went on and on, the wrong way. Which brings me to River Oaks Boulevard, eons away from my destination.

At this point I shall witness a shooting. When I am on the witness stand, the attorney will glare at me and demand, "Just *why* were you on River Oaks Boulevard at 5:30 on a rainy afternoon?"

Gulp.

"Do you live there?"

"No, sir."

"Do you work there?"

"No, sir."

"Do you have any reason whatsoever for being there?"

Silence. Sweaty silence. Then I shall break down completely. "I did it and I'm glad! Glad, do you hear me? He had it coming."

"It was a she."

"Don't quibble!"

This situation of being where you don't want to be happens in Houston because it is so easy to go the wrong way, even when you know where you are going. And we have so few through streets that it's impossible to go back again. Not long ago, I was on a bridge over some railroad tracks near the Ship Channel while trying to park downtown. I knew that I would be splattered by a drunken gravel truck driver and no one in my family would ever figure out what I was doing over there.

"But he was going downtown."

"Why was he on that bridge?"

"You got me."

Freeways are notoriously bad for this. You miss your exit and you are in Waco.

"Why was he in Waco?"

"You got me. He was going to the Galleria."

People understand that. We have all missed freeway exits and gone far beyond our destination. But just prowling around town on city streets and winding up in an unfamiliar spot is difficult to explain to others. Still, it happens to me time and time again. I go right to avoid the line of traffic and discover I'm in a "Left Turn Only" lane, which neatly feeds me into Allen Parkway, which deposits me on Memorial, which leads to the West Loop and drops me off at the *Post*. I was trying to leave the *Post*. That is where I started 20 minutes earlier.

Late one Saturday night I was coming back to Houston on I-45. Traffic was murder. I got off and slipped down a service road. So long, suckers! Suddenly I hit a dead end, turned off, down a street, around a corner, and found myself in the midst of a most exotic neighborhood. Suffice it to say that I was the only college graduate on the block. One flat tire and it was good-bye, pilgrim.

"Why was he there so late on a Saturday night?"

"You got me. He was supposed to be picking up a TV set near Westheimer."

There should be a word in the English language, I am sure there is one in some other tongue, for a person who is not really lost but is not where he planned to be, where he simply wound up because of detours, "Left Lane Ends," and "El Paso — 790 miles." "Lost" is not right. "Confused," perhaps. Or "totally incapable of getting there." In any event, I am trying to go west while madly hurtling east. Somewhere this side of Lake Charles a Peterbilt will inhale my VW and my family will be asking, "Why was he in Louisiana?"

"You got me. He was supposed to be picking up a TV set near Westheimer."

At the Age of 33

Good grief, it is a shattering thought. I have been around for a third of a century — 33 years and four months. It is a terrible burden to bear. Sort of postadolescent purgatory, that obscure time of life when a man is too old to get away with childish pranks and yet too young to command respect.

When I say something, no one smiles and says, "Out of the mouths of babes . . . ," nor do they nod with appreciation and note that I am older and wiser. At my age it is termed "spouting off" and is thus answerable with a swift kick to the groin. Sigh. Thirty-three is a bad time. A time when one must suffer both acne and baldness — the worst of both worlds.

But what is really humiliating is that I have so little to show for my one score and 13 years of existence. At the age of 33, William Howard Taft was solicitor general of the U.S., Jesus Christ was crucified, and Thomas Jefferson was putting the finishing touches to the Declaration of Independence. I have trouble with adverbial clauses.

But in all fairness to myself, let me make it perfectly clear that it took Jefferson time to write the D. of I. He didn't just hack it out one night. And it doesn't have many adverbial clauses.

His archenemy, Alexander Hamilton, was a lieutenant colonel in the Continental Army and Washington's aide-de-camp at the ripe old age of 22, having already distinguished himself as an artillery officer. When he was 32, Hamilton wrote about two-thirds of *The Federalist*, which explained and interpreted the new Constitution. To this day it is considered one of the great works of American intellect. Sulk-sulk. I got a C in government.

Washington, himself, was an early bloomer. He was the surveyor of Culpeper County at 17, a colonel in the army at 22. One of his friends and aides during the war was young Lafayette, who got married at 16, and at 19 years, four months, was a full major general in the Continental Army. Of course, it always helps when you bring along your own army.

After four years as a private first class, the Marine Corps finally made me a lance corporal and somehow still survived. Lafayette, I have arrived! Major general, indeed.

Then there was George Armstrong Custer, a brigadier general at 24, a scalp at 37. And *that* to another young man in a hurry. Ha! But perhaps the fastest rising star in these 33 and a third revelations per minute is the late and lamented Alexander the Great. He was regent of Macedonia at 16, a general at 18, a king at 20, and he conquered all the world he could find (this did not include Seabrook) when he was 33. Then he caught a fever and died. There is a moral there somewhere.

Attila the hun, that fun-loving gadabout, became king of the Huns when he was 27, although he had to share the power with his brother, Bleda. Attila, always the one-upmanship type, simply had his brother killed and reigned alone as the Huns ravaged Europe.

Alfred the Great was king of England at 22, but William of Normandy didn't become William the Conqueror until he was 39, so I have six years left to defeat the Saxons. And we must not forget the ladies. Cleopatra was queen of Egypt when she was 20, while Joan of Arc never saw 18.

Martin Luther was 34 when, on October 31, 1517, he nailed his Ninety-Five Theses to the church door at Wittenberg. Mozart had his first sonatas for piano and violin published when he was seven, two years after making his musical debut in Munich. At 12 he was commissioned by the Austrian emperor to write an opera but didn't finish it until he was 13, clumsy adolescent. He made do by conducting his "Solemn Mass" at court for the emperor. By the ripe old age of 13 he was recognized throughout Europe as an established composer and musician.

Napoleon, as a 24-year-old artillery officer, drove off the British ships in the Toulon harbor. At 26, Paris hailed Napoleon as her savior after he seized the insurgents' cannons and mowed them down in the city's streets. A year later he married Josephine de Beauharnais, then killed the following years and several thousand troops by beating armies in Italy, Austria, and Egypt. It beat hanging around Corsica squeezing grapes.

Always the irrepressible youth, Napoleon went back and whipped the Austrians again, caused Russia to pull out of the anti-French alliance, then returned home and made himself emperor of France. He brought Pope Pius VII to Paris just to make it all official. But just as the pope raised the crown to place it on Napoleon's head, the young Corsican grabbed it and crowned himself. Then Josephine was crowned empress. Napoleon was 35 at the time.

Closer to home, we had our own upstarts who didn't know their place. James Madison helped write the Virginia state constitution at 25. In 1834, Abraham Lincoln was a 25-year-old member of the Illinois legislature. Theodore Roosevelt was president of the board of police commissioners of New York City when he was 31.

Lyndon Johnson was teaching school in Houston when he was 23, but six years later he was a U.S. congressman. Jack Kennedy had to wait until he was 30 to go to Congress.

Judge Roy Hofheinz passed the bar at 19, was a practicing lawyer at 20, a state representative at 22, and county judge of Harris County at 26. Bobby Fischer was a grand master at 22, while Van Cliburn won the International Tschaikovsky Piano Competition in Moscow and a ticker-tape parade in New York City when he was 23.

A pox on you all. Taft, Custer, Attila, Alfred, even you, Napoleon. Think you're so hot. Bet you can't wiggle your ears like this. So there.

Early Bird Gets the Screwworm on Suburban Weekends

THE FRONT WINDOW—There goes another. That is the last of the lot. It is the weekend, and now Running Rats Acres is totally deserted. Except for me. You see, all my neighbors have weekend places — farms and ranches in the boonies somewhere, or lake homes, or beach homes, or something out of town.

Every Friday afternoon I can see them rushing home from work early, happily tossing hoes, picks, buckets of paint, and sacks of cement into the backs of their cars. Then they race off to spend the entire weekend joyfully performing manual labor.

"Put in 50 fence posts," the oil magnate boasted late one Sunday evening as he gingerly got out of his Mercedes.

"That's why I went to college," I answered.

"So you could put in fence posts?"

"No. So I wouldn't have to put in fence posts."

He looked at me with a condescending smile. "That's 'cause you don't have a weekend place," he said, turning to pull out an empty spool of barbed wire. "You need somewhere to get away from it all — a place where you can chop cotton, dig water tanks, mend gates, a place to take it easy."

It occurred to me that if I wanted to spend my weekends doing manual labor, I sure didn't need to drive 110 miles each way to do it. There is more than I can handle at my home right here in Houston. I told that to a corporate lawyer as he was loading air conditioning ducts into the back seat of his car one Friday afternoon.

"You don't understand," he said, "It's a lot different, working for yourself. Here, hand me that jackhammer, will you?"

The orthodontist hitched his boat to his back bumper, tossed in two pitchforks, a plumber's helper, and a sack of sorghum seeds. He was hurrying. "Got to get out before the Friday afternoon rush," he said. "All those campers and boats jam up the roads."

"But it's Thursday morning," I noted.

He paid me no mind. "It's as bad on Friday afternoons outbound as it is on Sunday nights inbound."

"How do you avoid Sunday night traffic?"

"I come back on Tuesday morning."

He attached a trailer to the back of the boat and a cement mixer to the trailer then left for the weekend.

The situation eventually got to where I was the only person left on the block. Then I was the only one left in the neighborhood, Friday to Sunday.

"Would you mind getting our mail?" the doctor's wife asked. "I hate for the house to look unlived in."

"Say, old sport," the veterinarian asked, "would you mind collecting our newspapers? I don't want . . ."

"Right," I said, marking it down on my clipboard after I answered the door again.

Knock-knock. "Please put out the pot-plants and water the cat."

Knock-knock. "Just sprinkle the bushes, don't bother with the grass."

Knock-knock. "If you'd just put out the garbage cans . . ."

Knock-knock. "Since you'll be here this . . ."

"Yeah, the goldfish," I say, checking it off.

At neighborhood gatherings (never on weekends, of course) I thought my newfound position would make me invaluable to everyone. They'd be nice to me at Christmas or the pipes wouldn't drip during the next cold weekend. But my role had just the other effect. The conversations would always center on screwworms, water tables, and the price of an acre outside Round Top. No one wanted to discuss the mosquito fogger, cracked slabs, or chinch bugs.

Eventually I noticed that the conversation would stop completely when I walked up:

". . . fungicide the backhoe . . ."

". . . ovulate the corn fritters . . ."

"Well, *my* rustler says . . ."

"Uh-oh. Watch out. Here he comes with his usual stupid comments about cracked slabs."

It wasn't too long until I was ostracized completely. My lists of duties were simply slipped under the door. There was only one thing to do. Midafternoon the next Friday, I backed out of my driveway with a rake and a pick sticking out of the open trunk, a wheelbarrow tied to my car roof, and an open bag of roofing nails in the back seat between the ice chest and the trowel. I tipped my John Deere gimme hat to the neurosurgeon, who was backing out the drive towing a tractor, and drove off.

After leaving my car in a U-Tote-M parking lot over the weekend, I slipped back home. Each night at precisely 6:32 I would turn on all the lights. At 11:18 I would turn them off. Late Sunday I drove slowly back up my driveway, then painfully got out and walked across the yard to the newspapers I had left scattered around. With a grunt and a groan, I bent over and picked them up, then shuffled to the postbox to retrieve the mail.

At that point, two neighbors stopped by to invite me over for a pitcher of martinis so we could talk about screwworms.

Improved Image for Washington
Not Easy Task

As you may have read, our nation's capital is trying to brush up its image and lure more tourists. To this end, city leaders have (what else in Washington?) formed a Committee to Promote Tourism. In addition, $100,000 has been set aside to pay an advertising company to come up with an ad campaign and a nifty slogan as good as "I Love New York," which has been immortalized on bumpers around the nation as "I♥NY."

Now, $100,000 isn't much money in Washington, but out here in the hinterland, that seems like a lot. So in an effort to cash in on the cash, I think we should come up with a slogan, at least. That would immediately save them $50,000. It has to be cute, short and worthy of a bumper sticker. How about:

Washington Is Real George

Washington—A Capital Idea

Come to the Banks of the Potomac—Visit Your Money

All right, they aren't up there with "Thanks, Mean Joe." Or "If you don't have an oil well, get one." But it's a start. If "I♥NY" is considered such a winner, then the obvious one for Washington is:

I$D.C.

It doesn't really mean anything, which should fit right in with that city. Here's a good suggestion: "Baja Baltimore." That doesn't mean anything either, but sounds cute and should be worth a lousy $50,000. In Washington, they spill that much. Here's another: "Washington—Just a Footstep Away from the Presidency." Or perhaps: "Your Nation's Capital—Just Plain Bills."

I am also working on radio jingles, such as:

Ya load Washington and whattaya get?
Another day older and a billion in debt.

Or:

Join Rita Jenrette and find your thrill on Capitol Hill.

There are two distinct problems with this campaign. First, all sorts of otherwise intelligent people get "capitol" and "capital" mixed up. Second, and more complex, is the city itself really doesn't have an image. Most of us don't even think of it as being a city, certainly not since it lost its baseball team. Even Arlington, Texas, has a major league baseball team. The vagueness of any image is to Washington's advantage, though, because if you do think of it as just a city, you certainly do not think of it as one you would wish to visit. As Spiro Agnew said, "You've seen one slum, you've seen them all."

No, we visit Washington by the millions each year only to see the federal projects. Take away the goodies built in the District of Columbia by the taxpayers of Topeka and all you have is 100,000 unemployed lawyers and journalists — an idea that hits many as terrific. It is not the city we wish to see but that campus of offices and agencies, bureaucrats and museums. So it would be foolish in the extreme to paint Washington as anything else. Lead with your best.

On the other hand, just the word "Washington" gets groans, blame, and laughter. It represents all our problems, taxes, and turmoil. Our last two presidents were elected specifically because they had never worked a day in that town. So who wants to make a pilgrimage to such a place? Perhaps the problem could be turned around, however, by playing on the undisguised negativism most U.S. citizens have for their national capital. (For this reason, "Washington: The 51st State" might not go over too well in the other 50.)

Here are a few more I'm running up the flagpole to see if anyone burns:

"Catch Potomac Fever"

"I'd Rather Be Lobbying"

"Escape Reality, Visit Washington"

"Ask Me About My Grandscam"

And, of course, "Washing-Fun, D.C."

That last one is so stupid and so cutesy it will probably be the one the committee will pick.

You Can 'Tell Bell,' But Not Very Much

Hi, there again, beloved fans and listeners. It's that radio show you've all been waiting for. Yes, it's time to Tell Bell. So just dial right up and let me know what you think, because your opinion is the only opinion that matters, and that's my opinion. This is your show. I'm just here to listen. Ah, yes. Our first caller. Hi, Bob.

Am I on?

Yes, you're on.

I'm on the air?

Yeah, Bob. You're on the air.

Who am I talking to?

Who did you call, Bob?

I called up to Tell Bell.

That's what you're doing, Bob.

Gee, I never thought I'd be on the air.

Forget it, Bob. Hi, Cha-Cha.

Hi, Bell.

What kind of name is Cha-Cha?

It's a nickname.

It's a dumb nickname. A grown woman shouldn't run around with a name like Cha-Cha. What's on your mind?

Bell, it was about your guest yesterday.

Oh, that dummy. George Shultz. Typical bureaucrat.

Bell, he's the Secretary of State.

So he says.

Bell, every time he'd try to tell you something about foreign affairs, you'd inter—

Actually, I don't like to have guests on this show. They usually don't know anything.

Maybe you're just afraid they'll show you up.

Good-bye, Cha-Cha. Hi, there, LeRoy.

Hi, Bell.

What's on your mind?

It's about the way you treated that last caller, Bell.

She was a cretin.

You always have to have the last word, don't you?

It's my show. You want the last word, get your own show.

What I don't understand, Bell, is why anyone would call you up in the first place. Just to be humiliated, embarrassed, have their words twisted, all so you can look brilliant.

People are dumb. They like to step into the ring with me. They like to have their stupidity exposed to the world. It satisfies some inner need to be punished. They don't hang up. They just sit there and take it. You, for instance, LeRoy . . . LeRoy? Hi, Glenda.

Bell, I think I'm in trouble. You promised that . . .

Bye, Glenda. Hi, there, caller.

It's a nice day today.

No, it isn't, caller.

Day.

Night.

Black.

White.

Yes.

No.

Bell, you are so opinionated and contrary. Not to mention wrong.

That's the dumbest thing I've ever heard, you moron. Good-bye. Hi, there, next caller. You sound like you're a long way away.

Yes, Bell. I am.

What's your name, caller?

Just call me Lech.

That's as dumb as Cha-Cha. What's on your mind today, Lech?

Well, I've got to talk fast. I don't have much time. It's about Solidarity.

Let me tell you about Solidarity. Those guys in Poland just don't want to work, you know? So they get this patriotic front and . . .

Bell, please. I must tell. The Eagle is wounded, but the nest is safe.

Huh?

I said the . . .

I heard what you said, Lech. What the heck does it mean? I've had some weird callers but you are Fruitcake City. Now, about Solidarity. I'll tell you about that bunch. They . . .

Bell, they're coming up the steps. Please. Tell Dutch that Boris is moving at dawn.

You don't know what you're talking about, Lech. But fortunately for my fans, I *do* know all about Polish Labor unions and . . .

They're kicking down the door. Bell, inform Dutch that the Eagle . . .

Buzz off, Lech.

Ahhhhhg!

Boy, I'll tell you, we get 'em all here. Hi, there, caller. Who are you?

Dutch.

Say, Dutch, you sound long distance, too.

Uh, yeah. I'm calling from Washington.

So what's new on the Potomac?

Did that last caller, uh, ah, did he say something about Boris?

Oh, that kumquat. I dunno. Why?

What about Boris?

He's going home. No, he's moving.

When?

I forget. So what's on your mind? The price of gas? The Mideast? Let's talk about me.

No, Bell. Please. This is very important. Did Lech mention the Eagle's nest?

Boy, you're on the same wavelength as that last joker. So long, Dutch.

No, wait, Bell. This is very imp—

Oh, boy, what a bunch of idiots. Hi, caller.

Bell, you are an arrogant ass, a pompous, self-important jerk armed with a milligram of intelligence and a third-rate education trying to snow an entire city. You ought to be taken out and taught a lesson.

Mother?

Too Much Money — Those Were the Days

Alas, the Texas Legislature. It is heading toward the end of its biennial session still facing a raft of bills, most of which require state money. For example, the schoolteachers want more money. Then there are the roads, the prisons, the judges, and on and on. All the time State Comptroller Bob Bullock, who would very much like his present job to be a stepping-stone, keeps saying, "There's not enough money." It is a small point, but big enough to mess up everything else.

In such sessions, at such times, our lawmakers may be forgiven if they sit back in their deep seats, gaze at the ornate ceiling above their chamber, and think, "Sully, where are you when we really need you?"

Yes, Sul Ross. He was the one and only governor of Texas to call a special session of the Legislature to deal with a unique problem: the state had too much money. It was such a surplus that no one knew what to do with it all. Ah, those were the days.

The days were in the spring of 1888, and Ross was in the second year of his administration. (Some of this comes from a new book put out by Texas A&M Press called *Sul Ross, Soldier, Statesman, Educator,* by Judith Ann Benner. The rest is from various history books and the *Galveston Daily News.*) He was a most interesting fellow, Lawrence Sullivan Ross. The son of an Indian agent on a reservation near Waco, young Sully grew up with a greater understanding of Texas Indians than most. He loved the good ones, he killed the bad ones.

During a summer vacation home from college in Alabama, he led a company of Indians from his father's reservation against the dreaded Comanche. The next fall, that must have stopped the bull sessions in the dorm. "Hey, Sully, what did you do this summer?"

"Well, we were in the midst of a battle with the Comanches when four of us spotted a little white girl who was a captive. As we were getting her, we were jumped by 25 braves. Two of us were killed immediately. My gun misfired. I got an arrow in my shoulder and was then shot point-blank by a brave. It was Mohee, a Comanche I'd known since we were children together. As I was lying on the ground, Mohee whipped out his scalping knife and was about to scalp me when his chief called him away to kill someone else. My Indian friends rescued me and nursed me back to health. What'd you do this summer?"

"Oh, not much."

Ross eventually joined the Texas Rangers, and at the ripe age of 21 was made captain of a Ranger company. In yet another battle, Ross caught up with Nacona, a Comanche chief who was responsible for much of the savagery against whites. Ross shot Nacona and rescued another white woman, who turned out to be Cynthia Ann Parker.

When the War Between the States broke out, Ross joined the Confederate Army as a private. He came out a brigadier general. Ross took part in 135 engagements, including 112 days of fighting around Atlanta. He was a lucky man. After the war, Ross took up farming near Waco, then got into politics. He became sheriff of McLennan County, a state senator, and, in January 1887, was inaugurated governor. He was the first to use the new capitol.

That is when he had to tackle the problem of too much money. Part of the trouble was that most of the taxes came in during December and January. The money sat around until it was spent during the rest of the year. Then the U.S. government, acting on the advice of the army, paid Texas $927,177.40 as restitution for Indian depredations and expenses incurred by the state.

You see, in the 20 years after the war, Texas Rangers—not the U.S. Army—did much of the fighting with both Mexican bandits and hostile Indians. In addition, Texas patrolled its own border with Mexico. Texas was the only state to run up such expenses (mainly because it was the only one with its own army). Washington reimbursed the state for the cost and made good such losses as cattle rustling by the bandits and Indians.

It all came to a tidy amount, particularly in those days. A reporter went to the state vault, which held $2 million in cash, 20 percent of all the money in the state rendered for taxation:

> The vault contained a large burglar- and fire-proof safe, in which $1,250,000 in paper money was neatly arranged in packages, forming a compact square mass, ten by twenty four inches, and eighteen inches high. In the same money chest about $25,000 in gold in bags was resting secure from moth and rust. Outside the safe a pyramid of silver in bars was built from the floor nearly to the ceiling, resting against the west wall of the vault.
>
> Another safe was covered nearly to the ceiling with boxes of silver. Several tons of the precious metals were in view. In the corner was a pile of money bags containing silver quarters, halves and nickels. In the safe first mentioned, in addition to the cash, were shown in packages some $7,000,000 in bonds, viz, $2,991,900 of state bonds and $2,276,000 of county bonds, $1,753,817 of railroad bonds, besides $79,400 of public debt certificates.

On March 27, 1888, Ross complained to a press conference that he couldn't sleep the night before, worrying about what to do with all that money. "I don't feel authorized to keep so much money locked up fully a year if deferred until the regular session." So he called a special session and suggested that some funds should be set aside to pay the state's bills for the rest of the year, some should go to raises for schoolteachers, and the state should repay $96,000 borrowed from the university fund. Then the new capitol had to be furnished, the state needed new asylums, and so on. What was left, Ross said, would still be considerable, and that should be returned to the taxpayers.

Yes, those were the days.

A Low-Grade Case of Skool Daze?

THE STREET CORNER—Hey, it's my old friend Miss Frisbee. "Hi, Miss Frisbee."

Miss Frisbee walks over, smiling. "High, their," she says.

"How are you?" I ask.

"I'm fine, thanks. But I was fired from my last job sense I saw you."

"What was that?"

"I was John McMullen's mole among mortals."

"Then why are you so happy?"

"Got a new job this past spring. The pay is lousy, but the vacation time is great."

"Doing what?"

"I'm a teacher for the HSDI."

"You? A teacher? Well, that sure explains those grades the HISD chalked up when the teachers took those competency tests."

"Oh, those."

"The grades were terrible."

"Yeah. It's a shame, alright. But they were nesessary to weed out the bad one's. But remember, not all the teachers took the test."

"Just a third of them."

"Right. So 25 percent is not a fare measure."

"How did you do on the tests?"

"Excellentally in english."

"I saw where 62 percent of the HISD teachers who took the test failed the reading portion."

"And no wonder. It was unfare. They wouldn't let us use a dictionary or even a catharsis."

"I can see the problem."

"And the test asked things like 'Who was Hamlet's uncle?' "

"So?"

"They shouldn't bring religion into the classroom. I'm going to file a protest with the ACCUL."

"What else did they ask?"

"Oh, dumb things like 'What is wrong with this sentence: John ain't got no smarts.' Do they think were stupid?"

"Yeah, that is pretty obvious. I hope you corrected it."

"Of course. 'John *hasn't* got no smarts.' But me and all the other teachers were really insulted by that kind of putdown and insinuendoes."

"Well, I keep hearing that we are having trouble getting good English teachers."

"Where'd you get that idea at?"

"Just a rumor going around."

Miss Frisbee sighs. "I can't get to excited about those test grades. Like Mark Twain said, 'Nice guys don't finish first.' "

"That was 'Nice guys finish last.' And it was Leo Durocher."

"He finished last?"

"No."

"I didn't think so. All my friends voted for him."

"I saw where about 45 percent of the HISD teachers who took the math test failed."

"Look at the bright side. That means 75 percent passed."

"How did you do on the math test, or should I ask?"

"It was as dumb as the english part. I mean, if a farmer has eight cows and loses two, how many does he have?"

"Six?"

"Who told you?"

"I used this pocket calculator."

"Yeah, well, what do I know about agriculture and fraterization? Do I look like a county agent?"

"It sounds to me, Miss Frisbee, as though you didn't do real well on the tests."

"It don't make no difference."

"Why not?"

"You see, my brother works at the printting plant where they ran off the tests, and he gave me a copy of the answers which I took with I to the testing."

"That's cheating."

"Cheating is when you steel answers from the person sitting next to you. I was engaged in research."

"I think that it was a good idea those test grades weren't released while the Legislature was in special session debating teachers' pay raises."

"Hey, what do those lawmakers in Waco know? Governor Bentsen promised us a 24 percent pay rise so we can get a higher quantity of teacher."

"Miss Frisbee, I suspect that if we start paying more to get better teachers, you will be the first to go."

"You think I should push for lower celeries?"

"That's the only way people like you will keep your jobs."

"Look, teachers as me are worth more, and you get what you pay for as sure as two and two equal . . . uh, two plus two is . . . can I borrow that hand calculator a minute?"

Lighter's Side

The American serviceman has always been a rather uncomfortable animal. He is a cynic and a griper, an impatient shortcut specialist who must smile, keep quiet, and do things by the numbers. He comes from a civilization that beknights the rugged individualist, yet demands that he get in step with the program.

So, traditionally, he has turned to humor to vent some of his frustrations. No doubt the soldiers huddled around fires at Valley Forge thought up dirty limericks about George III and perhaps even about another George. Far along the line, during World War II the ubiquitous "Kilroy Was Here" signs popped up everywhere. These days, in a more complex war, the slogans and jargon to break the tedium and tension of being a target take on more complex – and deeper – meanings.

"Over here," writes a brother from somewhere southwest of Da Nang, "everyone has a cigarette lighter, on one side is written his name and unit, and on the other side is some saying or proverb. I'm sure some of these have been kicking around the Marine Corps and elsewhere for quite a while. But they were new to me."

Indeed, some of the slogans are veterans of other foreign wars, and the fact that they are considered new only testifies to the youthfulness of the troopers. For instance: "And when I get to heaven, to Saint Peter I will tell, another Marine reporting, sir. I've served my time in hell." That, I believe, was first seen scribbled on a new grave at Guadalcanal, before any of the current crop was born.

Some are aimed strictly at the current fracas: "If I had a home in hell and a farm in Vietnam, I'd sell my farm and go home." Others are more inclusive: "You'll wonder where the yellow went, when you napalm the Orient."

It must be true that there are no atheists in the foxholes, for so many of the etchings deal with God, hell, and heaven: "Marines don't die, they just go to hell and regroup." Some recall those early days of Sunday school and bring them up to date: "Yea, though I walk through the valley of the shadow of death, I will fear no evil. 'Cause I'm the meanest man in the valley." And some are really more of a prayer than a boast: "You and me, God. Right?" One of the best of the lot in the booby-trapped world of the infantrymen touches all the bases: "Walk with God, but let God walk ahead."

Alas, the chaplains still have their work cut out for them. For instance, this chilling inscription seen on a lighter carried by a young American: "All I feel when I kill is the recoil." The job at hand appears to have given some a swaggering, romantic view of themselves; then, again, maybe not: "Oversexed, underpaid, teenage killer." It is hard to determine if it is a boast or a complaint. Perhaps the owner himself is unsure.

No military group in the world has more self-esteem than the Marine Corps, but even the Corps is not shielded from the brickbats of angry leathernecks. Some day the gunny sergeant is going to hold a cigarette lighter inspection and then march the entire platoon over to the provost marshal to face charges of high treason. Certainly leading the pack will be the young jarhead with the lighter that reads: "Fighter by day, lover by night, drunkard by choice, Marine by mistake." He will be joined at the Leavenworth rock pile by the one who carries around in his pocket the immortal words "If you kill for pleasure, you're a sadist. If you kill for money, you're a mercenary. If you kill for both, you're a Marine."

Finally there is the short but sweet "Eat the apple and to hell with the Corps." Now, the commandant might take offense at some of these complaints from the ranks. On the other hand, it would be interesting to find out what is inscribed on *his* lighter. Probably a nasty dig at troops who carry lighters with nasty digs at him.

Still, there are some whose loyalty charges on like a Tet offensive, although they, too, seem to have a testy edge to their slogans: "Marines have done so much with so little for so long, that now we can do anything with nothing forever."

Certainly one of the great quotes of the Vietnamese War goes to the officer who explained to a group of reporters looking at heaps of rubble and smoldering ruins: "We had to destroy this village in order to save it." There is no evidence yet that this quote has been elevated to immortality on the sides of cigarette lighters. Quite to the contrary, many of the troops seem rather dovish: "When the power of love overcomes the love of power, then there will be peace." The inevitable joker in the battalion pursues the same goals, but in a more colorful manner: "Fighting for peace is like making love for virginity."

This is one of the few inscriptions that mention sex, a rather strange phenomenon among young men. Even when it does pop up, it is put down: "If you think sex is exciting, try incoming mail."

No, most deal with weightier matters — the difference between here and there and the fact that some may not appreciate it: "When you go home, tell them of us, and say that for their tomorrow we gave our today." And there is the point that war gives one a new perspective on life: "You haven't lived until you've almost died," one infantryman's inscription reads.

"My favorite," the letter concludes, "is the motto of the 1st Marine Division: 'For those who fight for it, life and liberty have a flavor the protected never know.'"

They've come a long way from Kilroy.

Daddy's Home

THE BACK DOOR — It is, perhaps, altogether fitting that the man of the house, the breadwinner and master, should enter his castle each evening through this portal, the same one used by the egg man and the plumber and the children's playmates.

Yes, this is where he belongs, for — although he may labor all day in the factory or fields to turn a buck — this is where he must return to earth. And it is here, right here, where the most important moment of his day takes place. For it is here that he is greeted with the real reason for his existence, his wife and family. But how few women and children realize the true importance of this moment.

Let us recall the situation. The man of the house has been fighting all day. He has pushed steel through a foundry at the Cameron Iron

Works, or rammed a truck down the freeway, scattering small cars and large chickens. He has run a bank through the maze of SEC inspectors who do not fully appreciate his ingenuous method of bookkeeping. He has reattached the bottom of a left leg to the top of same. He has bought short and sold long, struck out twice and walked once, held up liquor stores or chased those who did.

And through it all, his boss has been complaining, his secretary has been using the WATS to talk to her mother in Longview, his competitors have been running away with next quarter's profits, and that idiot summer intern has just been hired as his assistant. Through the day the phone has rung, the door has opened, the mail has piled high on the desk, and the letter from New York — the one with the advance tip on the stock split — has been unread.

The poor fellow somehow staggers through the day and finally, a half-hour after everyone else in the office has left, he begins his drive home only to discover that all of Houston is waiting in the freeway lane ahead of him because two trucks filled with turnips tried to squeeze into a lane built for one. OK, he limps home an hour late and forgot to stop by to pick up a doorknob for the bathroom, but that is no matter, for — after one long string of disasters and putdowns and complaints through the day — he is finally home.

Thus we come to this most important moment. How is he greeted? Is it with a litany of disasters and putdowns and complaints? Did the washing machine overflow and the pillow rip and the check to the butcher bounce? If so, chances are he will find out about it before he gets both feet in the door. If the price of lettuce is up, he will be told the history of lettuce from A.D. 45. If Junior kicked the teacher, he will know. If there is a lump in the mattress and a dent in the fender, he will know. He will know before the door closes behind him. Oh, yes, and did you remember to pick up the doorknob for the bathroom?

All right, there is no getting around the fact that he should know. But do not hit him in the face with it before the drawbridge is down. No, there are ways to handle every situation, and certainly there are ways to greet father upon his return from the wars. I, myself, prefer to get my car in the garage, which sometimes takes several minutes, since there are usually six bikes and at least one skateboard in the driveway. That done, I find it accommodating of the family if they will let me fully turn off the ignition before pouncing on me with assorted emotional earthquakes.

Once inside the house, of course, I am steeled for the onslaught, but in all fairness I must say that my wife goes to great pains to protect me for up to 30, even 40, seconds after my arrival. Indeed, there are times when all is pleasant. The children are fed, the kitchen is scrubbed, the soft music is on, and a nippy-poo is waiting on the drainboard. In the winter there may even be a fire chirping along, preferably in the fireplace. It is at that moment that I am most content. Father is returned home safely, all is well with the world. Well, if all is not well, I am sure to find out in a few minutes, but for one brief shining moment this is Camelot.

Thus I have drawn up a few dos and don'ts for families to follow when the old man comes home:

DO allow him out of the car before saying a word.

DO make sure the first words are upbeat. "Junior hit a home run." Later you can add that it was through the Millers' $350 front window.

DO have a drink ready. On the other hand:

DON'T lock the back door.

DON'T, when he knocks, ask, "Who is it?"

And finally, DON'T leave cigar butts in the ashtrays — he may not congratulate you for giving up cigarettes.

The I's of Texans a Matter of History

Recently Sound-Off ran this letter from our reader in Katy:

"Mr. Lynn Ashby apparently did not grow up in Texas, or he would surely know we are 'Texans,' not 'Texians' as called by some people."

Two errors in one sentence. A record even for Sound-Off.

I will not bore you with childhood recollections or a trip through my family tree, but to set the record straight, I was born, raised, educated, married, and have lived in Texas most of my life. Except for visits to some relatives in Louisiana, I never set foot out of the state until I was 19. We go back to the Republic. Indeed, even at this time, my mother, who fought at the Alamo, is enrolling me and mine in the Sons/Daughters/Children of the Republic of Texas. So much for that.

But now to the major charge: "We are 'Texans,' not 'Texians,' as called by some people." Yes, indeed, *we* are Texans. Who, pray tell, said we were not? But the letter is obviously in reference to a column I wrote about the Republic of Texas in which I called the inhabitants of said nation Texians.

Not to get all bent out of shape over the simple use or nonuse of an *i*, but when someone corrects me in public, at least do your homework. Let me explain:

Residents here were once citizens of Mexico, which made them Mexicans. (Or Spaniards, if you wish to go back that far.) But eyeballs have a direct link to the brain, and if you scanned over the colonists coming in from the U.S. and elsewhere, common sense indicated that these were not your usual Mexicans. The gringos were different. So, the Anglo settlers in what was then the northern part of the state of Coahuila eventually became known as Texicans. This came to be of some importance during the Revolution, when Mexicans and Texicans sounded much too similar.

"Hey, Billy Bob, here come a bunch of Texicans."

"Mexicans, you say? Fire, boys."

Eventually, as best as anyone can tell, Texicans became Texians. Frederic Leclerc, a young French physician, visited Texas in 1838. A translation of his observations explains, "Throughout the text the settlers are referred to as Texians, since this form was current usage during the days of the republic."

In the introduction to their novel *The Texians*, authors David Larry Hicks and Dan Parkinson write, "Incidentally, there were no Texians prior to 1830 — they were Mexicans until then. And after 1836 the Texians were no longer. They were Texans from then on. This point is significant. The differences go far beyond words."

Significant, yes. And wrong. Because the term Texians was used long after 1836. Examples:

A visitor described the city of Houston and the huge amount of drinking going on here, concluding, "so that the Texians being entirely a military people, not only fought, but drank, in platoons." (*Hesperian; or Western Monthly Magazine*, October 1838.)

Charles Hooten, an English novelist, came here to gather material for a book, then returned to England to write *St. Louis' Isle, or Texiana*, in 1841.

Texas' ambassador to Britain received this formal card: "The Lord Chamberlain is commanded by The Queen to invite the Texian

Chargé d'affaires to a Ball on Monday the 19th of May at ½ past 9 o'clock. Buckingham Palace. Full Dress." That was in 1845.

Yet it wasn't only others who referred to the residents of Texas as Texians. The inhabitants themselves did. Or as Pogo said, "We have met the enemy and they is us." In Austin there was a newspaper, the *Weekly Texian*. In Houston there was another weekly, the *Texian Democrat*. A newspaper in Nacogdoches was the *Texian and Emigrant's Guide*. And on and on.

Many of those early emigrants came from Missouri, Kentucky, Tennessee, Georgia, and the Carolinas. When they moved here, they called themselves Texians. During the years of the Republic, that title was widely and popularly used. (French immigrants used the title Texienne.)

After Texas joined the Union, however, the newer newcomers began calling themselves Texans. This tended to chap the old newcomers, many of whom still ran the government. What you called yourself—Texan or Texian—was more than just a title. It told something about you. Officially, the change did not occur until 1860, but the old-guard Texians continued to use the term well into the 1880s.

Anyway, reader in Katy, get your facts right before popping off about me and my home. Just remember, the *i*'s of Texans are within us.

Mileage Tests

To: Administrator, EPA
From: Felix T. Mildew, Investigative Agent
Subject: EPA's MPG

Sir, as per your instructions, I have thoroughly investigated the policies and methods used by the Environmental Protection Agency in determining its miles-per-gallon estimates for new cars. You know the estimates. They are printed out by some computer in Tacoma and plastered on the inside windshields of new cars. Right next to the other big sticker that tells you how much the car costs plus the optional extras like a drive shaft. That sticker.

As you noted, there has been a lot of unrest among the car-buying public. Many have written to you, complaining that the EPA MPG estimates are off the mark.

A breakdown of the complaints are as follows:

> 24 percent say they get half the gas mileage listed on the EPA sticker.
> 55 percent say they get less than half the gas mileage.
> 14 percent complain that their gasoline bills are higher than their car payments.
> 4 percent called your researchers "charlatans."
> 2 percent called them "cretins."
> 2 percent opted for "shysters."
> The final 2 percent stuck with either "lackeys of Detroit" or "owners of oil company stock."

You may notice that this comes to 103 percent, but the EPA statistician assures me it's all right.

My next step was to investigate just how the EPA gas mileage estimates are determined. Your researchers took me to the EPA test track to watch as an Octane Guzzler was put through its paces. For the City Driving part of the gas mileage test, the car is relentlessly:

> Put into neutral down a 10-degree incline for four miles.
> Shoved through a wind tunnel with a 75-mile-per-hour wind at its back.
> Towed 12 miles by a wrecker.
> Pushed another grueling 18 miles by an M-278 tank.

Researchers explain that these are normal driving conditions for a car that is driven down Pike's Peak during a hurricane and rammed into a parked bus in the midst of an armed uprising. They have film to prove it.

The Highway Driving part of the test was even more severe. The car was:

> Strapped to a flatbed trailer from Fort Worth to Omaha.
> Pushed by 34 fraternity brothers from Omaha to St. Louis.
> Completely disassembled and mailed to Indianapolis.
> There it was reassembled and driven on the Speedway

under normal highway conditions for 48 miles at speeds of up to 32 miles an hour.

This gave the Guzzler an average gas mileage in town of 56, while the highway MPG came close to 98. As you know, the EPA always averages out these two figures to give the prospective car buyer an additional insight into the car's gas mileage. Like most people, I assumed that they simply added the two figures together and divided by two.

But the statistician noted that this would not be an accurate figure, since it would not take into consideration other driving conditions that affect gas mileage but were not used in the tests.

As he explained it, added mileage is often evidently due to weight loss, such as sideswiped fenders and stolen rear seats. So the average MPG must be increased accordingly.

More and more motorists are using gas-saving devices, such as sails. Other motorists have discovered that in rush hour traffic on the freeway, they can cut off their engines altogether and be pushed along by the crowd.

Lesser mileage occurs on rare occasions, such as when the air conditioner is used. (To avoid complication, the air conditioners are removed during the tests. There was no explanation about the absence of the radio, spare tire, grill, and hood.)

When all factors are fed into the computer — generously supplied by GM — the official EPA average figure for an Octane Guzzler under normal driving conditions comes to 121 miles per gallon.

Just to make sure there were no variables, EPA scientists insisted that at all times the vehicle was driven by the same 112-pound jockey.

Finally, to make certain that this governmental watchdog agency is totally above suspicion, I checked on the researchers themselves. I found that:

No more than 2 percent of them actually own oil company stock. The other 98 percent refused to answer.

I hope this investigation will put an end to complaints by the driving public.

Yr Ob't S'rv't
Felix T. Mildew
Investigative Agent

Battle of the Bugs Rages 'Neath
Facade of Peaceful Garden

THE GARDEN—And how does your garden grow?

Mine is doing splendidly. The leaf lettuce is sprouting like a forest of oaks. So is the iceberg lettuce. The tomatoes are starting to plump out. A few are the size of golf balls. Big plants, little plants. All of them must be fantastic, because the bugs are lined up to take a bite.

Alas, my garden seems to be the target of every hungry creature in town. The leaf lettuce, for instance. Usually it withers and dies the first week or so. Not this year. It is growing so fast I can't keep it back. But every leaf looks as though it was an innocent bystander in a shotgun battle. The leaves are holier than thou.

And the tomato plants. I am told that the actual tomatoes spring forth from the little yellow buds that grow here and there. True to tradition, my little yellow buds pop out, I admire them, and the next day they are gone. A nubby stub is all that's left. Some creature comes in and nibbles at my flowers.

The bell peppers are yet another example. My bell has been rung by a gang of night robbers. The parsley has been plundered. The roses and daffodils are war brides from the losing side. And some bulbs I planted have yet to make their entrance at all, in any fashion. I fear there is no reason to send a search party down the mine shaft to see if there is any sign of life. Get the padre.

Every farmer knows the dangers of bugdom. In the good old days we could fight back: a crop duster would spray something that would make the plants look good for the counter even if it caused acne on your toes. But now all of those dandy chemicals have been taken off the market due to pressure from the bug lobby.

Alas, the same problems that face the farmers also plague those of us who plow the peat of a cracked pot. The great old goo we used to use has been declared unsafe. Discipline has broken down completely, so we must try to get by with a slap on the wrist.

I bought a bag of something that sounded terrible but really didn't work against bugs. It only whetted their appetite. "A dash more, if you please," they would yell up at me between bites.

Gad. Look at this feast for beasts. Perhaps if I laced the powder with Tylenol, or added a dash of jalapeño. I've got it. Liver. Of all God's curses on humanity, the smell of liver ranks right up there with swarms of locusts, hurricanes, and the Oilers front office. Yes, liver. But wait. What if bugs groove on liver? They probably love it. Bugs from as far away as the Heights will get the word that I am serving up liver-flavored poison. I'll be knee deep in voracious vultures.

There are organic gardeners who believe that insecticides are harmful not only to bugs but to people as well. There are also people who believe the earth is flat, Congress is wise, and if you borrow a trillion dollars from your grandchildren it really isn't borrowing. My poisons are harmful to me but not to my bugs. I think I've got things reversed. Maybe I opened the wrong end of the bag.

My caladiums are not here. They are rotting down there in the ground somewhere. I bought and planted them last year and it was a veritable forest of caladiums I had. Come the fall I was told to dig up the bulbs, dust them with some sort of powder (a box for a mere $4.96), and hang them in my attic, in a set of panty hose. It seems that panty hose are great for ventilation, strength, and supple support. I will not tell you what the air conditioning repairman said.

After all of that work to save my caladium crop, I dutifully replanted them in the garden this spring. By actual count, 32 bulbs were planted. I have two sprigs. Two lousy spring sprigs to show for my work. It must be the bugs, for I know way down deep it couldn't be me.

Yes, the bugs. They are out there even now. I caught one the other day, a short, green caterpillar, with a napkin tied around his little neck, a small bottle of Lafitte Rothschild breathing next to the hot rolls. I stomped him flat.

But he has friends. At night I can hear them singing and munching and telling a waiter, "The next round is on Ortho. Munch-munch."

"A good lettuce, but not a great lettuce."

"A pretentious tomato, yet with an alluring bouquet of clever withdrawal."

"I'll have one from row 2 and two from row 1."

"Do you have something in a '44 fungicide?"

All right, enough is enough. I am waiting out here at midnight, knowing full well that the gang of gnattily attired pests will come out from their cocoons just about now. They will scan the menu, then tackle my garden. But I'm ready. No more Mr. Nice Guy.

Locked and loaded, lieutenant.

Aha! There's the little nipper. Blam! Take that! And that! That's for ol' Sarge, and for Stinky and Tex and the kid from Brooklyn! Blam! Gotcha!

The smoke is clearing as the lights go on around the neighborhood and the wail of a siren is heard. I carefully check my crop. Yep, here's one of the enemy. Half of another. Nailed that ol' bugskin to the wall. The bad part is, I'm too late. My garden looks like it was an innocent bystander in a shotgun battle.

Head Aches

Good headline writing, like good lovemaking, is more difficult than it looks. Oh, anyone can go through the motions, but actually capturing not only the facts, but the spirit, of the situation is a challenge indeed.

For one thing, you've got to tell what happened in a very few words, since, by their very nature, headlines have to be short. For instance, Henry Kissinger was reportedly, but not necessarily, drawing up a peace treaty for the Middle East. You can't say:

HANK 'WRITES' PACT

That's short, but not clear and far too cutesy-pie for a serious matter. So what did the *Houston Post* do?

KISSINGER ALLEGEDLY
FORGES MIDEAST PACT

That caught the spirit of the story, but somehow was not a clean hit. Here are some more, again noting that it's a lot easier to criticize heads than to write them yourself. This one appeared in a Houma, Louisiana, paper:

NEGRO CHARGED
WITH BATTERY

From the *Post* a few years ago:

NUDITY IN FILMS STILL SPREADING,
BUT SLACKS OFF WHERE IT BEGAN

The *Dallas Morning News* ran this gem:

FRIENDS NOTICED CHANGE
IN SLAIN DENISON MAN

The *Macon*, Georgia, *News* readers must have taken notice last August when they read:

DEAD EXPECTED TO RISE

Sometimes a two-line headline will get one line from one story and the second from another. Thus the *Daily Oklahoman* came up with:

CROPS, STOCK PRICES DIP
TO HONOR SAM RAYBURN

If you think these are wild, you should see the ones that never make it to you. Not long ago here at the *Post* some headline writer suggested:

EUELL GIBBONS DIES
OF NATURAL CAUSES

Another one that never made it off the drawing board was:

QUAKE RATTLES CHINA

One of the biggest problems in headline writing is when the person's name might have another meaning. When an educator named Shaver died, the *Houston Chronicle* came up with:

RITES HELD FOR FORMER
SCHOOL HEAD SHAVER

An AP story about an English lord being arrested was headlined in one paper:

LORD HELD IN THEFT

Ah, yes, the old headline game. Every journalist has his favorites, most of which are too dirty to put in a family newspaper, even though they once appeared in a family newspaper. There is a great double entendre about a fast-zippered former Oklahoma governor that I can't use, so how about this one instead?

LOUISIANA GOVERNOR DEFENDS
HIS WIFE, GIFT FROM KOREAN

Considering the vast number of words in any newspaper any day, the wonder of it is that there aren't more typographical errors than there are, but there are enough, and sometimes they pop up in headlines:

THE PUBIC RECORDS

Here's another, which caused a certain amount of snickering around the *Oklahoma City Times*:

VATICAN RITES
BEAUTIFY FIRST
AMERICAN NUN

And one that appeared in the *Amarillo Daily News* was:

GIANT QUACK SHAKES YUGOSLAVIA

Needless to say, some journalists get rather uptight about these headlines, although all I have been using have been given to me by journalists, many of whom wrote them and, today at least, find them all rather amusing. At the time, they were a bit testy about it all.

Columbia Journalism Review each month runs on the inside of the back cover a little item called "The Lower Case," which is a compilation of errors in the industry, and many of them are headlines. From recent issues, we have:

COLD WAVE LINKED TO TEMPERATURES

That came from the *Daily Sun-Post* in San Clemente, California. And the *Norwich Bulletin*, which came up with a catchy headline:

MARITAL DUTIES TO REPLACE
BOROUGH AFFAIRS FOR HAROLD ZIPKIN

We must hope that Mr. Zipkin once worked on a copy desk and thus realizes the built-in pitfalls of headline writing. If so, he will have sympathy with the *Chicago Daily News* editor who noted:

WOMAN BETTER AFTER BEING
THROWN FROM HIGH-RISE

Or the *Detroit News* copy-desker who proclaimed:

ADMITTED KILLER OF 4 WOMEN
GETS 93 YEARS IN WASHINGTON

It all goes to prove, as the *Indianapolis Star* so proudly hailed:

NEWSPAPER IS AMERICA'S MOST
VALUABLE EDUCATIONL AGENCY

Foiled Again

Harold Wilson, the former prime minister of Britain, has discovered the true reason for his nation's economic difficulties.

No, it is not the balance of payments problem, nor runaway inflation caused by spending more than it has, nor the labor unions, nor the oil shortage, nor even the welfare state that changed that once proud and mighty land into, in Prince Philip's words, "a third-rate nation." The villain is the United States.

Right. Us. We are to blame, and I, for one, feel it is certainly an inarguable conclusion. To get specific, Wilson lays the blame on the World War II Lend-Lease program, which provided Britain with a watch to time its finest hour.

He noted that, as one example, the jet engine was a British invention, yet the idea was given away scot-free after the war to pay off Britain's debts. "If we had got 100 pounds ($170) for every jet engine that was built, we would have had a terrifically favorable balance of payments," Wilson said. Indeed, that very sentence shows just how right he is. "We had got 100 pounds ($170)" used to read, only a few years ago, "we had got 100 pounds ($450)."

All that has changed. It changed when those Yanks arrived, Coke bottles and nylon hose in hand, and fleeced the Brits of their best ideas. We had no pride. We looted in the fields. We stole in the villages. We ripped off their blood, sweat, and tears, marked them up 10 per cent, and sold them back. Even their own jet engines were shrewdly stamped "Made in USA," then sold back to Britain to be used in a perfectly fantastic idea that we somehow overlooked: the Concorde.

From 1946 until 1976, we systematically loaned Britain $6,222,200,000 in our diabolical plot to steal their jet engines. It was such a secret operation that even today many British don't know about it, and get along with the Yanks better than they get along with Harold Wilson.

Yet Wilson is right, and it goes even further than he knows, for we did not limit our greed to that one unfortunate country. No, we went through the world from 1946 to 1976 fleecing countries at every chance, handing out money for inventions like so many gun traders dispensing firewater and rifles for land and pelts.

We loaned money to Afghanistan, Albania, and Algeria. To Kenya, Korea, and Kuwait. Norway got almost $1.5 billion, Pakistan almost $5 billion, Sweden more than $231 million. We showed no mercy. Mexico reluctantly took more than half a billion, South Africa $34 million. Spain bit the bullet and accepted more than $2.4 billion, knowing all the while that the Americans were making off with the family jewels.

Harold Wilson, you have caught us at last. How we spread over the globe like a postwar horde of locusts, ramming more than $12 billion in aid on poor, unsuspecting Korea. Demanding that the Philippines take almost $2.5 billion, pouring $1.5 billion on Jordan, more than $2 billion on Egypt, and almost $7.5 billion on Israel.

We played both sides of the street, we did, showing no favoritism. And when other nations dug in their heels and adamantly refused to take another dollar from our slimy hands, we used cover men, such as CENTO ($52 million) and other assorted worldwide cover organizations ($30 billion).

Here is $1.2 billion for the Russians, $2.1 billion for the Dutch, $4.3 billion for the Greeks, and $5.4 billion for the Italians. South Vietnam was the big loser, with more than $22.7 billion showered from Washington in our futile attempt to steal Saigon's corporate secrets. Rubbing salt in the wound after World War II, we flaunted our victorious might by forcing $3.7 billion on the Germans and $3.3 billion on the Japanese. It was certainly one of our low points, making the exploits of ITT and Lockheed pale into insignificance.

It seems that in the last 30 years we have given out $181 billion to other countries as part of our diabolical plot. The UN and other such groups got almost $8 billion, while the funds for guns to Korea, Vietnam, and the Middle East came to $161 billion. Then there was the interest paid on what we borrowed for this program—$185 billion.

It all comes to $536,672,567,000, or more than half a trillion dollars. Frankly, considering the size of our national debt, I think it would have been cheaper to have given Harold Wilson that $170 per jet engine.

Putting on Heirs

It all began when I discovered that I was not bettering myself. I needed to change my approach to life.

"What you need," my career consultant told me, "is a new job."

"What kind of new job?"

"Become a doctor."

"I tried that for two years in college. Didn't work."

"Be a lawyer."

"I have my pride."

"Then there is just one thing to do. You've got to be an heir."

"An heir?" I repeated. "You mean not work for the money, just inherit it?"

"Of course. It's the American way."

The idea sounded all right, so I started checking into my father's fortune, only to discover that he had sunk everything into a six-pack. So I asked my mother.

"I gave at the office," she said.

"But Mom, my career adviser says I should be an heir. It's the only way I'll ever amount to anything."

"Then check the family tree," she said. "Maybe the family fortune is hidden in there somewhere."

I began my search immediately. Grandfather Ulysses Ottawa Ashby had been a land agent during the oil boom. No doubt he had slipped a few deeds to the Kilgore field into a shoe box. By now the stack of royalty checks must be enormous.

"Ulysses Ottawa Ashby," said the clerk, shuffling through the shoe box. "Yep, sure did."

"I knew it!"

"Sold out, though. Some guy named Sid Richardson, for $5.50 plus a slightly used vest. You can see it's signed right here."

My mother's father was a railroad man. Well, actually, he and Jay Gould weren't exactly drinking buddies. But it was obvious that Grandfather Lynn Cox had squirreled away in his trunk vast amounts of railroad stock.

"Controlling interest, he had," said Cousin Elmo, poking through the trunk.

"I knew it! In what?"

"The Houston, Galveston & Havana Railroad."

"Never heard of it."

"Went broke building the bridge."

"I guess you had to be there."

"The key to the family fortune," Aunt Effie said, "was Nimrod Ashby."

"Which Nimrod?" I asked. "We had five."

"Nimrod the Weasel. He ripped off the rest of the family and reportedly hid the treasure at the family homestead. Refused to talk, even when they fastened the rope."

"Where?"

"Winchester, Virginia, naturally," said Uncle Ed Joe. "That's the first town in the New World we were run out of."

More digging in musty libraries, hot on the trail of my rightful fortune. Alas, it turns out Nimrod hadn't kept his fortune. He had lost everything in an attempt to franchise Aaron Burrgers.

I found this bit of family history:

> Clarke County: The great road to Belhaven [Alexandria].
> Along this old road were brought the Hessians — prisoners
> captured by Daniel Morgan at Saratoga and elsewhere. A
> party of Hessian prisoners were passing along the old moun-
> tain road. They halted for rest near the home of Thomas
> Ashby. The men-folk were all away in the Continental Army
> and Mrs. Ashby and a couple of her younger children came
> out to see the prisoners.
>
> In the party was a Major Greene, an Englishman, who
> was also a prisoner. He asked Mrs. Ashby for a drink of
> water, which she gladly gave him, saying that she was
> pleased to furnish him with it under the circumstances; also
> that she would like to furnish all the British Army, if those
> would come along in that way. The major, who was a
> gentleman, saw the point and laughed, and asked if her hus-
> band was in the American Army. "Oh, yes," she said. "My
> husband and oldest son helped to capture Burgoyne," and,
> pointing to a little fellow 10 or 12 years of age, said, "My
> other boy is going to help take Cornwallis next year."

I'm rich! Gentleman Johnny always lived well. We must have liberated the silver tea service, jewels, and pay chest. But more digging in official records determined the full amount of the fortune:

> Thomas Ashby, 2nd Virginia State Regiment. On 15
> March to 1 May 1778, he drew $10 for one and a half months
> duty. April 1778 at Valley Forge he enlisted for three more

years. May at Valley Forge, pay for that period six and two-thirds dollars; month of June at Brunswick, pay for June six and two-thirds dollars, month of July at White Plains, same pay, August at White Plains, same pay, remarks: "three days fatigue."

That's it? Thomas got a lousy six and two-thirds dollars a month? How could he have done that to me? More digging further back: Captain John Ashby of the 2nd Virginia Rangers went to Kentucky to fight with Daniel Boone against the Indians in the French and Indian War in 1774. "In consideration of military service rendered to the Colony of Virginia by John Ashby in the Indian Wars," he was granted a large slice of Kentucky and was given a silver watch by the House of Burgesses for gallant service. I'm the king of Kentucky!

Going back earlier, here's a copy of an entry from 1748. "Saturday, March 12th. This Morning Mr. James Genn ye surveyer came to us we travell'd over ye Blue Ridge to Capt. Ashby's on Shannondoah [sic] River, Nothing remarkable happen'd." That is out of a diary written by a young surveyor and family friend, G. Washington. Four years later to the day, he stopped by and spent the night at "Col. Ashby's." Quick promotions in those days.

More research revealed that we lost Kentucky in a horse race, someone stole the silver watch, and to his dying day G. Washington denied he ever slept there, but did admit that Colonel Ashby was his spelling coach.

"I'm not hacking it as a professional heir," I told my career consultant. "I'm thinking of changing jobs."

"Funny you should mention that," he said. "I'm thinking of doing the same thing."

Pigskin Report

Some of you may have missed this UPI dispatch from Vienna, so I bring it to your attention because it is too important to be overlooked.

American football is heading for Europe. A group of U.S. businessmen plans to field a football league in Europe, with teams scattered from Turkey to Scandinavia. But what about the iron grip of soccer, you say? Alas, it appears that soccer is out. Julius

Ukraincyk, Europe's number one soccer promoter, flatly predicts
"the death of soccer."

And Jakob Reisner, former manager of Austria's greatest team,
Rapid S.C., agrees: "Soccer is a game with 19th-century rules played
before crowds with 21st-century minds. Present-day crowds are
looking for something new, more dramatic, more dynamic—just
the kind of thing United States football can offer."

Actually, such a move is not so mind-boggling as it may first
appear. It is a well-traveled road—in reverse. For instance, Reisner's
former right wing at Rapid, Toni Fritsch, now suits up for the
Houston Gamblers. Each year even more top soccer starts try out
in this country as kickers. They have seen the handwriting on the
scoreboard—not to mention on the paycheck.

But such a plan is fraught with peril. First, what language would
you use when the Dutch play the Italians? The Turks take on the
Swedes? They get along well enough today when they play soccer
because everyone knows the rules. But starting out new like this,
well, it's going to be a sticky AstroTurf.

A simple word like "hike," for instance. The Spanish would call
it *el hiko*, the Dutch would spell it *hykkej*, and the French, who
are busily throwing out English words, would rather die than use
it at all. Perhaps *l'snappe* would work in a pinch (pronounced
"peench").

There might be no objection in West Germany to an official throwing out a red flag to mark an infraction of the rules, but would the
communist bloc see it as a political statement? It would seem a shame
for a clipping penalty to start World War III. Or imagine how it
would sound to click on your radio in time for the announcer to
scream: "Finland's defense is crumbling and Russia is going for the
long bomb!" That would spin your spine.

Let us assume for a moment that a German team would not mind
100,000 frantic Frenchmen screaming, *"Geaux, l'team Geaux!"* But
would fistfights develop over whether it is the *dix, diez, d'ehsuht,
dez, deka,* or *dieci*-yard line? Or perhaps, when in Rome, the
X-yardline?

There is also the problem of national animosities creeping into
the games. So we must pity the poor officials who try to keep
gridiron peace when Russia plays Germany, not to mention Turkey
vs. Greece, or Canterbury vs. Dresden. At least when the Ulster
Protestants take on the Ulster Catholics everyone can cheer for the
Fighting Irish.

No doubt headline writers would move in to fan the flames of nationalistic passions:

LONDON PLASTERS PARIS

BERLIN BLITZES ROTTERDAM

STONEHENGE SHATTERS GLASGOW

DUTCH DAM UP GOAL FLOW

And one can only shudder at the culinary headline concoctions when Hamburg plays Frankfurt. Or after a hard-fought battle of the Leningradiron, *Pravda* might report PEOPLE'S PACKERS 19, RUNNING DOGS 14 after Crazylegs Ivanovich caught the winning pass from Red Square Joe Namitski in the last three seconds of the game. Crazylegs had dropped the 10 passes thrown to him during the preceding three seconds.

So, as one can see, there are still some details to be worked out before Europe really gets the hang of American football. How can we explain to the Commissar for People's Sports that when an American is down and out he's not really down and out? It is doubtful that a Scottish seamstress would understand the accurate definition of a fly pattern. And Lord help the BBC sportcaster who tries to imitate Howard Cosell.

But this will not be the first time that Europe has seized upon an American import with joy and gusto. Levi's, Coke, chewing gum, and gang muggings are now part of the Continental way of life. When the 3-M Company can sell Scotch tape in the Highlands, we've nothing to fear. So it should not sound too strange for a Madrid fan to run through the Plaza del Toros waving his pennant and shouting, "We're *número uno!* Hook 'em!"

One final job before the first kickoff should be relatively easy: names for the teams. Most are obvious. The Roman Gabriels, the London Bridges, the Moscow Mules. Some towns may opt for rhymes, such as the Munich Eunuchs. (You are probably one of the wiseacre types who say that they pronounce it "*Munch*-en," but I happen to know that eunuchs can't pronounce anything right. So there.)

I personally like the Buda Pests, although Hungary might not. Then there are the Istan Bulls, the Venetian Blinds, the Brussels Sprouts, the Bergen Edgars, and the Geneva Conventions. But the

final stamp of approval for this new export to the Continent will
be when there is grumbling along the Riviera after the Nice Guys
finish last.

In any event, it's going to be a whole new ball game.

Remembering

"I have a grand memory for forgetting," Robert Louis Stevenson
wrote in "Alan Breck." And don't we all?

Remembering anything for very long is an anguishing experience.
To aid us, we have schools and magazine articles and books, but
they don't always work. Like the fellow who had such a
photographic memory because he went to the Sam Carnegie
Memory School.

All of them rely heavily on memory aids, called mnemonics. That
is, you tie things together so when you remember one, the others
follow naturally. For instance, if at a cocktail party you are introduced to a fellow named Small, and he is four-foot-nine, remember
that Small is small. If he is six-foot-seven, tough.

In an effort to solve the problem, a fellow named Scott Morris,
writing in a California publication of Mensa, and reprinted by the
Gulf Coast chapter's monthly newsletter, *InforMensa*, goes into it
a little deeper. Morris notes that most people use mnemonics simply
to remind themselves of two concepts and two names that get confused. Dichotomy mnemonic, it is called. For instance, do you set
your clocks forward or backward in the spring at the beginning of
Daylight Saving Time? "Spring forward, fall back" is the old tried
and true.

Stalactites and stalagmites are another. One is up there hanging
from the roof, the other comes up from the floor. Morris always
remembers which is which because the *c* in stalactite stands for ceiling and the *g* in stalagmite stands for ground. He has a friend who
pictures the *m* in stalagmite as a pair of them rising from the ground.
Another friend recalls that a stalac*tite* must stick tight up to the
ceiling while the stalag*mite* rises mightily from the floor.

Then there is the confusion over whether it is the Indian or the
African elephant that has the big ears. Morris remembers the *A* for
African—a big *A*, triangular, like an elephant's ear. That's it! The
African elephant has the big ears.

All of which does no good at all in telling the difference between an alligator and a crocodile, a turtle and a tortoise, a seal and a sea lion. You have to ask them.

There is also the mnemonic series, a more complicated form using initials. The best known is the one to remember every other note on the musical scale used for making chords: "Every Good Boy Does Fine." The initials correspond (E, G, B, D, F). The nine planets, from the sun outward, can also be remembered by the initials: "Mary very easily makes John send us news promptly." (Mercury, Venus, Earth, Mars, Jupiter, Saturn, Uranus, Neptune, Pluto.)

Some mnemonics are more trouble than whatever it is you're trying to remember. This solar system code, for instance: "My Victrola ensconces marijuana joss sticks, unless nepotism palls." On the other hand, it's so outrageous that it sticks in your mind.

Some lists can be remembered in more ways than one. The colors of the spectrum in order could be Roy G. Biv (red, orange, yellow, green, blue, indigo, violet) or Morris' own, more colorful version going in the other direction: "Very interesting: buxom girls yell out rape."

In pre-war (the Two) days, Washington bureaucrats could remember the cabinet officers in order of their rank with "St. Wapniac"—State, Treasury, War, Attorney General, Postmaster General, Navy, Interior, Agriculture, and Commerce. These days, it would be St. Dapiaclhewhudt, which would probably get you in trouble with the feds, not to mention the Vatican.

Naval officers occasionally refer to "Timid virgins make dull companions," which is the basis for all navigational works, and is handy to remember during shore leave, too. It stands for "True course + Variation = Magnetic course + Deviation + Compass course."

In his novel *Arrowsmith*, Sinclair Lewis quotes an old medical mnemonic to sort out the main nerves of the head, something about "On old Olympus' topmost top, a Finn and German viewed a hop." I haven't the foggiest idea what it means, but it sounds important.

I used to have a terrible time separating the NAACP from the NCAA until I remembered that NAACP could stand for Never Attack Adam Clayton Powell. I could differentiate between starboard and port because of a long drinking story that ended, "They had some port left." A quicker way is to remember that both port and left have the same number of letters.

Outdoorsmen remember to avoid coral snakes because "Red and yeller kills a feller." Unfortunately, this also creates havoc at traffic lights. Some tough ones can be reduced to simplicity with the use of a good mnemonic. For instance, to spell Connecticut just remember, "To Connect I cut." This does me no good with Cincinnati, however.

And my kingdom for a good mnemonic gimmick to remember whether it is John Adams or John Quincy Adams, all together or altogether, Jack Parr or Jack Paar. Flammable or inflammable are easy because they both mean the same thing, but is Breckenridge a park in San Antonio or a town in West Texas? And would some timid virgin please step forth to remind me when it is heroine, not heroin?

We can only take comfort in remembering that Nietzsche said, "Many a man fails to become a thinker for the sole reason that his memory is too good." At least I think it was Nietzsche, if he's the fat, triangular-eared German who ensconces marijuana. Then again, maybe it was St. Dapiaclhewhudt.

Why Do I Spend Christmas Morn With the Pope and 5,000 Parts?

THE FLOOR—It has become an annual tradition in my happy home, not so much out of design as out of demand. It is early Christmas morning and I am sitting here on the floor desperately trying to insert Part 27-C into Part 27-D.

This happens every single Christmas dawn no matter how hard I try to circumvent the inevitable. I may start right after Thanksgiving to put together a bicycle or Ping-Pong table or whatever, but things never work out. The gift is too obvious to leave lying around, or too big, or I am afraid that some small one will trot into the room just as I am hammering the left-wing rigor into the right-flap stomtang. So I can't begin my work. I have to wait.

A week or so before Christmas, panic sets in. I peep under the bed, into the closet, back in the pits of the garage, and there squats a big, brown box. "This Side Up." "Product of Japan." "Sweat 'R' You."

No matter how I try to get a jump on things, it always boils down to this time, this place, and these background sounds. The time is late Christmas Eve or early Christmas morn, the place is here on the bedroom floor, safely behind closed and locked doors. And the background sounds are always the same. From Rome, specifically, Vatican City, where the pope and hundreds of churchmen are holding Christmas mass in Saint Peter's Cathedral before thousands of parishioners and a few hundred million watching on TV.

I don't watch much, for I am too busy thinking un-Christian thoughts about Japanese toy designers who probably have "I'd Rather Be Invading" bumper stickers. My problem is the instructions. They are always folded into a tight square and put in the plastic bag holding all the small pieces. Once you get the instructions unfolded and spread out on the floor, you see a drawing of the toy, its various pieces unjoined and suspended in midair, with little arrows pointing to where each part goes. There is a coded inscription beside each item.

"Step 32. Adjust please the 55-J comsrat to line up the YU-76 benchlid to on the level." The designer smiles a wry smile and hums the love theme from *Tora, Tora, Tora!*

"Insert to the tri-bar, upwards the C-16 nutt," the instructions read. "Complete to Step 3, then backwards thread A-0 bolt into again rewind the Bar 45." OK, I can handle that. Insert the tri-bar. Where is the tri-bar? *What* is a tri-bar?

It is midnight or past, and in the background, from the TV set, a BBC announcer is giving a description of the pope's actions in breathless, hushed tones. It always reminds me of a golf announcer. "The pontiff now faces the congregation," he whispers. I half expect him to add, "and takes out a nine-iron."

"Into the gilthor insert the Bolt 43." There is no Bolt 43. There may be one back on the floor of an assembly line in Osaka, but there is not one here. And at 1 o'clock on Christmas morning, my chances of securing another one are minimal.

Why is it that when I buy a spatula, I walk out of the store with a spatula? When I buy a radio, same thing. But when I buy a toy, all I actually get is a box full of toy parts. The rest is up to me. It is a toy I have never put together before, so it takes me a long time. I could assemble the second one in record time, but that never comes up.

"Part 7 the axel into wheels please push. Use mamar if necessary." Mamar? Must be hamar. Close.

At the store they didn't show me a box of toy parts. No, they showed me a toy already put together, ready to use. It saves the manufacturer a buck, making the customer do all the work of assembly. My wife says that if and when we ever buy a new car, she fully expects to go around to the dealer's loading dock where a forklift will bring up a big box stamped, "Sedan, blue," and dump it in our trunk. The rest will be up to us.

"And now the Bishop of Rome faces the altar and lifts up the cup of wine and speaks," a whispering British voice tells me.

I face Wheel 3 and lift up a socket wrench and repeat slowly, "Wheel 3 which snaps place into, please, the Axel 90-90."

And on the other side of the world, a toy designer faces the rising sun, lifts up his voice, and shouts, "Banzai!"

Sharpening City's Image
Without Losing Our Focus

The word was out, whispered in the back halls of the various city bureaucracies, muttered over gin and tonics in the country club bars, slipped quietly into conversations in Turning Basin beer halls: Mayor Kathy Whitmire wants to change Houston's image. "Get away from the cowboy image," she more or less said, "and reflect Houston's true and diversified image."

That raised several questions: What is the mayor up to now? What, pray tell, is Houston's true image? And, specifically, what will be our new sales campaign to lure tourists and conventions to Houston?

As your intrepid reporter, I set out to find out. My first stop was my mole in the mayor's office, Deep Chic.

"You don't understand the wine and cheese crowd at City Hall," he said when we met at 3 a.m. in a pothole on Fannin. "They're absolutely embarrassed about anything that isn't trendy. You know that the NOW chapter doesn't groove on John Wayne and longnecks."

"So what is the city doing?"

"First, we're designing a new city seal. It has crossed jogging shoes over a field of quiche. Below is a profile of Sam Houston in a turtleneck. Also, to show our many diverse qualities, the seal shows a computer printout of a hospital bill to represent the Texas Medical Center, tiles falling off a nose cone to show NASA, also the Astrodome, an oil slick, a billboard, police pickets, and three illegal aliens. Below is the new city motto."

"New city motto?"

" 'Today Montrose, Tomorrow Telephone Road.' "

"Sounds fine."

"The only problem is that the new seal is so big and ornate, it won't fit on anything but city gravel trucks."

"It's a commie plot," said my next source, Billy Bob, as he sat in the back booth of his beer hall. "I got it straight from the Grand Kleagle himself. He has a list of 34 known leprechauns in City Hall. At least Pasadena is still safe for God-fearing Americans."

"I take it you're against any change in Houston's image."

"Naw. We gotta keep up with the times. But if they're gonna spend all that money, then they ought to do it right. You know, show the rest of the world what Houston is really like. Take out ads showing that in Houston you can build anything you want anyplace you want, without some birdwatcher meddling into your business. And we need a snappy new slogan. 'Six Packs and Gun Racks—No Place But Houston.' "

"Not bad. Or, 'Houston—The Big Grapple.' "

"I don't get it," said Billy Bob.

The trail led to a source in the City Image Bureau who told me the town had long since become a modern metropolis. "We don't have cowboys and shootouts and all that. Why, I can walk down any street in my neighborhood and be safe. I never see any of that 'pioneer aggressiveness' and good-ol'-boy stuff people keep talking about. We dropped that long ago."

"That's great. What part of town do you live in?"

"Like most City of Houston employees, I live in Conroe."

After directing four tourists from Chicago to the Simonton Rodeo and a busload of California vacationers to Gilley's in Pasadena, I dropped by a local public relations firm, Flacks 'R' Us.

"When you think of Pittsburgh, you think of steel," said Angelo "Three Lunch" Martini. "When you think of Salt Lake City, you think of Mormons. Los Angeles is Hollywood and Disneyland. San Francisco is the Golden Gate and cable cars."

"Right," I said. "And when you think of Houston?"

"You think that it's only 50 miles to Galveston."

My search was narrowing down. I stopped by the city's ad firm, Smokescreen, Snow, & Fogg. The vice-president in charge of imagery, Bill Board, agreed to talk off the record. "As with any $500,000 ad campaign, the first thing we had to do was justify the cost. That meant a four-volume study with lots of graphs, scales, and pie charts that no one will read. I didn't spend three years with the MTA for nothing."

Board continued: "Our research found that Houston's image is one of oil, cattle, cowboys, and Texas culture. So the mayor was right. We had to change that. Our next survey found that what visitors want to see when they come to Houston is oil, cattle, cowboys, and Texas culture. As you can see, the situation was even worse than supposed."

"I'm not sure I understand this," I said. "If that's what we project and that's what people want, why this big move to change?"

"You're right. You don't understand the ad game," Board sighed. "If our studies had shown that everything is fine, we'd never get to map out a new ad campaign. The big bread is the new campaign. And, of course, the follow-up."

"The follow-up?"

"Sure. After we go through the first half-million to change Houston's image, showing its true diversification, we do a study to find out why tourism has fallen off."

"Then?"

"Then we map out a second campaign. I've already got it thought through."

"What do you do?"

"We launch a multimillion-dollar media blitz to sell Houston as a city of oil, cattle, cowboys, and Texas culture."

Rebellion, Indeed

June the eighth has come and gone without a mention of the Great Pamphleteer, Thomas Paine. You see, that was the anniversary of his deathday, June 8. He died in 1809 in a rooming house at 59 Grove Street in Manhattan and no one missed him, then or now.

He left as he lived — alone. Only one newspaper even mentioned his death back then. The *New York Post* gave it one paragraph, which included the comment "He had lived long, done some good and much harm."

Paine would not have been surprised at his obit, although he could have done much better, for he was a genius with the written word, a propagandist, a man whose reasoning was second to none in the country. George Washington said that Paine "worked a powerful change in the minds of many men," and John Adams said that "without the pen of Paine the sword of Washington would have been wielded in vain."

But if Paine was brilliant, he was also a troublemaker, a boat rocker, an angry zealot, a drunk and a smelly one at that. He made enemies with the same relish that he made friends. He turned on Washington in his later years, calling his onetime good friend and fellow soldier "treacherous in private friendship" and "a hypocrite in public life." Theodore Roosevelt called Paine a "filthy little atheist" and a coach driver once refused to take Paine aboard, saying that he was damned if he'd give a ride to that "infidel."

As you might imagine, Paine lived up to his name. He had a way of touching off strong emotions and spent most of his life being either hailed as a great man or bumped from coaches. In other countries, he was leading parades and drawing up constitutions or languishing in a dungeon awaiting execution. But he dearly loved a cause, and if he couldn't find one, he'd drum one up.

Paine was born abroad, as were 10 other Founding Fathers. In Paine's case it was England, where his father was a Quaker and a corset maker. Paine spent his early years knocking around as a sailor, teacher, and such. He was happily married, but his wife died. He remarried and wished he hadn't. Finally, bankrupt and separated, he came to America in 1774 when he was 37, carrying with him letters of introduction from the American colonial agent in London at the time, Benjamin Franklin.

For the next 18 months he edited the *Pennsylvania Magazine* and mingled with the colonies' small group of intellectuals. And he sensed something in the air: rebellion. Ah, that was Paine's cup of tea (or brandy, actually, although in a pinch, rum and water would do).

Rebellion, indeed. What a splendid boat-rocking idea. But it was an incomplete idea, for no one could really agree on what needed to be done or how. There was a great deal of disorganized emotion running around, so Paine gave it some thought, and this is what he did best. He had a way of reasoning out everything, simple, strong, neat, and clean.

He got it all together in a 47-page pamphlet he called, naturally enough, *Common Sense*. The cover even broke down the matter into four separate categories:

I. Of the Origin and Design of Government in General,
with concise Remarks on the English Constitution.
II. Of Monarchy and Hereditary Succession.
III. Thought on the present State of American Affairs.
IV. Of the present Ability of America, with some
miscellaneous Reflections.

The pamphlet laid it all out in apple-pie order, so that even the thickest backswoodsman could understand that independence from the British crown was the only logical solution. On January 10, 1776, it hit the streets like gangbusters, selling 120,000 copies the first three months and eventually a half-million.

One Philadelphian sent a copy to a friend of his down in Virginia, a planter who was recovering from his own illness and the recent death of his mother. "A present of 2 [pence] worth of Common Sense," the friend wrote, and Thomas Jefferson gave it a reading. "O ye that love mankind! Ye that dare oppose not only the tyranny but the tyrant, stand forth!" Up until then, Jefferson had not made up his mind, but this pamphlet showed the way. Rebellion it would be. It only made, well, common sense.

The fuse that Paine had lit exploded on July 4 into open rebellion, and Paine joined the fight. Not that he was much of a threat, this 39-year-old scholar who was out of shape and rarely sober. He became General Nathanael Green's enthusiastic and voluntary aide-de-camp, and was kept out of harm's way.

But war declared and war won are not the same, and the Revolution went straight downhill. Paine found himself, musket on shoulder, in retreat after disaster, marching across the frozen countryside in an army of scarecrows. In December, the tattered command stopped briefly at Newark and Paine broke out his ultimate weapon. Using a drumhead as a desk, he sat down to write:

> These are the times that try men's souls: The summer soldier and the sunshine patriot will, in this crisis, shrink from the service of his country; but he that stands it Now, deserves the love and thanks of man and woman. Tyranny, like hell, isn't easily conquered; yet we have this with us, that the harder the glorious conflict, the more the triumph.

But the love and thanks of man and woman were not to be Paine's.

Essays and Exits

It was noted that the anniversary of Thomas Paine's deathday went by unmentioned.

This is not so surprising, for he is the least remembered of the Founding Fathers. No one even knows where Paine is buried, or if he is. But it's all part of a pattern. Indeed, he published many of his pamphlets anonymously. In the preface to the third edition of *Common Sense*, Paine explained that the author's true identity really made no difference, since it was "the Doctrine itself, not the Man," that was important in this case.

His famed essay on "the times that try men's souls" was called "The Crisis," and was the first of a dozen by this title. As the Revolutionary War mucked along, the newness of it became jaded and not a few Americans began wondering aloud whether it was the right step. Enter Tom Paine unshaven, obnoxious, brilliant, and smelling like a bar floor. He worked better after a few nips; somehow Demon Rum was needed to oil the wheels of logic. And he would write on. At each crucial juncture, when the colonies were undecided, a new issue of "The Crisis" would sweep the land to lay it all out, simply, logically, showing that there was really only one course of action to take, old shoe. Onward.

In 1780 Paine took a look forward and decided that the Articles of Confederation wouldn't work. What this country needs, he decided, is a strong federal system with safeguards for states' rights. It should be put in writing—a constitution, perhaps. Paine's pamphlet *Public Good* once more hit the mark.

But Paine couldn't stand success. He was his own worst enemy. He kept pushing the nation toward such unwanted goals as abolition of slavery, free public education, equal rights for women, all that sort of troublesome stuff. Paine was wearing out his welcome, even if his arguments did make sense. So in 1787 he returned to England to peddle a new invention of his, a pierless iron bridge. But it wasn't long before he got a new and better idea for a new and better British government—a republic. Simply topple the king, toss out the House of Lords, and be done with it. He put it all down in a new pamphlet, *Rights of Man*, which made such good sense that Paine was indicted for treason.

It was time for another quick exit—Paine was getting experienced at this sort of thing—and he hopped over to France, where a simp-

ly terrific revolution was under way. In short order Paine was trium-
phantly elected to the revolutionary convention, led demonstrations
through Paris, and was sent to the dungeon for explaining so clearly
that Louis XVI should not be executed, only exiled.

Paine figured that his old friend George Washington would bail
him out before the guillotine fell, but Paine was wrong. Finally,
the American ambassador in Paris, James Monroe, rescued Paine
so he could get back into hot water in short order. First, he wrote
Age of Reason in two parts, setting forth his logic for believing in
God without the trappings of organized religion. This was quickly
misconstrued to be an advocacy of atheism, although it was nothing
of the sort.

Next, Paine whipsawed his old friend who had left him in the
French clink, writing a blistering *Letter to Washington.* Tact was
not Paine's strong suit. In any event, after taking on both
Washington and God, Paine returned to America in 1802 something
less than universally loved.

He ended up on a farm in New Rochelle given him by the State
of New York in better times. Paine's lot fell so low that once he
sued a newspaper publisher for libel. The publisher lost the case
but was commended by the court for libeling such a scoundrel. Finally came the ultimate insult. His neighbors in New Rochelle refused
to let him vote because he had served in the French National Convention. Paine argued logically and brilliantly as ever but was refused the vote. After all, he was nothing but a drunken atheist.

The Great Pamphleteer finished his days in Greenwich Village
rooming houses, where he finally died at 72, unmourned. But his
troubles were not over even then. The Quakers refused to bury him
in New York City, so he was taken back to New Rochelle, where
his former housekeeper and her two sons dug a grave and buried
him.

But there's more. In 1819 — 10 years later — a nutty British political
journalist named William Cobbett figured that Paine would be more
honored in England, and stole his body. But Cobbett was wrong;
nobody in England cared either. He willed the bones to his son,
who went into bankruptcy. The remains were passed around and
eventually lost for good.

Paine's fellow Americans felt so bad they composed this little ditty,
as reported by John Deedy in the *New York Times*:

> Poor Tom Paine! here he lies,
> Nobody laughs and nobody cries;

Where he's gone and how he fares,
Nobody knows and nobody cares.

Yank-ed Out

THE FRONT YARD — Hey, there's my new neighbor. The fellow who just moved in. He's standing out by his curb, wearing a raincoat and carrying an umbrella, even though there's not a cloud in the sky. I'll go over and introduce myself.

"Hi, there. Welcome to the neighborhood," I say.

"Hello. Just moved in here. Came from New York City. Name is Ulysses S. Sherman. Stocks and bonds. The wife's into macrame. Transferred here from our Manhattan office."

"That's nice," I say.

"Is it?"

"Huh?"

"Being transferred to Houston. I should be getting hardship pay."

"I don't understand."

"No subways, no Broadway, no Met, no Mets, and your cab service is awful. I've been standing out here for half an hour, and no cab. It's like 44th Street right after show time."

"Well, Mr. Sherman, in Houston we really don't have cabs cruising out here in the neighborhoods. Most of us drive. Just get in your car and drive."

"I don't own a car," says Sherman. "In Manhattan, you don't need one."

"But this isn't Manhattan," I explain.

"You're telling me. I saw one of your buses. Not a bit of spray-can graffiti on it. Not one. And when, might I ask, was your last blackout?"

"Gee, Mr. Sherman, I don't know. But let me ask you something. Why are you wearing that raincoat and carrying that umbrella? It's not supposed to rain."

"Yes, it is," he says, pulling out a newspaper. " 'Rain expected.' That's what it says, right there."

"But Mr. Sherman, that's the *New York Times*."

"Of course it is. Do you think I'd read anything else?"

"It's a great paper, but not much help in the weather forecast for Houston."

"I get it by mail. It's two days late, but I figure that Houston is at least that far behind New York."

"I take it you are having a bit of trouble getting acclimated to Houston."

"It's not that I haven't tried. I've even been learning your language. Listen to this: Y'all hurree back now, y'heah? Smile when you call me that, sodbuster. Bugler, sound the charge! Take *that*, you commie pinko hippie. I've been taking Texan lessons at Berlitz."

"Mr. Sherman, I think maybe you've got us all wrong. You should learn a bit more about Houston."

"I've been learning. Have to. My company has a policy of getting to know the natives. In Bangladesh, the Ivory Coast, Kuwait, Houston. I've been drinking the water. Even put my children in your local schools."

"Which ones?"

"Kinkaid and St. John's."

"They're fine schools, all right, but not exactly the average."

"Of course not. Your public schools are at least a generation behind ours. I read all about it in *New York Magazine*. Or was it the *New Yorker*? Maybe it was one of your local papers like the *Wall Street Journal*."

"Mr. Sherman, I think you're going through culture shock, coming from the Big Apple out here to Pit City. Maybe you should do it a step at a time."

"Tried that. Wore my three-piece Brooks Bros. tweed suit to work. Wrote angry letters to the editor about Con Ed and the decline of Off Off Broadway. I even had a four-by-five terrace built onto my upstairs bedroom so I could go out and squint into the smog."

"Now, that sounds great. Just like you're back in Manhattan."

"Yeah. So much so that I got homesick. In a burst of emotion I went out to a park to get mugged. All I got was funny looks from joggers."

"I'm really sorry. Maybe you didn't try the right park. I just know you can get mugged if you try hard enough. In Houston we pride ourselves on our muggers."

"About ready to throw in the towel. What can you expect from a city with a balanced budget?"

"Don't give up all hope yet, Mr. Sherman. We'll get worse. Just you wait and see."

"Hope so. But I'd give anything to see an Ed Koch bumper sticker."

"We've got others, Mr. Sherman. Like: 'The Yankees Are Coming Again — Only This Time They're Staying.'"

The Name Game

This morning we are going to sharpen up our wits, hone our minds to a fine edge, brush aside the cobwebs, and shape up. All of which is hard to do while wrestling with the DTs, but we must try.

Take out a pencil and get your scissors. Because we are going to write down the answers and then cut out this column and stick it on the front of the refrigerator with one of those ridiculous little magnets that fall off every time you shut the door after getting a beer and then you spend the rest of the hour on your hands and knees . . . but I digress.

In each case, the answer is a name. Or two. Or three. Names you have read and known and discussed, but they are stuck down there in the nether reaches of your mind, and now you have to recall them. Old friends, long forgotten, ready for a last hurrah. Let us begin.

Who were the Four Horsemen of Notre Dame? All four. (I'll give you a hint. They played in 1923-24. They weighed in at 151, 160, and two at 162. Those Four Horsemen.)

Who was the Man Without a Country?

Who did Humphrey Bogart play in The *Treasure of the Sierra Madre*? Now, think. Bogart repeated his name several times.

Here's an easy one — name the U.S. Attorneys General under President Nixon. Not the acting ones, just the more or less permanent types.

Who wrote "The Night Before Christmas"?

So far, so good. OK, another sports question. Everyone knows that Hank Aaron hit his record 715th home run, but who pitched it to him?

Who ran for vice president on the same ticket with Barry Goldwater in 1964? Who ran on the Democratic ticket with James Cox in 1920? (Think, now. It's easier than it looks.)

You are quite probably batting .1000, so let's dig a little deeper. Who said:

"This generation of Americans has a rendezvous with destiny"?
"In two words: im possible"?
"Every dog has his day"?

Moving right along, name the Hardy Boys.

Back in that same era, who was the head football coach at the University of Texas before Darrell Royal?

We all know that the assassination of Archduke Francis Ferdinand of Austria-Hungary touched off World War I. But who shot him?

What was the name of the Army sergeant that Phil Silvers played in the TV show of yesteryear *You'll Never Get Rich*?

Who invented the crossword puzzle?

Who were the first two men to climb Mount Everest? Come on, now, it was big news not so very long ago. Rack your brain. You know the names, they are just back there in the dust somewhere.

Here's an easy one: name the Three Musketeers.

Who was the first Texas governor to be elected to three full terms?

Hey, you're really scoring today. So, no doubt, you will also know who was the first governor of Texas. Oh, come now. Think. No it wasn't Sam Houston. Think again.

Who rode a horse named Copenhagen and who rode Marengo?

Absolutely astounding, the way your mind pierces to the very truth. OK, everyone remembers the first men on the moon — Neil Armstrong and Edwin "Buzz" Aldrin — who were in *Apollo 11*. But who was next? They were in *Apollo 12*, if that's any hint.

Obviously you are also a Biblical scholar, so which of the Disciples was a medical doctor?

One final question. Everyone is excruciatingly full of Watergate information, but to begin at the beginning: who was caught planting bugs in the Democratic campaign headquarters that night of June 17, 1972? Come to think of it, where were you the night of June 17, 1972?

That does it. Now cut this out, put it on the refrigerator door, and tomorrow we'll see how quick, bright, intelligent, and shifty you really are.

Toe-to-Toe Stand

As you recall, yesterday we all took a test to see if we were well versed in a multitude of subjects and could stand toe to toe with the encyclopedia salesman.

First were the Four Horsemen of Notre Dame — one of the best-known groups in the history of American sports, and no one remembers their names. They were Harry Stuhldreher, Jim Crowley, Elmer Layden, and Don Miller.

The Man Without a Country was one Philip Nolan, a U.S. Navy officer, in the story by Edward Everett Hale.

Bogart played the role of Fred C. Dobbs in *The Treasure of the Sierra Madre*.

Now we come to the U.S. Attorneys General in the Nixon administration. First was John N. Mitchell (1969), then came Richard G. Kleindienst (1972), next was Elliot L. Richardson (1973), and finally, former Ohio senator William B. Saxbe.

Who wrote "The Night Before Christmas"? Well, no one, if you want to get picky. Its official title is "A Visit from St. Nicholas," and it was written by, of course, Clement Clarke Moore.

Where were we? Oh, yes. The poor fellow who served up Hank Aaron's 715th home run was Al Downing of the L.A. Dodgers.

Barry Goldwater's running mate on the GOP ticket in 1964 was William E. Miller of Buffalo, New York. They got 52 electoral votes, out of a total of 486. The fellow who ran for the vice presidency with James Cox in 1920 was one Franklin D. Roosevelt, who lost and was never heard from again.

Ah, yes. The quotes. The "rendezvous with destiny" statement was made by the self-same FDR, in his acceptance speech for renomination in 1936.

"In two words: Im possible" was Samuel "Include Me Out" Goldwyn, of course. And "Every dog has his day" is from *Don Quixote* by Miguel de Cervantes.

The Hardy Boys are Joe and Frank.

The head football coach at UT before Darrell Royal was Ed Price, who was removed in 1956 after posting only one victory all year, a 7–6 win over Tulane.

Ah, yes, who shot Archduke Francis Ferdinand? Gavrilo Princip, 18 years old. He planned to kill himself, but the poison he took only made him nauseous. Some days nothing goes right.

Phil Silvers played the part of Master Sergeant Ernie Bilko in *You'll Never Get Rich*.

Crossword puzzles were invented by Arthur Wynne in December of 1913, to fill up some extra space in the *New York World Sunday Magazine*. He called it "Word Cross."

Up atop Mount Everest first were Sir Edmund Hillary and Tenzing Norgay.

The Three Musketeers were Athos, Porthos, and Aramis.

Allan Shivers was the first Texas governor to be elected to three full terms.

The first governor of Texas was the ever-popular J. Pinckney Henderson: February 19, 1846–December 21, 1847.

Now to the horses. The rider of Copenhagen was the Duke of Wellington. The fellow on Marengo was Napoleon—when he could ride (he had a bad case of hemorrhoids).

The second set of men on the moon were two Navy commanders—Alan L. Bean and Charles Conrad, Jr.

The Disciple (one of the 70, not one of the original dozen—just seeing if you're on your toes) who was a doctor was Luke, or Luther if you want to be formal.

And finally, the Watergate eavesdroppers caught in the Democratic offices were James W. McCord, Bernard L. Barker, Frank A. Sturgis, Virgilio R. Gonzalez, and Eugenio Martinez.

Buttered Out

It is a cornerstone of the Reagan administration that social programs will be reduced while defense spending will be increased enormously. More guns, less butter, or in human terms, children will go without lunch so that generals can have more punch. This has come to us so wrapped up in red, white, and blue that I felt rather unpatriotic for even questioning it. Perhaps I was suffering from a military-industrial complex. So I set out to find the truth.

"We need an extra $32 billion right away," said a general. "The commies are gaining on us."

"What will all my money be buying for the military?" I asked.

"Well, for one thing, this," he said. "It's the state of the art. A biological weapon, very hush-hush, if you know what I mean."

"What does it do?"

"It takes on any fungus, bacteria, slime, and dissolves it on contact."

"Sounds fantastic. Where do you use it? In the jungle?"

"Well, no," said the general. "We sprinkle it in the swimming pool at the officers' club."

I checked with an admiral I knew, who assured me the defense budget needed increasing. "Do you realize the benefits a retiring Soviet admiral gets after only 20 years?" he asked. "With our bigger budget, we can have this baby—a pension-sniffing missile. It seeks out and destroys anyone who gets between a retiring admiral and a job with Texas Instruments."

My next stop was at the Agency for More Benefits for Buddies.

"Look," said the former colonel in charge. "I joined the Marines when I was 18. I never took a nickel in unemployment insurance. If I got sick, I didn't get on Medicare like those welfare widows with five kids who are bankrupting this country. No, I went straight to Bethesda Naval Hospital."

I called at the Procurement Agency, U.S. Army. "This is the latest," said the general in charge. "With our new defense budget, we can have one in every military outpost."

"What is it?"

"This is the ice-seeking swizzle stick. A must for every regimental happy hour. It's a steal at $54 each."

"What's this?" I asked, looking at a strange instrument.

"Ah, yes. This is a recoilless double-dipper. It allows you to draw a government paycheck and two government pensions at once while voting against a rampaging bureaucracy and a large federal budget."

"And this?"

"This is one of our most effective weapons. It's the anti-epistle missile. It lets you write angry letters to the editor on government time and stationery questioning the loyalty of reporters you don't like."

My next step was with Hawks, Inc., a defense contractor. "Of course we need the bigger military budget," said the chairman of the board, a retired general. "Else how could we develop this?" With a dramatic wave, he lifted the canvas off a tracked machine with antennae sprouting all over.

"Fantastic," I said, looking at the large boring bits. "It digs foxholes by remote control, right?"

"Eh, not exactly," said the chairman. "This is for desert warfare. It digs sand traps at our golf course."

"Bunker mentality," I said. Further digging located the top-secret Project Banana—whereby a minor civil fight, if properly nursed, causes panic in Congress, which approves billions of dollars for missile systems. "Are we going to launch one of these on a village of 24 cane cutters?" I asked.

"It's commie-symps like you who dilute our vital bodily fluids," explained the project's commander.

Soon I called on an air force captain I knew. "With a bigger budget, we can finally build this MX-23 troop carrier," he said, rolling out the blueprints.

"But it looks like it only carries six people," I said.

"Of course. An executive Learjet isn't big. We try to hold down costs."

"But it's got armchairs and a foldout bar. Where's the armament?"

"It holds six shotguns in the rear, plus rubber boots and duck calls."

I finally got past the Assistant Secretary of Defense for 6th Fleet Basketball Tournaments and the General in Charge of Bugles and Braid and visited the Defense Department Command for Lots of Goodies (COMGOOD).

"I'm not sure you really need all this money," I said. "Particularly considering that health, food, and clothes are going to be taken from the poor."

"Of course we need the money," the colonel replied. "These funds will go to the Three B's, as we call them."

"Bombers, barracks, and bayonets?"

"No, bands, barbecues, and bowling alleys."

Later, over a martini with the admiral in charge of the Pentagon's Office of What to Call the Next Aircraft Carrier, the commander of Fort Palm Springs, and the Assistant Secretary of Defense for Pastry Chefs, I inquired, "Does any of this money go directly to learning how to fight?"

"Fight? What's that?"

"I mean, the top-heavy Defense Department's featherbedding would pale any civilian governmental agency. I've met admirals who never got wet and generals who never fired a shot. Do any of my hard-earned tax dollars go to showing people in uniform how to fight?"

"We've got a splendid new uniform in the works," said the air force colonel in charge of Wild Yonder Blue.

"No, I mean *fight*. Like in, defend our country."

"Dear chap," said the officer in charge of Officers in Charge, "we have the poor to do that."

Stuck Again

THE DEN — All I need is a dab of that glue to attach this part of the front porch lamp to the rest. It should be right in this drawer. I put it here. But it's gone. "All right!" I yell. "Who took the glue?"

Silence from throughout the house. Total silence. It's right here somewhere. I put it in this drawer.

"Daddy?"

"Oh, so you took it. Give it here."

"I didn't take it, whatever it is. I need to know what's an equator."

"I don't care about equators. I'm looking for the glue."

"I need to know. For homework."

"The equator is a line around the earth."

"Which way?"

"Back and forth, east to west."

"Why?"

"I've got my problems, you've got yours. Look it up."

"I did. It says, 'A great circle of the earth lying at right angles to its axis and equidistant from the poles.' "

"Right. That's what I said."

"It doesn't say anything about 'back and forth.' Why did you say that? You said 'back and forth.' "

"Who are you, Racehorse Haynes? Go do your homework." Now where was I? Oh, yes. The glue was in this drawer. I put it here. Now it's gone. Maybe it's here in the . . .

"Daddy?"

"I get rid of a kid and another one pops up. What?"

"Who's Crispus Attucks?"

"He was the first black man killed in the American Revolution."

"Why was he killed?"

"Because he hid the glue from his father." Maybe it's in the tool chest. Yes, it must be there.

"Daddy?"

"Look, your brother and sister have already been in here asking ridiculous questions. You, too?"

"No."

"Good."

"Name two countries named after individuals."

"That does it!" I yell. "*I* am not in school. *You* are in school. Do your own homework."

"Miss Frisbee says it's OK to get your parents' help."

"I do not pay my exorbitant school taxes so that I can answer questions."

"Every child should have the support of his or her parents. We are the hope of tomorrow."

"Who said that, Crispus Attucks?"

"What's a Crispus Attucks?"

Maybe I put it out in the garage. Yes, it's probably on the workbench. I always put my glue in this drawer, but it must have wandered out there by itself. Now I am in the garage, poking through boxes of junk and bundles of stuff.

"Daddy?" comes this call from the house. Sigh. One more who-was-the-third-king-of-Prussia and I shall strangle the school board. I trudge back into the kitchen.

"Don't tell me. There's a phone call from the White House. Amy wants to know whether the Guelfs were members of the medieval political faction in Italy supporting or opposing the pope."

"It was the Ghibellines who supported the German emperors. The Guelfs supported the pope."

"I really don't care, unless they have some glue."

"Why would they want glue? They were descendants of Welf I of Swabia."

"Welf the Sticky? Certainly he had lots of glue around. Maybe you know where he left some."

"You're weird, Daddy." He stalks off.

"All right. You've made me feel guilty. What did you want?"

"Nothing. I didn't want anything. I just came to tell you something."

"What?"

"Rhodesia and Bolivia."

"Are they at war?"

"No, Daddy. Those are the two countries named after people."

"What about America? Named after Amerigo Vespucci."

"There's no such country as 'America.' Miss Frisbee told us."

"She's a traitor. 'America' is the past nominative case of 'United

States.' Look it up. And while you're at it, look into Miss Frisbee, too. She's probably a communist. Or a Louisianan."

It's probably in the glove compartment of the car. Yes, it's got to be there. Glue is always there, and has been ever since King Frederick II conquered the Goths in 1237.

Tips on Houston Floods, or How to Behave While Tide Up in Traffic

THE STREET — It's raining in Houston, which is rather like saying it's snowing in Buffalo, foggy in San Francisco, or slow in Fort Worth. It often rains here. Thus far this year we've received 11.97 inches of rain at the airport, almost 3½ inches less than normal for this time of year.

Rain is nice. It keeps the plants green and the streets clean, but it can mess up things. It can ruin parades, picnics, family outings. Sometimes it even cancels baseball games. That's right. On July 26, 1979, it rained so hard that the Astrodome was marooned in a sea and the game had to be postponed. There is probably an asterisk in the record book on that date.

While the rains are nice, flooding isn't. More and more the rains create flooding and more and more we hear people say, "It's getting worse." That is not quite true. It is worse now than a few years ago, but the flooding situation is much better than it was several decades ago.

There are vast numbers of people living in Houston right now who remember the bayous overflowing into downtown. Houston's last major floods were in 1929 and again in 1935. That last one flooded 20 blocks south of Buffalo Bayou and two-thirds of the county. It left seven people dead and caused $2.5 million in damages. In my own neighborhood I met a resident, since deceased, who recalled when her second story got wet. That would have put my front yard about 10 feet under water. So let us not go off half-cocked by saying how much worse flooding is getting. It only shows you haven't been here long enough to compare.

Still, that's not much consolation when you see the waves lapping through your den. So I shall now pass on to you newcomers ways of knowing when and where to buy your house, where to work, and how to survive a heavy dew in Houston.

Never work in an office building that has lifeboat drills.

Never buy a house that the Realtor refers to as "a dandy place at low tide."

Be careful of neighborhoods where the building inspectors use glass-bottomed boats.

Tips for knowing when to worry:

When animals at the Houston Zoo start lining up two by two.

When NASA gets ready for a splashdown — and the capsule is landing at Hobby.

When your neighbors begin putting wipers on the *inside* of the windshields.

When the Houston Symphony strikes up "Nearer My God to Thee."

When you own lakefront property in the Heights.

When a coworker looks out your fourth-story office and says, "Surf's up."

When you go to sleep on a Beautyrest, but wake up on a water bed.

There have been some complaints that the city is not doing enough to combat flooding in Houston. This is, of course, a political accusation. Actually, much has been done to solve the problem. For instance, the City Council has demanded that the Army Corps of Engineers draft little Dutch boys. It has appointed cruise directors for MTA buses. The new city planner is Lloyd Bridges. Finally, most of the City Council has invested in Brenham.

Much of our trouble comes from the west. The vast reservoir and bayou channeling plan to drain all the rainfall into the Gulf has been neatly undermined by extensive building in western Harris County and even up to Montgomery County. Every square foot of concrete poured in those places is one less square foot to absorb rainfall. Unhindered by such silly notions as land control, retaining ponds, dikes, or even responsibility, developers have made those areas aquatic freeways eager to dump a tidal wave on the rest of us. They, of course, will remain dry and thus will be able to watch us grabbing for a passing Wendy's.

Fortunately, if you live in the city of Houston itself, you are lucky, for you could live in Kemah or Friendswood or League City. Every expert who has looked at the matter says that the next hurricane to come into Galveston Bay will solve most of the civic problems of those areas simply by doing away with those areas. The only survivors will be the Vietnamese boat people who stayed that way.

Hurricanes not only blow down everything around but touch off tornadoes and create extremely high tides. Then a foot of rain falls on everything. It is a one-two-three punch guaranteed to increase your insurance rates and give excellent training for the National Guard.

Not to paint too black a picture of all of this, look at the bright side: you can be buried at sea and never leave home. In any event, I should like to point out several steps that can be taken to avoid appearing on the 10 o'clock news:

First, next flight listen to the flight attendant explain how to inflate your life preserver.

Store a three-day supply of food in your wallet.

Buy a condo atop Mount Houston.

And stick close to the Houston Rocket of your choice.

Well, that covers most points. I hope I have made the flood plain. Venice, anyone?

Innocent Days

Nostalgia is all the rage these days, as we look backward in search of times past that will ease the burden of times present. How fun it is to recall those innocent days of yore, and our pitiful little worries over the atomic bomb, Joe McCarthy, and the Depression.

The problem is, however, nostalgia is so popular it is almost impossible to find a decade not already claimed. *American Graffiti* has seized the '60s, and the '50s are totally overrun with claim stakers. The Andrews Sisters are back on Broadway with the '40s, a new TV series called *Manhunter* is set in the '30s, and Gatsby has a copyright on the Roaring '20s. So with all these archeological gold diggers working the pits, a mere amateur is hard put to find a virgin decade.

Yet, after much work, I have discovered one. The '40s, those gay, mad '40s. What a war. What elections. Yes, the 1840s, when President William Henry Harrison delivered the longest presidential inaugural address (8,441 words) during a driving rain, promptly

caught pneumonia, and died. When the U.S. population jumped
from 17 to 23 million, including 1.7 million immigrants and 3.2
million slaves.

Fifty-four Forty or Fight! The cornerstone is laid for the Washington Monument. Texas joins the Union. And in Richmond,
Virginia, two newspaper editors agreed to a duel with the traditional pistols. When both fired and neither was killed, they went
at it with bowie knives, tomahawks, and, finally, broadswords. The
survivor was brought to trial and quickly acquitted.

Ah, yes, those fun-filled '40s. Quite a few people were born then,
including Buffalo Bill, Carry Nation, Thomas Edison, Alexander
Graham Bell, the Czar Alexander III. To make way for them, several
died, as well. For instance, John Jacob Astor, Beau Brummell,
Frederic Chopin, 1,733 U.S. troops fighting the Mexican Army—
another 11,000 died from disease—and John Chapman. The last,
as you may recall, lived in the Ohio River valley, mostly in rags
because he gave away everything he had. (He had been a little weird
ever since he was kicked in the head by a horse.) Chapman died
in 1845, but his memory lives on in the form of thousands of apple
trees he planted. Today John Chapman is better known as Johnny
Appleseed.

The good ol' '40s, how we recall with fondness the "Tippecanoe
and Tyler Too" slogan of Harrison and Tyler, and the slanderous
attack on President Martin Van Buren: "Van, Van Is a Used-Up
Man." Harrison carried 19 of the 26 states, showing a dirty politician is an elected politician.

Culturewise, the 1840s saw *Two Years Before the Mast*, *The Gold
Bug*, and *The Communist Manifesto*. But the high point was certainly May 10, 1849, when fans of Edwin Forrest, an American
actor, voiced their resentment over an appearance by his chief rival
for the limelight, a British actor named William Charles Macready.
Once the militia got through with the groupies, there were 22 dead
and 36 injured. They just don't make fans like that nowadays.

This golden decade was when the world first heard Emerson's "A
foolish consistency is the hobgoblin of little minds" and Thoreau
proclaim: "If a man does not keep pace with his companions, perhaps
it is because he hears a different drummer."

The decade also gave us the Donner Party, the California gold
rush, and the Mormons' arrival at the Great Salt Lake. And we saw
the first, faltering steps of the civil rights movement when blacks

aboard the slave ship *Creole* mutinied during a trip from Virginia to New Orleans and forced the officers to land at Nassau. The U.S. government was not amused.

This was when we first used anesthetics as Dr. Elijah Pope yanked a tooth from the head of William E. Clarke, a medical student. Charles Thurber invented the typewriter and Samuel F. B. Morse tapped out "What hath God wrought" over a line from Washington to Baltimore. The U.S. government, which financed the invention, was not interested and dropped its rights. But the big scientific breakthrough of the decade came July 1, 1847 — the very first adhesive U.S. postage stamp went on sale.

Overseas, during this glorious time, there were revolts in Ireland, Venice, Denmark, and France. And although there was no revolt there, the Antarctic was proclaimed a continent. Pope Gregory XVI, a former monk, ran the Vatican like a monastery, and was succeeded by Pope Pius IX, who was supposed to be more liberal. Unfortunately, Pius took the wrong side in Italian politics and had to flee Rome.

Yes, the 1840s are my decade. For where else could one find a New York farmer, William Miller, predicting — according to careful Biblical calculations — the end of the world will come precisely at 3 a.m., March 21, 1843? Some 50,000 of his followers waited on hilltops — the closer to heaven, the shorter the ride — but nothing happened. Miller reluctantly gave the world another chance, and reset the Day of Destruction for 1844.

Austin Revisited

AUSTIN — Hooray, hooray. Kill the fatted halfback, the alumnus is returning. Here I am to see my first football game in Austin since the UT Board of Regents personally threw me out of school and mailed me a diploma six months later.

The campus has changed a bit. All the old courting places are gone. The grass and babbling brooks have been supplanted with concrete buildings and asphalt parking lots. Ah, but the student body is as beautiful as ever. Some things never change.

To get into the true spirit, one must go to Scholz's beer garden for a few drafts before the game. Sing the old songs, remember those good old days. The day we tore the goalposts down, we will have these moments to remember. Dripping with nostalgia, the old grad returns to Scholz's to sit in the yard beneath the trees and harken back to those thrilling days of yesteryear.

Here we are. But it is raining. No sitting in the back yard, we must go inside. Well, no problem, wait, yes, there is. The place is packed unbelievably tight. Hundreds of other old grads intermixed with an equal number of students poking one another with umbrellas, stepping on one another's muddy shoes. The waiters are busier than a Secret Service agent in Floresville.

Out into the night. So much for those moments to remember. We finally find another bar, too crowded. Even a nearby sandwich shop is packed. Here we are now, huddled under the covering of a deserted storefront, dripping wet. Standing up. Hungry. We look rather like those woodcuts showing Napoleon's retreat from Moscow. This is not the way I remember those moments to remember.

Here come the crowds slogging toward the stadium, and it is time to join them. First, one must check out his ticket to see where he sits. I am in 8U, which, according to the little map on the back of the ticket, is underneath the new upper deck. Now this is a mixed blessing. I will be dry, but on the other hand, that new upper deck has never been used before. Tonight is the maiden voyage, and if it sinks I'll be among the first to know.

Through the gate. To the 8U section, just follow the signs. Up steps, then a ramp, then more steps, and finally plunging out into the bleachers. Good grief, everything is changed. Metal benches instead of those wooden ones that left splinters in one's posterior through the following Tuesday. A new scoreboard and flags and everything is painted orange and white. In the classrooms they still pack students into lectures 500 deep, but spare not a farthing for football. Nothing's changed.

The usher eyes my tickets and motions me up the steps. And up. And up. Row 76, the ticket says, and we keep going. Puff-pant. I don't remember the steps being this steep. On row 40, my wife and I set up a base camp, then climb upward. Row 50, all is well, food supply lasting. Row 60. View getting better, air is thinner, weather looking ominous.

Onward. Maybe I should plant a flag when we get to the top. Row 75, getting closer. Hooray, row 76, champagne all around.

We, the Edmund Hillary and Tenzing Norkay of Memorial Stadium, have arrived.

Row 76, seats 19 and 20. What's this? Some interlopers are already sitting in our seats. "You, out." The fellow looks at his tickets then gets up to check his seat number. He is sitting in seats 17 and 18 and has tickets to prove it. Mine must be across the aisle. Of course. "My mistake, I'm sorry." But across the aisle are others sitting there. "You, out." Yet once again they check. They are sitting in seats 23 and 24 with tickets to prove it.

The seat numbers stop with 18 on one side of the aisle but pick up with 23 on the other side. It comes like a thunderbolt that I have been sold tickets to nonexistent seats. Numbers 19 and 20. I have heard of two on the aisle, but this is ridiculous. Even after all these years the UT Board of Regents is still having the last word—probably laughing themselves silly in their 50-yard-line seats.

Down but not out, I seek the services of an usher. He patiently takes my tickets and leads me back, only to make the same discovery: no such seats. He sends me to his superior, who—in turn—sends me to his superior, Paul Goertz, who goes through the same routine only to make the same discovery."This has never happened before," says one usher, looking again and again at my tickets, then at Section 8U.

Mr. Goertz sends me down to find the Big Boss—Mr. Lundstedt (whose name is on the tickets) or Mr. Bolt. I follow route instructions to the office only to find myself outside the stadium, clutching two already-used tickets to two nonexistent seats. By smiles and guiles I get back into the stadium and into the office, where, fortunately, there is a radio so I can hear what's left of the first quarter.

Comes the Big Boss. "Are you Mr. Lundstedt or Mr. Bolt?" I ask. "Neither," he says. That explains everything. I was sold two phantom tickets by two people who aren't. He hears my tale of woe, then writes down numbers for two more tickets that, he assures me, do indeed exist. Then, clutching my piece of paper like a note from my mother, we hit the trail again, this time crawling up to row 60, in section 8. Oddly enough, row 60 is by the 8U entrance. We sit down just in time for the halftime festivities featuring a Boy Scout rope bridge.

A burglar was busy when we returned from the game and the car's water pump blew out in Smithville, giving us even more moments to remember. Dear Mom, send money. Nothing's changed.

A Call to Danger

MYKAWA AND ALMEDA-GENOA ROADS—"Most journalists are restless voyeurs who see the warts on the world, the imperfections in people and places," Gay Talese wrote in the opening paragraph of *The Kingdom and the Power.*

"The sane scene that is much of life . . . does not lure them like riots and raids, crumbling countries and sinking ships, bankers banished to Rio and burning Buddhist nuns—gloom is their game, the spectacle their passion, normality their nemesis."

Thus when the word came at 1:46 p.m. Tuesday that fuel-laden railroad tank cars were on fire at this lonely spot, the restless voyeurs flocked to the scene, each taking with him the tools of his trade: the reporters with their notepads and pencils, the photographers with their little black boxes and film cases hanging from them like ammunition belts, the television cameramen with their motion picture cameras and tape recorders.

These were the visible means of support, but somewhere along the line each had been issued another tool—an undying desire to find out just what is happening. And there is only one sure way to do it.

They came up this road toward the fire. "Journalists travel in packs with transferable tensions," Talese wrote. At about 2:10 p.m. the pack was laid low by a second explosion. The blast split the steel tank and threw it out to end up lying peeled open and lying flat on the ground, looking like a slice of soggy pizza. The area is littered with railroad cars without wheels and wheels without cars. There are lengths of crazily twisted tracks and neatly rolled-up fire hoses.

People were caught in the blast. They were burned up and knocked down, they were scattered along the road and tossed into that rain-filled ditch. Firemen had their hats and coats and boots ripped off their bodies. And the reporters, to whom life is a spectator sport, suddenly found themselves out there on the playing field.

Now, casualties in the ranks of the Fourth Estate are not terribly common. Indeed, workers who make felt hats pay higher insurance premiums. Yet, as in any job, there are occupational hazards such as Vietnam, Mayor Daley, Mafia leaders, and city editors facing a deadline. One of the most insidious enemies of all, however, is the open bar at press conferences. Statistics show that journalists as a group have a high incidence of alcoholism.

Problems of the job occasionally mount to the point that making felt hats actually seems safe. A New York City paper a few years ago was rent by a contract fight between the paper and the Newspaper Guild over the size of pensions, which would begin at age 65. The entire fight became moot, however, when one reporter noted that in recent years only 10 per cent of the staff had lived to be 65. It is no accident that many newspapers keep up-to-date photographs and biographies of their reporters.

Still, none of this should be construed as a complaint. Journalists are volunteers, pure and simple. When curiosity was passed out, they took one step forward. They have sold their soul to the First Amendment. They have sought out a life of shiny suits and questionable acquaintances, of strange hours in obscure places, because, in the last analysis, they are idealists and romantics who will deny it to their last cynical breath.

Many of their colleagues have gone on to advertising and public relations, where the money is better and the hours are shorter. But journalists take a sly pride in their position. They know things no one else knows. They know who is stealing from whom and who is sleeping with whom, and they know it before you do.

They carry little cards in their wallets that allow them to go places and do things — like approach a chain of burning railroad tank cars. Word of mouth is no good. Viewers and editors complain if the 10 o'clock news only shows the smoke from afar. So, the volunteers take a little more than one step forward.

There is also the possibility that the other fellow is up to no good — that you are standing there, safely behind the parapets, and are being soundly scooped by a more adventuresome colleague.

A while back, reporters from several newspapers and television stations were headed for a party given by a colleague. One by one they would pass by a newly opened guardrail on an expressway overpass. There, at the bottom, was an overturned car.

The party house was only a short distance away, so singularly and suspiciously each would race to the host's home. Soon it became a standing joke as the doorbell would ring and another heavy-breathing guest would announce "Hi, can I use your phone?" then plunge down the hallway with coveted notes in pocket or purse, there to call in what must have been the best-covered car wreck in history.

But when the flash hits the pan, they tend to forget briefly about competition and the First Amendment, and hew more to the law of self-preservation. And so *Post* reporter Jim Bishop beat a hasty retreat, saying to himself: "God, why was I here?" The answer, of course, known only to mountain climbers and newsmen, is simply: because it is there. If this fails to make much sense, it is suggested that you stay away from mountains and burning tank cars.

Out in El Paso

EL PASO—Debbie Reynolds was born here. Omar Bradley lived here. Bum Phillips coached here. John Wesley Hardin is buried here. El Paso is Texas' westernmost area, and its oldest. People have lived in this area for at least 11,000 years.

This is one of the fastest-growing major cities in the United States, much of it from south of the border. It is estimated that El Paso is now about 70 percent Mexican American. (In 1859, there were 44 Americans and 300 Mexicans.) In 1970, the official census counted 322,261 persons in this city. The 1980 census put it at 424,522, up one-third in a decade. That growth makes El Paso the 28th-biggest city in the country, passing Fort Worth to be the fourth-largest in Texas.

Actually, El Paso is simply reclaiming its ranking, for at one time it was not only the largest town in Texas, it was the only town in Texas. We tend to think of European culture and settlements spreading across America from east to west, but in this area it moved from south to north. A century before the first pilgrims landed at Plymouth Rock and only 15 years years after Hernán Cortez captured the Aztec civilization, Spaniards came through here. They had begun their trip looking for Cuba.

I can see this might take some explanation. There was a shipload of conquistadors who went searching for Florida in 1528, but that didn't work out so they attempted to sail to Cuba. A storm blew them off course and the ship eventually crashed into the Gulf Coast of Texas, where Indians killed or captured the lot of them.

Eventually, their numbers were pruned to four—Alvar Núñez Cabeza de Vaca, Alonso del Castillo Maldonado, Andrés Dorantes, and a Moor named Estevanico. After six years of slavery under the Indians, the four escaped in 1534 and spent the next two years wandering across Texas and at one point passed through here.

Cabeza de Vaca and his crew heard stories from the Indians about the fabulous Seven Cities of Gold to the north, which they duly reported to the Spanish viceroy upon their eventual arrival in Mexico City. That, as any history student knows, touched off vast Spanish exploration for God and gold, not necessarily in that order.

The gold never panned out, so to speak, but God arrived accompanied by padres sent to convert the Indians. This place was about the only spot around where travelers could pass through the mountains and continue north, thus it became known as El Paso del Rio del Norte. Since Spain, and later Mexico, owned both sides of the river, there was no particular differentiation as to which side was actually the town of El Paso until 1848, when the Rio became an international boundary between Mexico and the United States. Even then, what was called El Paso was often what is today called Juárez.

If you let it, things can get confusing around here. For example, the town south of the Rio was called El Paso del Norte. It became the capital of Mexico when President Juárez moved there following the French takeover of Mexico City when Maximilian was installed as emperor. Fortunately, in 1888, they changed the name of that town to Juárez, so that left only one El Paso.

Yet this town used to be called Franklin, and part of it was known as Magoffinsville. Then there are Ysleta, Socorro, and San Elizario, which used to be in Mexico until the meandering Rio put them in El Paso. And, of course, there is the Chamizal, which has belonged to both countries and is split down the middle, with each claimant getting a part.

By any name and any man-made changes, El Paso is high. The general altitude is about 3,700 feet, but the top of Ranger Peak overlooking the city is 5,632 feet above sea level. It is dry — precipitation averages about 7.7 inches a year. The TV weather forecasters each night give the rainfall not in the past 24 hours as they do back in Houston, but thus far this year.

This is a long way from anywhere and, erasing all the man-made boundaries, sits squarely in the middle of a desert, miles and miles from anything else in any direction. It's the only part of Texas in a different time zone. We traveled all night and half the next day to get here from Houston, never leaving Texas. If we had traveled the same distance heading east instead of west, we'd now be 20 miles on the other side of Tallahassee, Florida. El Paso is closer to Las Vegas than to Houston. From here, Los Angeles is 15 miles nearer than Brownsville, 28 miles nearer than Texarkana. During the Civil

War, El Paso was captured by Californians, and today on the TV cable, four of the stations are in Los Angeles.

Just to the north and west is New Mexico, causing one resident to comment: "We feel a closer community of interest with New Mexico than with Texas." This is borne out by the newspapers' sports sections. When the headlines refer to the Aggies, they mean those in Las Cruces, not College Station.

Out in the West Texas town of El Paso, William Howard Taft and Porfirio Díaz met in 1909 in the first conference between leaders of the two nations, and since then it has become a tradition. Pancho Villa lived here in exile, eating ice cream at the local confectionery. Wernher von Braun tinkered with his rockets here. Bat Masterson, Billy the Kid, George Patton, and other gunfighters lived in El Paso for brief times.

Yes, this is an interesting city. The television stations run recruiting ads for both the Houston Police Department and the Mexican Army. And there are not many towns in Texas with an Indian reservation and a permanent command of the West German Defense Ministry.

Hail, Sherman

THE FRONT YARD—"Cab! I say, taxi!" someone is yelling.

What the heck? Who's calling for a cab? Gad, I should have known. It's my new neighbor, just moved in from New York, Ulysses S. Sherman. Still out on his front curb, trying to hail a cab.

"Morning, Mr. Sherman."

"Howdy, pard," he says.

"Huh?"

"How y'all doing?"

"Mr. Sherman, why are you talking like that?"

He looks around furtively, then comes over. "Don't you know that it's real 'in' in New York to be Texan? That Broadway show about the Chicken Ranch, and the Lone Star Cafe, and everyone on Wall Street these days is wearing 10-gallon hats and pointed boots. Or is it 10-gallon boots and pointed hats? And, of course, there's all those Texans living in New York we've just discovered. Some of 'em have even *been* here. It's super-chic to go cactus in the Big Apple."

"Yeah," I say. "I've heard the rumors, Mr. Sherman. But I came over here to remind you that cabs don't cruise around Houston the way they do in Manhattan. I mean, you could stand here in Running Rats Acres all day and not see a cab. Or a police car either, for that matter."

"My good man," he says, "I wrote the *Times* a stiff letter about the cab situation in this town. You'll see some quick changes — would have been sooner, but they have been on strike."

"Mr. Sherman, I don't think a letter to the *Times* about the cab situation in Houston will have much stroke. Anyway, a minute ago you mentioned boots and hats, which makes me want to ask you about those galoshes you're wearing. And the ski mask."

"It's going to snow, my good man. Don't you watch the evening news?"

"Yeah, I watched it. Didn't say anything about snow."

"You don't watch the proper channels. You should be on the cable, as I am."

"Cable?"

"Indeed, I get all the New York channels."

"Mr. Sherman, I don't know how to break this to you, but you're not *in* New York anymore. You're in Texas. Houston, Texas."

"I'm trying to forget that. It's not easy being a missionary to the savages. I should have taken Bangladesh when the company offered it. I'll wager you can get decent bagels there."

"No doubt."

"By the way," he says, "do you think I could get a Stetson in my old school colors?"

"If your old school colors were young beaver underbelly."

"Think I'll get some Tony Lamas. Ha, that would make them green with envy at the Harvard Club. Pop around there in my Tony Lamas. Or do I ride around? Can you actually walk in those things?"

"Slowly, in the beginning, Mr. Sherman. And don't try to handle steps the first week or so."

He takes out a pad and jots that down. Suddenly he frowns. "I was making a list of a few items for going Texan. Do you drive a wagon on the left- or right-hand side of the prairie?"

"Left. But never over 55."

He jots that down. "Is it acceptable to actually keep a gun in your pickup gun rack?"

"No, indeed, Mr. Sherman. I mean, we're not that barbaric. We keep guns out of sight, like on the seat beside us."

"Check," he says, writing it down. "And exactly which way is thataway?"

"Usually it's whichever way the posse goes. This, of course, depends on such variables as Indian uprisings, outbreaks of screwworm, and the Fortune 500."

He puts up his book. "Well, ciao. I'm off into the sunset to hail Wells Fargo. Y'all hurry back now, ya heah?"

"Gee, Mr. Sherman," I say as he departs, "it's really funny watching you trying to be one of us."

He slowly turns back to look at me. "My good man," he says icily, "I am *not* trying to be one of you. I am trying to be one of *me*, and the trendy thing among people like me is to be people like you."

Texpatriates

From 1961 until 1968, I lived in New York City. Manhattan, to be exact. I was the sole survivor.

In those days, to be a Texan in New York City was to be a Martian in Mexia. We were strange creatures from an alien world, suspected of racism, conservatism, backwardness, and mayhem. The suspicions were proven. "Now you've done it!" a fellow in a Manhattan stockbroker's office yelled to a friend of mine who was visiting there, doing some business one November afternoon.

"Done what?" he asked.

"You've killed Kennedy!"

And we had. Clearly we had held a statewide referendum and had chosen overwhelmingly to shoot our president. A popular editorial cartoon of the day was entitled "Deep in the Hate of Texas." To argue otherwise in those dark days was fruitless.

You must remember what it was like back then. Civil rights were in the air, marches through Georgia, dogs and fire hoses, Bull Connor, JFK's assassination, Charles Whitman in the UT Tower, LBJ's unsuccessful effort to follow Camelot. And everyone had plenty of heating oil.

I bring all of this up today because it strikes those of us in the Old Corps a bit strange, even funny, to find that New York has suddenly discovered Texas. Today, I am told, it is chic, even proper, to be a Texan in New York. There are Texas bars and Broadway plays and books, even a Texan-in-NY newspaper that does not have to be sold in a plain brown wrapper. How the times have changed.

My own introduction to Gotham was not at all a shock. True, it was a fairyland for one who had never been out of Texas save to visit grandparents in Minden, Louisiana, and to serve in the Marines in California. But New York seemed nice enough.

A day or so after my arrival with a friend, we noticed that the New York football Giants were going to play the Dallas Cowboys in Yankee Stadium. The Cowboys were pretty bad back then, and the Giants were in first place. There would be no contest, but it was a chance to see Yankee Stadium, fully stocked. So we walked up to the box office that Sunday morn and requested two tickets.

I remember well the look on the clerk's face. Finally, he allowed that there had been two tickets turned in. We took them, looked at where they were — on the front row in an end zone — and asked for something better. Once again we got a strange look, with the dry statement that there was nothing else currently available. Only later did I learn that every seat at every Giant game was sold well beforehand. Entire wills and estate battles loomed over who would get the Giant tickets.

Well, Texas hats atop our heads, we sat there on the front row and cheered for the Cowboys, despite odd looks from our neighbors. The Cowboys won, 17–16, before 60,252 shocked fans and two delighted hicks. We got into our car with the Texas license plates, and the seas parted before us through the parking lot. One guy came up and congratulated us. Then asked for a ride. Gee, New York's not so bad.

Beginners' luck soon changed. I got a job with the *New York Times* as the token Texan, and for the next six and a half years had to put up with the usual good-natured gaff. And some that wasn't. Constantly the *Times* carried stories datelined Tuscaloosa, Meridian, Poplar, Selma, and other combat zones. I would translate, since I spoke fluent Dixie. On Christmas Day, a copy editor hunted me down to find out exactly what the first family was eating at the LBJ Ranch. It was a weird concoction called cornbread dressing. What's that?

And one evening, a wirephoto came across the desk, showing students huddled on the UT campus "behind the base of a statue" while a sniper fired from the campus tower. Any Teasip would know the statue was actually a flagpole base, but then, back then, there weren't any others. So it fell to me to point out the mistake. The only bright side was that for some time afterward my coworkers' tended to give distance to my steely eye and quick right hand.

Yes, it wasn't much fun. They had great sport about my boots, chortled at my hat. (I wore them only when it snowed—intimidation is a terrible thing.) And although I don't have much of an accent for some unexplained reason, it was thick enough to rejoice the rejoiners. Such as one day at work, when I answered the phone with just "Broadcast desk." But it was enough for the voice on the other end to say, "Well *dooooo* tell, pardner." My emotions were tempered by the fact that I am a Southern gentleman, and the voice on the other end was that of my boss's daughter.

We were a hardy lot, Texans in New York in the '60s. We few, we happy few, we band of brothers.

Current Texpatriates, riding the crest of hype, watching smugly as the Cowboys thump the Giants into the mud, can they appreciate what it was like back then? Now everyone wants to go back to Luckenbach, even though they've never been there before, and New Yorkers pack into the Lone Star Cafe to sip a cool one with Waylon and Willie and the boys. So how can the Texas Foreign Legion respond when told that once the military commander on Governor's Island—a Texan—ran up the Lone Star on Texas Independence Day and it was front-page news? And everyone thought it was cute, since no one else had the foggiest idea what their state flag looked like.

Those were the bad old days. And we pioneers through the outback of Manhattan can only pity today's replacements, for to fully appreciate something, first you have to suffer.

ABC's 'Nightline' Toes a Tight Line

THE TUBE—Good evening, I'm Ted Koppel and this is *Nightline* on ABC. Tonight, we are going to discuss the history of the world, the true meaning of life, and urban blight. But first, here is Frank Blair with the news. Frank, we've just got a few minutes, so try to keep it brief.

Right, Ted. In Washington, the president held a news conference, there was more fighting in the Mideast, a flood washed away Denver, and the stock market collapsed.

Thanks, Frank. Now, as I mentioned, *Nightline* will take an in-depth look at the history of the world. On the right of our split screen from Oxford we have Dr. Morgan Organ, noted historian, lecturer, and deep thinker. Dr. Organ, could you summarize the history of the world for us?

Well, Ted, the world is several billion years old, so it is hard . . .

If I might break in right here, Dr. Organ. On the other side of the split screen we have Dr. Dusty Wracks, curator of the Library of Congress. Dr. Wracks, could you respond, briefly, to Dr. Organ?

Respond to what, Ted? You didn't give him . . .

If we might move on, gentlemen, in the middle of the screen now we have the U.S. Congress, which, as you know, appropriates funds for the Library. Gentlemen, not to be trite, but have you read any good books lately, and could you tell us about them? Concisely.

Ted, I'm Representative Dewey Decimal, Republican from Indiana, and I just read *War and Peace*, which . . .

Representative Decimal, we've got to close this segment of the program, so could you briefly summarize that book?

It's about war and, of course, peace.

Thank you.

Thank you, Ted. If I might . . .

And now: what is the true meaning of life? To take a probing and detailed view of this matter, this evening on *Nightline* we have the Department of Philosophy from the University of Chicago. Gentlemen, exactly what is the true meaning of life?

That's such a complicated . . .

Excuse me, could you identify yourself for our audience?

I am Professor . . .

Could we summarize that to just "Prof."?

I suppose. Anyway, Theodore . . .

"Ted" on this program, just to keep it brief.

All right.

"OK" is briefer. We've got to move along. Thank you. In today's America, urban blight has been a nagging and growing concern. To take a detailed look at this problem, *Nightline* has Detroit standing by. Now, Detroit, could you, very quickly, sketch the problems you are facing?

I'm a cab driver, Ted. Name's Hack. Howard Hack. One problem in the inner city is . . .

Excuse me a moment, Mr. Hack. Since *Nightline* always tries to balance out any program, no matter how much it messes up everything—I mean, if we've got someone on the show saying night is day, then, by George, we're going to have someone else on the show saying day is night. So, to speak for rural blight, we have the state of Iowa standing by. Iowa, would you like to respond to Mr. Hack, briefly, please?

Mr. Koppel, I'm Cy Lowe, an Iowa farmer, and this is the dumbest format for a show I've ever seen. I get exhausted just watching. You're always telling everyone to hurry, hurry, hurry. You got too many people on trying to handle too big a subject. If you'd just . . .

If I might step in here for a moment, Mr. Lowe. Standing by in New York are the ABC stockholders, employees, and board of directors. How would you respond to Mr. Lowe's charges? We have about 30 seconds.

Ted, the nice thing about *Nightline* is that it allows us to take subjects and explore them in depth. For example . . .

Could you identify yourself, please?

I'm . . .

Thank you for watching. This is Ted for *Night* on AB. Good eve.

Toy for Santa

SAN JACINTO—This is the time when we remember what it was like back then, what happened and how. And it is the time when we raise a tankard or two to all who passed this way: Houston, Lamar, Deaf Smith, and, yes, even the Napoleon of the West, General Antonio López de Santa Anna, who modestly signed his name "A. L. Sta Anna."

But it is high time that we honored another Texan, a woman, who did her bit for the cause: Emily Morgan, our first undercover agent. You won't find her name on the bronze plaque inside the monument listing all the Texans who fought here. The files inside don't even have any material on her. But she was here, and she served Texas well.

This is where Santa Anna was camped 139 years ago today. He set up breastworks of trunks, baggage, packsaddles, and such, then dug his army in behind. Right here in the center—the safest slot— the general put up his tent. He always went first class, so he had a big silk-and-canvas rig, with heavy carpets on the ground.

At the door he had stacked several crates of champagne, and inside he had silverware, china of white with a green rim and a Mexican seal in the center, medicine chests full of opium (he was addicted), a sterling silver chamber pot, and Emily Morgan.

Emily was not exactly a willing "serving girl," as the historians euphemistically put it. She was a fine-looking woman, a mulatto girl who belonged to one James Morgan of New Washington, which today is known as Morgan's Point. When Morgan came to Texas about 1830, the place still belonged to Mexico and slavery was prohibited. So Morgan simply freed his 16 slaves, then bound them as indentured servants for 99 years.

When Santa Anna came through New Washington a few days earlier, he was feeling lonely. On every previous war outing he had left his frumpy wife back in Mexico City and had lived off the land, so to speak.

During the siege of the Alamo the Napoleon of the West had discovered a 17-year-old San Antonio beauty named Melchora Iniega Barrera and had tried to seduce her.

But Melchora had a mother who would put up with no such ideas, even from El Presidente. So Santa Anna discovered a sergeant in his army who was a former actor and spoke Latin. The sergeant became a temporary priest, performed the marriage, and the two lived happily ever after, or at least until the Guadalupe River at Gonzales.

The river was so high that the general's carriage couldn't get across, forcing him to send it and Melchora back to Mexico City to await his triumphant return. Thus when Santa Anna hit Morgan's plantation, it was love at first sight, on his part. Just to keep peace on the ol' plantation, the general looted the place, then burned it to the ground.

At about 3:30 on the afternoon of April 21, Sam Houston mustered his force and began walking up the slope, from where the USS *Texas* is today up to the monument. The Santanistas were snoozing, lying about, apparently with no sentries out. The general said later that when the Texians hit camp, he had been asleep "from fatigue and long vigils" and the "din and fire of battle awoke me. I immediately became aware that we were being attacked and that great disorder prevailed."

Others disagreed with that version, noting that not all the action was outside the tent.

An English ethnologist named William Bollaert later interviewed both William Morgan and Emily and wrote: "The Battle of San Jacinto was probably lost to the Mexicans owing to the influence of a Mulatto [Emily] belonging to Colonel Morgan, who was closeted in the tent with General Santana [sic] at the time the cry was made, 'The enemy! They come! They come!' and detained Santana for so long that order could not be restored readily again." In any event, Santa Anna was slightly out of uniform for the battle, wearing only his drawers and red slippers.

Martha Anne Turner, who has written extensively on Texas, concludes: "Whether or not the mulatto girl wittingly detained Santa Anna—she had little choice—she deserves to be elevated to her rightful place as a heroine of Texas history."

And in a way, she has, because a song began to spring up about "Emily, the Maid of Morgan's Point." There are several versions, one of which is in a yellowed, mysterious letter to "E. A. Jones" from "H.B.C." It's not a letter, exactly, but a poem, which begins:

> There's a yellow rose in Texas
> That I am a going to see
> No other darky knows her
> No one only me . . .

The Warpath

BRENHAM—There is a sudden tenseness in the winter air. Oak leaves, poised to plunge headlong into space, stop and listen. The winter grass covering these rolling hills goes into instant hibernation. Small animals and large men halt in their tracks to hear the message, then drop everything and run, pale and shaken.

It is the drums. The drums beat-beat-beating their awful message: hide your daughter, nail down your wallet, and send a rider to the nearest Ranger troop, the Indian Guides are coming.

Up and down the Brazos River bottom the word spreads like streptococci. And, as usual, the tom-toms do not beat with forked drumstick. For it is true, the Apache Tribe of Indian Guides—those Oilers of the Outback—is descending on the settlement, intent on its usual unspeakable crimes.

As Brenham draws its wagons into a circle around Gus Mutscher, we must pause to take a look at how it all began. The Apaches ("Pals Forever") are a collection of fathers and sons. Our noble leader is Sleeping Turtle.

Others include the local veterinarian, Foaming Mouth; our tribal cook, Greasy Spoon; then there are He-Who-Cheats-At-Cards and the neighborhood surgeon, Running Sores. I am Scratching Bull, for some incomprehensible reason. All together, there are 11 little braves and seven big braves, which means we're outnumbered.

We had decided that since all the lawsuits were settled from our last outing, it was time to take on another. We had heard about Amtrak, but unfortunately Amtrak had heard about us. After rejecting an attempt to reroute us in a Santa Fe hopper car, we finally secured booking as far as Brenham with the distinct understanding that we would take the bus back.

Thus we departed last Saturday morning at a ridiculously early hour. So early, in fact, that Sleeping Turtle was still meditating with the Great Spirit when the first braves arrived at his tepee. We finally got to the train station and boarded Amtrak, only to find it over-run by Cub Scouts. The Indians and the Long Knives scowled at one another, but there was no violence. We still remember who won at Wounded Knee.

Promptly at 9:50 the iron horse departed and at 9:51 the wise tribal elders gathered the little braves around for a meeting. "Scatter out, even unto the four corners of the iron horse, tossed asunder like snowflakes by the great wind of the prairie, and find the bar car."

"So we can get a Slurpy Sloppy or so you can get blottoed on firewater?" ask the little braves.

"Little braves seek to find fat lip," said Sleeping Turtle, returning to his meditation.

Soon, our scouts were back to report that while the bartender was not used to filling an order for firewater at 10 a.m., he would comply. And thus the Apache tribe made its watery way across the prairie, communing with the flora and fauna of the great outdoors.

By the time we got to Brenham (a catchy song title, don't you think?) we were on familiar terms with the conductor, who bid us adieu with an old railroad saying, "Good riddance."

At this point, the tribe turned its attention to Brenham, Texas, which is a pretty, neat, prosperous little German farming town, although the action on a Saturday afternoon won't give Las Vegas any worries. Houston, probably, but not Las Vegas. Our first problem was finding a good place to eat, so we fell back on that time-tested way of the red man.

"Where do the truck drivers eat?" we inquired. "La Grange," the locals answered.

In any event, we fanned out through the town until we discovered a barbecue place. And thus began the tribal meal. We consumed vast amounts of barbecued beef, pork, chicken, sausage, plus German potato salad, beans, home-cooked bread, and several barrels of Shiner beer. Living off the land has its bennies.

The little braves, ever alert to each movement of the elk, each flight of the geese, found Schulz's bakery, which sells doughnuts for a nickel each. Then it was time to investigate the settlement, so the Apaches wandered about, absorbing, savoring, seeing, visiting, breaking and entering.

At last it was time to leave, and the community happily had two policemen see us off at the bus station. We shall remember Brenham, and no doubt, Brenham shall remember us. For it is a town far removed from any other Indians. Or as I was telling Kissinger only last week, we should seek a settlement without any reservations.

Ask Not What Texas Can Do for Students, But Ask What . . .

Almost one out of every 10 counties in Texas has no doctor. There is a shortage in our rural areas of schoolteachers and health officials. We have undereducated children in our city's ghettos. The lot of the poor in our towns and villages along the Rio is among the worst in the nation.

OK, now couple this with the fact that in Texas' state-supported colleges and universities are 620,286 students. Last year 75,396 graduated, and in a month or so we'll have at least that many more. And add in the fact that any number of them are out seeking jobs at this very moment, and won't get them. By now, no doubt, you are on my wavelength. We hook up the problem with the solution.

My idea is simply this: Texans are now supporting a vast and ever-growing higher educational system, because (1) we need it, and (2) we are willing to pay for it. But we have gone along with the idea that somehow students deserve this — it is their God-given right to a higher education and society demands that they should give back nothing in return. This is not the fault of students, for we have been telling them this since birth. But I say that it is high time they paid Texas back for what they have received: they work for the State of Texas for a year or so.

This is not such a revolutionary idea. If you go to one of the U.S. service academies, in exchange for an education you agree to serve your country for x number of years, and well you should. Hard-pressed medical students go into the military to continue their training and repay Uncle Sam by spending a few extra years in uniform. The Mormons expect — and get — two years' service from their young people. The Russians demand that highly educated emigrants repay the nation for their education before moving on to the West. France gets one year's service from its young men, in the military or in some Peace Corps–like pursuit. So this is no wild-eyed plan, you see. It is being done all over the place, but not in Texas.

What would the graduates do? I'm not talking about any make-work tasks, but still the list is endless. Let's start with a young doctor emerging from one of the several state medical schools. His training has cost his parents dearly, but the taxpayers of Texas have helped out, too. The average public university student in Texas pays between 10 and 12 percent of the cost of his education. You and I pay the rest. So it is safe to assume that by the time a medical student has gone through four years of undergraduate school in Texas, then four more years of medical school, his or her IOU to the state is considerable.

No big deal. We need doctors desperately, and they shall do Texas a lot of good over the years. But more immediately, they can help repay the staggering cost of their education by getting out to one of the 23 Texas counties that have no doctors at all, and working one year for considerably less pay than they would get in River Oaks. The same goes for lawyers. We are cranking out young lawyers at our state schools in record rates. At the same time we are hiring public defenders, assistant DAs, and a legal cast of thousands. I would hate to think how many lawyers there are on the state payroll, and how many more we could use in our prisons, backwater courts, attorney general's office, and so on. The solution is clear.

Check the state payrolls and you will find jobs for home economists and halfbacks, veterinarians, agronomists, and on down the line. They, too, can serve. Now, when you get down to English majors and philosophers, the problem is a bit sticky, so I suggest they work out their debt by cutting grass along state highways and picking up the litter. Not only will this plan spruce up Texas but it should have an immediate effect at the university registrars' offices. And don't forget our vocational schools, either. Texas can well use some good auto mechanics on DPS patrol cars, some bakers at our state schools, some plumbers in our state office buildings—all working one year for far less than those they replaced.

This, in turn, brings forth two immediate points. First, in answer to your question of how we would pay all these additional employees who go on the state payrolls, I point out that the program pays for itself, and may even save us money. A newly coined teacher in a Brownsville barrio will draw, say, one-quarter what a full-blown teacher would draw. And the second point is that the thousands—nay, hundreds of thousands—of current state employees would fight this plan with a lobbying effort to pale all others.

Of course, I'm not saying we replace all of our current crop of state employees. We need experienced people, and the State of Texas can't be run by on-the-job training. We must leave amateur hour to the Legislature. But we could replace some employees, and fill new vacancies, and make Texas a better place in which to live. In addition, it would certainly cut down on all the out-of-state students who falsify their addresses so they can pay in-state tuition.

So, that's my plan: a Peace Corps program, giving Texas taxpayers a little bit back for the $1,157,808,837 we are spending this year on higher education, not to mention the $3.6 billion the Legislature is considering spending over the next two years. The students might object, but a year's guaranteed job at a guaranteed wage—albeit ridiculously small—is a better outlook than most of them have this merry month of May. The parents should be relieved Junior's got a foot up on a career, even if it is planting pines in a state forest. And the people of Texas should be happy: in the long run, it will save us millions of dollars.

We've got the problem, we've got the solution. Plugging the two together makes such good sense that we'll never do it.

That First Cheering Letter

All right, you put the little nippers on the plane or train last weekend for camp, and you still haven't written them, now, have you? The first few days are the worst on campers, since that's when they are most homesick. Every mail call they rush eagerly to the counselor and depart empty-handed, their little cheeks tearstained due to your thoughtlessness.

Never fear! I have come up with an all-purpose letter to your son/daughter to save you the time and trouble. Just check it off, clip it out, and mail. They'll think it was your own idea, you big teddy bear. OK, here goes:

Dear Son/Daughter:

It has been:

☐ Hours

☐ Weeks

☐ Not long enough

since you left us, and we really miss you. Only today your mother/father said:

☐ We miss you.

☐ It seems so quiet around here.

☐ Yeah, too quiet.

☐ They'll attack at first light.

It has been very hot here in Houston. The Southwest Freeway buckled, the grass is dying, the air conditioning is going constantly, and HL&P has bought a controlling interest in all states west of the Mississippi. Houston is now about eight inches behind in annual rainfall. It's so dry that:

☐ Restaurant customers are requesting doggie bags for the glasses of water.

☐ Stamps are thumbtacked to letters.

☐ People who sweat a lot are invited to all the right parties.

☐ Spitting on the sidewalks is still a $25 fine, but it can be worked off by spitting on the grass in public parks.

Now that you have gone, your mother/father and I have had a little time to ourselves and have discovered that we have absolutely nothing to talk about. So we watch hours of repeats on TV. Your mother/father drinks a lot and wanders around the house mumbling to herself/himself. Oh, in all the haste of your departure, you left your room an absolute wreck. In cleaning it up, we discovered:

☐ The Thanksgiving turkey.

☐ Your trunk for camp.

☐ Three Baggies of a funny-looking leaf.

☐ Several items of clothing from the opposite sex.

☐ An escape hatch.

The Astros are still fumbling around and are in great danger of being arrested for impersonating a baseball team. The Rockets may or may not be here next year, and the Oilers plan to join the United States Football League.

In other news, Judge Noel has refused to take himself off the WISD case, so there's still hope. Andrew Young has called Richard Nixon and Gerald Ford racists, but Young added that he is a racist, too. There goes the neighborhood. Haldeman and Mitchell have been ordered to begin serving jail terms that would have been over by now if they had gone quietly. President Carter is still pushing his energy policy, which your mother's/father's boss says is:

☐ Insane.
☐ Communistic.
☐ Certain to put Ronald Reagan in the White House.
☐ All of the above.

Your first letter from camp arrived and we were most interested in the fact that it was:

☐ Addressed to "Occupant."
☐ Sent collect.
☐ Written before you left.
☐ A lousy little checklist which shows you don't think enough of your own parents to sit down and write a decent letter, you ingrate.

Have a good time at camp and be careful. Don't forget what happened to your uncle Otto when he picked up a snake to beat a stick to death.

Love,

☐ Dad
☐ Mom
☐ Next-of-kin

With-It Ash-By Out of In-Crowd

The problem began when I decided that I wasn't really with it. You know, on the inside. No one mentioned my name at the polo matches. No one cared whether I summered at St. Tropez and wintered at Greenland or the other way around.

"It's your clothes," I was told at a party. So I went to the with-it store and bought a with-it wardrobe. At the next party, I arrived fashionably late after I was told that absolutely no one who was with it arrived on time. I was so late, in fact, that the party was over when I got there. The cleanup crew told me that no one wore cuffs anymore.

To make it big in Houston society I tried cheating on my income taxes, opening a restaurant specializing in ox-tongue crepes, and writing a novel so dirty that it was banned in Juárez. Nothing worked. I became an urban cowboy just as everyone else went preppie. So I put on my Izods, called everyone "Chip," drank Perrier, and kept saying "Ciao."

"Are you still a preppie?" my hostess asked at the Viking party. "I mean, it's so in that it's out. Everyone today is going Viking."

At the next open house I remembered to order white wine, since everyone who is with it today drinks white wine. No one noticed me until one fellow came up and said to bring around his car.

Cars. That was with it. I borrowed a powder-blue BMW to go to my next party. "Powder *blue*?" my hostess observed when I drove up. "How camp. Everyone is driving steel grey these days."

"Steel gray?" I responded.

"No. Steel *grey*."

Next I got the proper haircut and opened a boutique on Westheimer, thinking that would make me with it.

"Everyone is on Richmond," I was told.

At a party of energy barons to celebrate the bankruptcy of San Antonio, I rubbed shoulders with them and commented, "Brought it in at 50,000 feet."

"How gauche," said one. "Everyone of importance is bringing it in at 25,000. I mean, really, *anyone* can hit it at 50,000."

So I told everyone my grandfather had ruined Kilgore to acquire the family oil fortune. Kilgore, I was told, is out. Giddings is in. "Get shot by your *sommelier* in a dispute over Moet-Chandon '65," I was advised by the host, who took me aside. When I explained that I didn't have a *sommelier*, the entire party erupted in laughter. "How quaint," my hostess said, handing me my hat.

That was the lowest point of all. Standing out on the curb, nursing a longneck—which, I was quickly told, is passé now that hip flasks are back—I watched as an old friend, Tony Smedley, got into his Winnebago. (Winnebagos are in.) "Hey," said the society photographers, "it's Anthony Smedley-Brown! Get his pic!"

"That's the ticket," said Billy-Bob John-Son, my barber, the next afternoon. "Your problem is that you don't have a hyphenated name."

"What's that?"

"You really *are* out of it," he sighed, clipping off my eyebrows after having told me that eyebrows are out. "Everyone who is anyone has a hyphenated name."

"That's pretentious," I said. "They're made-up names. Any American with a hyphenated name is just trying desperately to draw attention to himself or herself."

"Exactly," said Billy-Bob.

"But that's really reaching for attention. We always take our father's name."

"But I don't know who my father is," he said, whipping off some more eyebrows. "With two names, I've got a better chance of getting it right."

After checking around to see what would be most appropriate, I changed my name to Ashby-Occupant, but my mail got so enormous that I couldn't handle it. Then I tried Ashby-Houston, but got registered as a three-star hotel. My attempt at Ashby-Houston-Texas ended when I was struck by PATCO.

"If you were a woman, you could hyphenate your maiden name with your married name," said Le-Roy Wash-Ing-Ton, my bootblack. "It's all the rage at the NOW conventions."

"But I'm not a woman," I protested. "And even if I were, that's pompous and phony, too."

"You want to be with it or not?" he asked, shining the straps around my toes.

So I tried L. Ash-By, with no luck. Then I tried el A-Shby until I was recalled by the Kuwait embassy.

"What you need to do," said E-Z Carpen-Ter, as he was sacking my groceries, "is to host an expensive, tasteless blast which will make all the poor people jealous. That will get you in with the hyphenated crowd."

So I held an intimate party at the Sears-Roebuck in Winston-Salem for Pope John-Paul. No one came. As a final effort, I am working on the editors here to return us to the good old days so that we can all be with it. The *Houston Post* used to be the *Post-Dispatch*.

Gentle Sam Raised a Little Cane to Turn Things Around

Hear that? Like someone screaming, "Help! Help!" Now a loud "whack!" Grunting and thrashing. It sounds rather like a fight, and that's because it is.

If you'll look closely in the dark, you can see two men rolling around the street. The street is Pennsylvania Avenue, in Washington, D.C. It is late on the night of April 13, 1832. The fellow getting the worst of the battle is the Honorable William Stanbery, U.S. representative from Ohio.

But that's not why I've brought you here tonight. It's because the other fellow, the huge guy in the buckskin coat cussing and bashing Stanbery over the head with a walking cane, is one Sam Houston. Now that seems odd. Really now, Gentle Sam? Fighting? There must be a good story here, so perhaps we should find out more about the situation.

Sam Houston is 39 years old, but he has fallen on hard times. He had served as a soldier (he was made a major general in the Tennessee militia at the age of 28) and lawyer. He knows Washington well, having served two terms in Congress. He had then been elected governor of Tennessee but resigned and went to live with the Indians after that unseemly scandal when his wife left him. Rumor says he drank a lot.

Houston returned to Washington in 1830, a full member of the Cherokee Nation and dressed like an Indian. (That's nothing. Later, as president of Texas, he received his Indian brothers dressed in a red robe given him by the Sultan of Turkey.) He had wanted government contracts to feed the Indians but couldn't get them.

Now he is back again, two years later, accompanied by a delegation of Indians and still seeking those elusive government food contracts. He began knocking on doors, but suddenly trouble arose and Houston was back in hot water. On March 31, two weeks before tonight, Representative Stanbery addressed the House and declared: "Was not the late Secretary of War removed because of his attempt fraudulently to give Governor Houston the contract for Indian rations?"

When Washington newspapers reported the speech, Houston was outraged. He charged Capitol Hill and got as far as the House foyer when then-congressman James Polk of Tennessee stopped him, led him outside, and cooled him down. Houston was still out for blood, and sent another Tennessee congressman, Cave Johnson, with a note to Stanbery, the first step toward a formal duel. Stanbery refused the challenge, saying he wouldn't duel with a man he didn't even know.

This really hurt Houston's ego. "I'll introduce myself to the damned rascal," he declared. When this word reached Stanbery, he reached for two pistols. He might not have known Sam, but he knew *of* Sam. As for our hero, he put away his knife and borrowed back a hickory cane that he had given to a friend in Georgetown.

And there the matter stood until tonight, April 13, 1832. Houston and some friends have been visiting Senator Felix Grundy in his hotel room and now are heading back to Brown's Hotel. I do not know if that's where Sam is staying, and at this point in the evening, I'm not sure Sam knows where he's staying. With him are two friends, Senator Buckner of Missouri and Representative Blair of Tennessee.

Walking here along Pennsylvania Avenue, Blair sees a man passing under a streetlight and recognizes him as his colleague from Ohio, William Stanbery. Blair says so, then — no dummy he — quickly departs.

Houston walks up and asks: "Are you Mr. Stanbery?"

"Yes, sir," he answers.

"Then you are a damned rascal," Houston announces, and swats the congressman over the head with his cane.

Stanbery is yelling, "No, don't!" and fights back. He's not as big as Houston, but he's pretty large. They are rolling around the street, Houston still landing blows with his cane. One of Houston's arms hasn't been of much use since the battle of Po-ho-pe-ka, but he's managing. Stanbery reaches in his pocket, pulls out a pistol, points it right into Houston's chest, and pulls the trigger. Click. Nothing happens.

Now Houston is really steamed. He wrestles away the gun and whacks Stanbery some more. The congressman attempts to run away, but Houston leaps upon his back. Finally, Sam lifts Stanbery high into the air and hits him "elsewhere," as a witness delicately put it.

Well, the fight quickly becomes the talk of Washington. Stanbery has Houston arrested for attacking him over statements Stanbery had made on the floor of the House, from which a congressman is immune. Houston has a rather slim defense: he attacked Stanbery for what he was quoted as saying in the papers.

Congress holds its own trial. Houston's lawyer is a sometime songwriter, Francis Scott Key. But it is Houston himself—attired in a buckskin coat—who does most of the talking. And he does a fine job of it, for almost a month. Still, even such supporters as President Andrew Jackson feel Houston doesn't stand a chance.

On May 6, Sam is told to wind it up the next day. That night he has a few friends over to his hotel room, where they proceed to drink and pass out. At dawn, Sam is all alone. With an awful headache, Sam puts on his new clothes and walks up to Capitol Hill. The galleries, even the aisles, are packed.

Sam gives it his all. He begins softly, firmly, then, slowly rising in voice and feeling, he cites every tyrannical government since ancient Greece. He argues simply that he has the right of every American: to protect his good name, his reputation, his self-esteem. "When you shall have destroyed the pride of American character, you will have destroyed the brightest jewel that heaven ever made!" he concludes.

The crowd goes wild and Junius Booth, the nation's greatest actor of the time, rushes down the aisle to compliment Houston.

One week later, Speaker Andrew Stevenson—an unbiased observer who, coincidentally, had also partied in Houston's room the night before the summation—hands down the decision: a mild reprimand and don't do it again.

But here's the kicker. Later evidence showed Houston was, indeed, the favorite bidder on those government food contracts, and only a breakdown in plans prevented him from landing the contracts in secret and at an enormous profit—he might have made as much as $1 million. But it would still have been a good deal for the government.

The most important aspect of this all, however, was that it turned his life around. A fistfight changed him from an over-the-hill loser back into a dominating leader. As Sam Houston said himself: "I was dying out, and had they have taken me before a justice of the peace and fined me $10 it would have killed me. But they gave me a national tribunal for a theater and that set me up again."

So be careful whom you accuse. Tomorrow is San Jacinto Day.

"Will That Be Cash or Charge?"

THE COUNTER — "Will there be anything else?" asks the clerk.
"No, that's it," says the customer, two places in front of me.
"Cash or charge?"
"I'd like to write a check," he says, pulling out his checkbook.
"Is this a local bank?"
"Uh-huh," he says, filling out the check.
"The bill is for $13.25. So make out the check for $23.25."
"Why is that?"
"There's a $10 charge for all returned checks."
"But this check isn't returned. I haven't even signed it yet."
"I know. But if it is returned, we have to be sure we get our money back. And put down your phone numbers. Home and office. Your place of employment, too. And let me see your Texas driver's license."
"I don't have one."
"What?" asks the clerk. "You expect to sign a check without a valid driver's license?"
"It's valid. I just moved here from Louisiana."
"I'm sorry, sir," says the clerk. "But I can't accept an out-of-state driver's license without authorization."
"From whom?"
"In this case, the governor of Louisiana. Just return the merchandise to the shelves and go through the metal detector on your way out. Next."
The customer in front of me stepped up to the counter. "Here you go," he said, putting a bottle of mouthwash on the counter.
"Will that be cash or charge?"
"Charge. Here's my charge card."
The clerk picked it up and bent it slightly. "Are you 'H. Harlan Hardesty'?"
"Yes."
"You live at 123 Cottonwood?"
"Right."
"How long have you lived there?"
"Three years. What's that got to do with buying a bottle of mouthwash?"
"Not a thing. But you're charging it. We get a lot of stolen credit cards in here."
"Mine's not stolen. That's mine."

"Do you have any other form of identification?"

"Yes, here's my driver's license. It's a Texas license."

"So it is," says the clerk, eyeing the license carefully. "If two cars come to an intersection at right angles at the same time, which one has the right of way?"

"The one on the right."

"Place your hand over your left eye and read these letters," says the clerk, holding up a card.

"E-H-J-K-I."

"Very good. Now parallel-park between those two poles. I'll wait."

The customer sighs and heads for the door. "Leave the mouthwash here, please," says the clerk, signaling the guard at the door.

I'm next. I put a package of gum on the counter. "Do you have your claim check?" the clerk asks.

"What claim check? I want to buy this gum."

"See that?" the clerk asks, pointing to a sign. "It states very clearly, 'No Sales Without Claim Check.' "

"I don't have one."

"If you lose your claim check, there's a dollar penalty. So that will be $1.25."

"A dollar charge! That's ridiculous!"

"See that sign?" says the clerk, pointing to one reading, "Dollar Fine for Arguing with Clerk."

"Cash or charge?" asks the clerk.

"Cash," I say, putting a five-dollar bill on the counter.

"This is a five-dollar bill," the clerk says in shock. "We only take bills for the total of the purchase. You'll have to buy $3.75 more."

"Look, I just want the gum. Sell me the bloody gum!"

"Don't get testy," says the clerk, holding the bill up to the light. "Since the store manager isn't here, I can authorize that change be made in certain cases. Here, hold the bill right under your chin. Face this way. Now this way." Lights flash. "Now," the clerk continues, pulling out a form, "I need three credit cards."

"Here you go," I say, shoving three across.

"These won't do. They are all in the same name."

"So?"

"They might all have been stolen from the same wallet. Give me your thumb."

I stick out my thumb as the clerk rolls it on a black ink pad, then on a white paper. "Now the other. Do you have some more verification as to your identity?"

"Like what?"

"Your discharge papers from the military, if you were honorably discharged, that is."

"Yes, I was honorably discharged."

"Which side?" asks the clerk, filling out the form.

"Ours."

"Any scars, birthmarks, amputations, or identifiable saber slices?"

"No. Why don't we just forget the whole thing, OK?"

"See that sign?" I look up to see another sign: "For Your Own Protection, We Won't Forget the Whole Thing."

"Do you have your voting registration certificate?"

"As a matter of fact, I do," I say, pulling it out of my wallet.

"How did you vote in the last presidential election?"

"That's my business."

"Yes, but that's our gum. OK, I think that's all," the clerk says, pushing the gum and the change across the counter. "Here you are."

"Great," I say, storming out of the store.

"Have a nice day," says the clerk.

Media Mayhem

The press is under a lot of pressure these days to tell the truth without bias or favor so that the reader can read into the story his own bias and favor.

But one man's truth is another man's blatant falsehood. We don't seem to agree on even the most basic ingredients, which is, of course, why we have horse races, jury trials, and elections. Each man tells it like it is — to him. So let us take a look at how the same story — Jack and Jill — might be handled by different witnesses:

Associated Press

BULLETIN

THE HILL (AP) — A children's innocent errand turned into tragedy today when two youngsters fell headlong down a ravine while fetching a pail of water.

Authorities say that there is a great deal of similarity between this incident and the one that befell three handicapped mice. A farmer's wife has been arrested in that case, but so far no charges have been filed.

First reports from the scene are fragmentary, but usually reliable sources have identified the victims as a "Jack" and a "Jill."

Channel 13

Eyewitness Sports has just learned that a major disaster involving possibly thousands of waterboys and -girls may throw a damper into the Oilers' exhibition season. Here with that story is Eyewitness Dan. Tell us all about it, Eyewitness Dan.

Thanks, Dave. Say, Dave, that's a nifty tie you've got on there. A Christmas present?

Gee, Dan. Glad you like it. Which reminds me of the one about . . .

In Eyewitness Sports, first, here is some film of me skiing up in Colorado during my vacation. Isn't that just great? We'll have more film of my vacation tomorrow night, fans, but first this late bulletin from the Hill where . . .

That's Eyewitness Sports, thanks, Dan. We'll be right back with 27 petty robberies, gory film from a car wreck in Tulsa last month, and more funny comments.

Houston Tribune

Another insidious Kremlin plot was brought to light today— despite efforts to hide it by namby-pamby judges and do-gooder social workers.

Two known Communist agents, code-named "Jack" and "Jill," were spotted carrying a suspicious object up the Hill. In their flight from justice, they tumbled down the Hill, and Agent Jack broke his crown.

Sources in the FBI say the suspicious object was a pail of clear liquid substance, possibly chlorinated water, and was part of an overall plot against George Wallace. God bless America!

Variety—New Acts
Jack and Jill
Tumbling, Errand Running
3 Min.
Storyland

Jack and Jill, a new duo on the scene, opened briefly at The Hill, our town's w.k. nitery. An unusual act, this J&J, mixing the surefire stuff—sex and violence. Should have good appeal if it can get a PG rating. Stagesiders, particularly the femmes, groove on the biggie finish. In for a pair of frames.

Pravda

THE HILL—Lackeys of the Wall Street Warmongers today set upon two members of the proletariat, beating them senseless, then throwing them down the hill in a clumsy attempt to make it look like an accident.

Comrades Jack and Jill, members of the Gus Hall Marching & Nonviolent Bomb Throwers Brigade, were returning to their mud hut after an exhausting day toiling for their absentee landlord when they were set upon by fascist thugs.

There will be a volunteer rally—or else—in Red Square tomorrow to protest this new threat to international peace, followed by a march on the U.S. embassy. Leaders of the People's Government expressed shock and alarm at the massacre but said it should not harm future Soviet–U.S. wheat deals.

Resolution from the Texas Senate

WHEREAS Jack and Jill went up the Hill to fetch a pail of water.

And WHEREAS Jack fell down and broke his crown and Jill came tumbling after—

BE IT RESOLVED, that the Senate of the Sovereign State of Texas, in the year of Our Lord One-thousand, Nine-hundred and Eighty-four, doth proclaim: Serves you right, troublemakers.

White House News Release

The President today announced that Jack and Jill are being investigated for their part, if any, in publication of the Mother Goose Papers—a clear violation of national security.

The President acted immediately and decisively after learning that the aforementioned Jack and Jill went up Capitol Hill without a note from their mother. The President categorically denies that he ever knew of the event, nor did any member of his staff. And he has a note from his mother to prove it.

To Sound-Off

Why did your paper only run 17 stories on the notorious Jack and Jill affair? What are you trying to hide? Spiro Agnew is right! You're nothing but a bunch of left-leaning Nazis. And don't give me one of your snide answers, either.

A Friend

You mention the word "Nazi." Heinrich Himmler was a Nazi, so was Pvt. Hans Dowe from Bremerhaven, which is in West Germany.

So is Lower Saxony, which had a 1950 urban census of 4,261,681. As for S-O making a snide remark, S-O does not make snide remarks. That's the dumbest thing S-O has ever heard. You're pretty stupid, aren't you? Get out of my sight! — Editor.

We would like to thank you for your honest handling of our story.

Jack and Jill
The Hill Hospital

P.S. Why are we being trailed by the FBI?

Can't Paint Town *Just* Red

THE PAINT STORE — "I'd like some paint, please," I say.

"Certainly," says the clerk. "What kind?"

"I don't know for sure. What do you have?"

"We've got almost everything."

"Well," I say, "we were thinking of green for the bedroom."

"Could you be a little more specific?" he says.

"Specific?" I say.

"Yes, indeed. There are many different shades and hues of green. We've got Forest Green and Bowling Green and Envy Green. We used to have Lucky Strike Green, but it went to war."

"Gee, I dunno."

"Lorne Green is very popular, although it used to be even more so."

"Maybe. What else do you have?"

"Like I said, we've got almost everything. How about a blue?"

"Yeah, I like blue."

"Great. We've got Baby Blue and Royal Blue. We also have Ben Blue, Monday Blue, Cross Blue, and Print Blue."

"Do you have Norther Blue?"

"No, but Belly Blue is close. How about a Sacre Bleu?"

"I didn't realize there were so many colors for sale," I say. "I just thought there were red and green and blue and so on."

"There used to be," says the clerk. "But you can charge a lot more for a Riding Hood Red than just a plain old red."

"Riding Hood Red?" I quiz. "That's new to me."

"Oh, that's an old brand. Practically out of stock these days. You can get an even higher price for a Big Red or a Well Red, so that's what we stock. Here's a new one. Do your study in Newspaper."

"You mean?"

"Right. It's black and white and red all over. Most attractive. Then, of course, there's scarlet."

"O'Hara or Harold?"

"On second thought, I won't. Do you still carry Canary Yellow?" I ask.

"No, now it's Peril Yellow. We also have Anita Bryant Orange and Bowl Rose."

"This was supposed to be easy. I was just going to step in here and pick out a few colors and be off. Well, for the outside shutters I just need a simple black. There can only be one."

"No, indeed," says the clerk, flipping through the pages of a catalog. "We have Power Black, Beauty Black, and Banker's Heart Black. Then there is Shirley Temple Black and Alvin Van Black."

"I'll have to think it over. "Maybe I should just do it in wallpaper," I say.

"Oh, we have a large variety of wallpaper," the clerk says, heading for another counter.

"I was afraid of that. I just want a one-color job. A pastel."

"No, pastels are out. Designs are in."

"OK, show me something with a few lines."

"Lines are out. Pictures are in. Here's a repeated pattern."

"It looks familiar," I say.

"It should. This is an HL&P quarterly earnings report. Only, unlike the original, this one never gets bigger. A lot of people find it comforting for a bedroom. It induces happy dreams."

"What's this one?"

"An aerial photo of a Steak'n'Shake parking lot. This is a closeup of a 64-year-old woman's varicose veins."

"No, thanks," I say.

The clerk flips over to another design. "This is a big maze. On a dull day, you just whip out a pencil and work your way around the room."

"You got anything else?"

"I like this one. It's a musical score. You can pick out the tune right off the wall."

"What is it?"

"The love theme from *Dragnet*."

"Let's go back to the paint. What about a brown? Just a brown. And none of this Plain Wrapper Brown. Just brown."

"Cleveland or Buster?"

"Neither, now that you mention it."

"Not to worry," smiles the clerk. "I've got a lot more. Here's a Martini Olive, an Age Bronze, and a Hi-Yo Silver. How about a Hound Gray?"

"You're getting warm. What else do you have?"

"Here's one of my favorites," says the clerk. "A Silence Golden. Or this one. It's a Bombshell Blonde. This is a Bruise Purple. Here's a Lung Aqua. How about an Inthe Pink?"

"No, all of this is really too much for me. Just give me five cans of white paint. Just white-white. OK?"

"Certainly, sir," says the clerk, heading back to the storeroom. "We've got Klan White and Pearl White and Betty White and House White, which goes well with Budget Red and Glasses Tinted Rose. Then there's . . ."

Art? What's That?

Texas can justly lay claim to various assorted stars in various assorted fields.

People come here from all over the world to see our doctors, who have made medical history with their work. In law, we have had Percy Foreman, Tom and Ramsey Clark, Judge Sarah T. Hughes, and a courtroomful of lesser lights.

Business? Dallas bankers have made a name for themselves throughout the nation. Houston has given Howard Hughes to the business world. Conrad Hilton got his start in Texas. I daresay some of our businessmen are among the best there are, and if you doubt this, look at the skyline.

Oil? It's hard to know where to start. Texans got in on the ground floor and set the pace. Athletics? From Rogers Hornsby and Tris Speaker to Ben Hogan to Doak Walker. Today, should Texans have to play in Texas, the Super Bowl might well become a traditional match between Dallas and Houston.

So, why is it that Texas falls so miserably flat when it comes to the arts? "The *what*?" you ask, which only reinforces my question. Alas, Texas seems to be almost barren in the field of painters, poets, musicians, writers, and philosophers. We have to pause in our conversations and think for a moment when the subject even comes up, however rarely.

J. Frank Dobie is about the only Texas writer of things even recognized across the Red River. Most of them flee the state at the first taste of success. Now, part of the reason, of course, is that they must go where the action is in their profession. If you are an automotive expert, chances are you will wind up in Detroit. Steel will put you in Pittsburgh. So, the arts lure you to either New York or Los Angeles.

David Westheimer (*Von Ryan's Express, Summer on the Water, The Magic Fallacy*) was last reported living and working in California. Larry McMurtry (*Horseman Pass By*, which became the movie *Hud*, and *The Last Picture Show*, which kept its name when moving to the screen, plus *Leaving Cheyenne* and his latest, *All My Friends Are Going to Be Strangers*) is the only writer of note to spring from the Lone Star State, and he is now in Washington, D.C.

Katherine Anne Porter came from Indian Creek, south of Brownwood, but long ago left for the East, following the path of O. Henry—William Sydney Porter, who once labored on *The Post*. Willie Morris (*North Toward Home* and *Yazoo*) came from Mississippi to Texas, then hooked a left and marched northeast to rise to fame and fortune poking occasionally gentle fun at his Texas era.

Others who have stayed, or who left and returned, seem to feel that the best way to sell to a national publication is to play Stomp Your State. Thus did Bud Shrake ream out East Texas in his article "Land of the Permanent Wave." To read it, one gets the idea that East Texas is totally populated by idiots, bigots, and fascists. Hardly the type of place to give us Van Cliburn, who, incidentally, left Kilgore for New York City.

Gary Cartwright, another Texan, made several good points but went on to journalistic overkill in "The Tin Star State," which appeared in the February '71 *Esquire*: "I have always thought of Texas as a freak of geography, a mere reference point; a microcosm of national logic (get them before they get us) set on the fossils of a vanishing frontier."

It may or may not be true, but such attacks are obviously marketable on Madison Avenue. There's gold in them thar howls.

Janis Joplin came from Port Arthur, but she rarely had anything good to say about her home town, and today it is returned in kind. Kris Kristofferson grew up in Brownsville, but his songs don't seem to reflect much of his Texas background.

So, when you get down to it, Texas has not made much of a contribution to the arts. Our creative people are not too numerous, and most of them have fled. But why? Are we any the less couth than others? Probably not. But there is not exactly an atmosphere in Texas conducive to artistic creativity. Our emphasis is on things monetary and material. A great symphony does not add to the skyline. A good book is less appreciated in our state than a good steak.

Imagine the look on the face of a father when his small son comes in to announce that he wants to be a concert violinist, or a sculptor. The chagrin when one golfer tells another that his son is studying poetry, or is majoring in philosophy. Better he should run guns to Cuba. There's money in gunrunning.

We tend to emphasize concrete, not creativity. We put more faith in things we can see and touch than in things we can feel. This is why our football coaches make more than our college presidents. When was the last time you saw an enthusiastic alumni group wining and dining a good university chancellor, much less a crackerjack English prof?

And it all seems rather a shame. Certainly we must have the raw material in Texas to create pictures and words and thoughts, but it gets the back of our hand, the short end of the stick, the low end of our priorities. Why bother with writing a play when you could be paving a road? We need both, of course, but if the question even needs to be asked, then the answer is apparent.

Great Tags Needed . . . Well, Maybe Next Time

Have you people no class? No style? Well, at least you have imagination. Two out of three ain't bad. I am referring, of course, to your entries in our latest contest: Name the Team. It is based on the news that a new professional football conference is being created, called the United States Football League. Clearly these new franchises need fantastic names.

So I asked that you submit new names for these new teams. But what did you send me? The Mobile Homes and the Ogden Nashes (Jim Osborn), the Bessemer Muchos and the Pompano Circumstances (Kirk Lewis), the Bismarck Sinkers, the Pocatello Peccadillos, and the Alabama Coushattas (Robert Illgen). Greg Reilly came up with the Flatonia Bad Czechs and the Killeen Sweeps. Den-

nis Lund of the Criminal Justice Center in Huntsville should be in-
carcerated for the Turkey (Texas) Columnists.

Several names came up several times, so I took the first one to
enter. This included the Indiana Jones (Laurel Traeger of the Baylor
College of Medicine and Richard Brady of the UT Health Science
Center). And Odem Golden Slippers (Al Earnest). He also entered
the Sunnyside Ups.

Yes, it's the Marlin Perkins vs. the Splendora Grasses (W. C.
Daniels), the Thibodaux Raymees vs. the Milwaukee Talkies (Bil-
ly George, who also gave us the Lake Pontchartrain Soreknuckles —
that falls into a category by itself). Then there are Henry Ridgeway's
Stowell Minks and Don Murray's Domino (Texas) Theories, Karen
Elkins' Helena Handbaskets and Derry Airs.

Ohio Silvers would be a surefire winner, but Ruth Weber can't
remember if she thought it up or heard it somewhere else. I still
like it. How about the Boise in the Back of the Room (Betty Freed-
man)? Doug Freede came up with the Akron Nyms (as well as the
Hobbs Nobs), while Don Marshall had the Akron Isms. Both are
worthy contenders.

Right up there, or down there, we have:

Bryan's Song (Jo Ann Smith).
Lincoln Mercurys (Harry Lee).
Iowa Ewes (Alan Wiggins).
Denton Cooleys (Anne Couch).
Tatum O'Neals (William Cassin).
Eugene McCarthys (Joe Hendricks).
Forney Caters (Ray Beeze).

Since I am slow on the uptake, there were some I never did get,
and others that took me several attempts. Finally I discovered it
was best to say the names out loud. You might try it for:

Paducah Wellingtons, Orlando Plenty, and Topeka Boo (Jan
     Wattik).
Anaconda Miniums (Pat Manginelli).
Duluth Teeth (H. T. Cooley, who also gave the world the
     Plano Vanillas and the Kema Sobbies).

It is heartwarming to know that talent and originality are dying
in America. Thus we have:

Tempe Tantrums (Kai Jensen).
Bexar Aspirins (Foster Wick).
Oklahoma Sexuals (Norman Whitlow).
Raleigh Coasters (David Rudell).
Olton Johns (Mark Turk).

Unquestionably, the new United States Football League will field some fine teams. Onward we go, Dallas Stellas (Linda Nicks). Fight fiercely, Denton Fenders and Hannibal Pachyderms (G. F. Paskusz). Some you have to worry about, like the Eau Claire deLunes and Sweeny Todds (Sadie Stockwell), not to mention Dave Whiting's entries: the Dearborn Agains and the Lansing Boils. A special commendation goes to the Departments of Medicine, Cell Biology, and Pathology at Baylor College of Medicine for their entries: the Ledbetter Bedwetters, College Station Wagons, and, my favorite, the Virginia Wolves.

Then there are the Paducah Hazards (Richard and Karen Scott), the La Marque Getsetgos (Houston Apartment Association staff), and from M. A. Charlton the Encino Evil, the Eureka Whiskey, the Ithaca Tastrophe, and the Louisiana One-anna-Two.

Alan Bartczak offers us the Nacogdoches Roaches. Others had the same idea, but Bartczak gets the nod for observing that the Roaches' halftime band is the Texas Instruments. E. S. Daley offers us a prime-time team, the San Marcos Polos, along with the Mathis Johnnys and the Iraan Hostages. Grace Cole has a good one: the Livingston Seagulls. Martin Bryan submits the Broken Arrow Dynamics but says no one in his office claims the San José Canyousees. I should think not. David Broker shows excellent taste with the Lynn (Massachusetts) Ashbys, as does R. W. Clark with the Linash Bees, although I couldn't find Linash listed anywhere.

We're narrowing it down, now. Ray Jones fields a few fine teams: the Hale Center Folds, Manor Beasts, and Salina Tests. Jeff Davis of Turner, Collie & Braden gets honors on his own name alone, but he also has some good entries, the Butte Tifuldreamers, the Stowe (Vermont) Aways, and the Ill. Literates. Paul Flowers, with the Livingston Presumers, wins honorary mention. Peggy O'Connor is grounded for the week for coming up with the Mount St. Helena Ashtros, while Alan Dabney, famed winner of our last name-the-team contest (the Perth Snatchers) does well again. He entered the Temple Moneychangers, St. Louis Encephalitis, Llano Goshen, and Schenectady Thigh Bones.

It was hard to come up with a grand champion, but I knew I was getting warm when Kenneth Graham came up with the Marshall Dillons and the Kermit Frogs to make runner-up. If for any reason the winner can't—or won't—accept the prize, it goes to Graham. But the final envelope. The winners are Strode and Donna Manley of Missouri City, who get downtown Texarkana and that city's franchise, the Texarkana Worms, for submitting not only the Hempstead Exemptions but the—ready?—Tupelo Zeros.

Paint Reflections

UP AGAINST THE WALL—An archbishop of note once said he would not pray for anyone else, explaining that a man must blow his own nose, make his own love, and say his own prayers. Alas, added to that must be painting his own room.

These days, if you want your room painted, you must paint it yourself. Now there are, of course, others who will do it for you—painters, they are called—but they want your firstborn for a down payment and the Aggie Band's marching orders as collateral.

Thus I find myself standing before a wall, armed only with brush and paint can. The wall is white. The fresh paint is also white. I must live aboard the USS *Hope*. Stand by. Check supplies. Cold beer nearby. Cigar clutched firmly between the teeth. Little Dutch Boy, we who are about to die salute you. *En garde*.

Brush-brush upanddown.

The lone advantage to painting is that others leave you alone. An artist must have solitude, he must be left by himself to contemplate the broader horizon. Like Jamie Bray, not alone among the county commissioners, who has a $5,698 car plus $273.60 for a stereo tape deck et al., and his $204.50 electric wastebaskets. Maybe he's a graduate of the electoral college. Maybe Jamie Bray is electric. How much would a windup model cost?

Brush-brush upanddown. The paint keeps running into my shoes. It depresses a man, sometimes. The Pakistanis are slaughtering one another by the thousands, the Catholic Irish are killing the Protestant Irish and vice versa, and Lord knows who are shooting the New York cops. George Bush loses and John Dowdy wins. Hurricane season starts in a week. We seem to think children on welfare really don't get as hungry as our own, then blow almost a million dollars for a chancellor's house in Austin.

It makes a man wonder if there is any justice. Or as Woody Allen put it, "Not only is God dead, but have you ever tried to get a plumber on Saturday?"

Brush-brush upanddown. Strange, my white is not as white as the old white. Have they been busing my brush? Still, one must keep things in perspective. Benjamin Franklin, one of my heroes—he was a rich journalist—noted that the hardest trait for him to master was humility, because whenever he was humble he was immensely proud of it.

By the same token, the one fault I cannot stand is self-pity, so I find that I feel extremely sorry for myself every time I engage in it. No, we must look at the current situation with a critical—but fair—eye, and there is room for optimism, even joy.

After decades of mutual snarling, American and Chinese leaders suddenly are saying rather nice things in public and perhaps are doing something about it all in private. I haven't the foggiest idea why, but then, that really doesn't make much difference, does it?

Then out of the clear blue, it seems that Washington and Moscow are interested in limiting missiles. They have even gone so far as to say that they want to talk about it. Now this, in the devious language of international diplomacy, could mean almost anything, but it sounds promising, and that is a major step away from the old sword-rattling days. Keep your trigger fingers crossed.

There are other points to be noted, such as the fact that this session of the Legislature is drawing to a close with no irreparable damage. And Gov Smith is no longer talking about running for a third term. Smile, too, because the Astros have a mathematical shot at finishing the season and the Oilers are tied for first place.

Now, that is a nicely painted wall, although it might look better if I hadn't painted the window, too. Brush-brush upanddown. No, things have been much worse before and may get that way again, but right now life appears to be worth living.

It is spring. The trees are green and the skies are blue, except Monday, when we finally got a rain. We can look forward to a long stretch of summer and swimming pools and beaches and bikinis and liquor by the drink and parties by the score and no man should ask for more than that. Meanwhile, we have an immediate future of cold beer and hot pants and that in itself is pretty good for openers.

We still have *Petticoat Junction* and Charles Manson and drive-in theatres that show *Wild Riders, Side Hackers,* and *Hell Cats* (all rated R) and proudly proclaim: "Tonight is Family Night!" But any civilization that has *Sesame Street* and "Doonesbury" and Margaret Rutherford and broiled shrimp can't be all bad.

There are still warts on mankind's face, but the old boy seems to be smiling—a most unfamiliar expression of late. God is not dead. How else would all those olives get in that little bitty jar? Indeed, there is hope. When Mr. Nixon can have a book overdue at the LBJ Library, there is hope.

No man should be condemned to painting his own room unless he lives in the Sistine Chapel. Brush-brush upanddown. Maybe Jamie Bray knows an electric painter.

U.S. Legation Site Needs Marker

TEXAS AVENUE—Once more it is the hunt. Ah, yes, the hunt. These many years you and I have kicked over stones and plotted intrigues and whipped unsuspecting peasants in search of almost everything: Nazi war criminals, God, the Twin Sisters, the perfect Scotch, an honest politician. Today we are off on another quest, looking for a small plot of land near the Rice Hotel.

The hotel now occupies the lot where the Texas Capitol once stood. According to early descriptions and drawings, our target might be right across Texas Avenue. At one time that spot, or one nearby, was the home of the U.S. legation, and someone should put up a brass plaque there to note what happened, and didn't happen.

I shall explain. Back in the early days of the Republic of Texas, it was not all joy in Mudville. To be sure, the Mexican Army had been thoroughly whipped at San Jacinto, and Texas was enjoying the first heady fruits of independence. But the simple fact was that there were only about 50,000 Texans—counting 20,000 Indians—compared to about 8 million people in Mexico, which still claimed Texas.

Life was not very easy back then. "Texas was heaven for men and dogs; hell for women and oxen," wrote a pioneer blacksmith by the name of Noah Smithwick. (He was also a tobacco smuggler, but let's not go astray.) In 1836, following San Jacinto, reports periodically swept across Texas that the Mexican Army was returning. The wild rumors continued throughout the next year and on Christmas Eve, 1837, the sleepy village of Houston, in the Republic of Texas, received a bulletin: 1,500 Mexican soldiers had retaken Bexar. Invasion was imminent.

Do not laugh. There was a lot of similar — and accurate — news going around. In 1836 the Mexican Army had conquered San Antonio and what is now Houston. In 1841 President Lamar sent an expedition against Santa Fe. The next year the Mexicans retook San Antonio. Twice. In late 1842 Texas sent an army against northern Mexico. Into late 1844 the border settlements were in "a State of excitements & rumors of Mexican invasion." Entire towns — such as Brazoria and Austin — were stripped of men as they rushed to join the army.

So when word hit Houston on Christmas Eve of 1837 that the Mexican Army was on its way, the fit hit the fandango. A resident of Houston, Mrs. Mary Austin Holley, six days later wrote:

> From that time commenced warlike preparations — all was business & bustle. . . . Meetings were called, money $2000 to $3000 subscribed, — men enrolled (600 in one day) all was excitement. From Mrs. Allens gallery we could over look the whole town in motion like bees swarming — clusters of men in confab — a rushing to the Presidents house next door — everybody in movement. Nobody was afraid, but everybody was busy. We were at the house of Mr. Labranche [the U.S. minister] . . . *a good cabin* — he promised us the protection of the flag if necessary.

And who, pray tell, was this Mr. Labranche? Actually, he spelled his name with a capital B. He was Alcee Louis LaBranche, born near New Orleans in 1806. His father, Alexandre, had sent young Alcee back to France to the Université de Sorreze to school. Alcee had returned to Louisiana to become a sugar planter and a member of the Louisiana House of Representatives. In 1833, he became the speaker of the Louisiana House.

He was described as a young man full of spirit, handsome and dashing. He was President Andrew Jackson's appointment as the first U.S. chargé d'affaires to the brand-new Republic of Texas. After serving in Texas, he returned to Louisiana and became a U.S. congressman in a campaign capped by a duel with a journalist. In the fourth round, LaBranche killed his opponent.

But let's not get ahead of the story. On December 24, 1837, the 31-year-old American diplomat was right around here somewhere, in one of the finer cabins in Houston. And, swashbuckler that he was, LaBranche offered the protection of the U.S. flag to safeguard some Texans from the rumored invasion of the Mexican Army.

But the invasion never happened. No Mexican soldiers marched on these streets. No terrified women and children fled to his protection. The gesture was needless because the report about Bexar being captured was false. But that's not the point. At that time, danger seemed very real and young Alcee LaBranche, waving his Stars and Stripes, might well have been gunned down in these very streets. Santa Anna's track record of POWs was not real good from the Alamo on.

Around here today, huge concrete trucks are lined up on Texas Avenue where there were clusters of men in confab. In the president's one-room house Sam Houston went without supper, as he often did, drawing up battle plans to defend the new republic. In the saloons and street corners, war money was being raised—one sailor gave $80 in silver, all he had. And somewhere around here, where a hole deepens or a tower rises, there was a very good cabin—the U.S. legation held down by a flag and a friend 143 years ago. We need to mark the spot. Considering how much separates us from the U.S., it's nice to have a remembrance of those events that join us.

If You Want Change, Don't Go to a Bank

THE BANK—"I'd like to break this five, please," I say, pushing a five-dollar bill across the counter to the clerk at the Money Changers window.

She looks at the bill suspiciously. "Do you have an account with us?"

"Yes, I do."

"What's the number?"

"I really don't know."

She pushes the five back at me. "You'll have to tell me your account number. Just go over there to Customer Service, and they'll give it to you."

"Customer Service? I just want this five broken."

She gives me a look that means I should go to Customer Service. There are three in front of me at the only window open. My time comes. "I'd like my account number, please."

"Is it listed under your name?" the Customer Servicer asks, turning to his computer.

"Yes, it is."

"Do you know it?"

"Of course I know my name."

"Not your name, sir. Your account number."

"Look, if I knew my account number, I wouldn't be asking you for it." The clerk turns away from his computer and looks at me. "Do you have some identification?"

"Yes, here's my driver's license and credit cards."

"No, I meant some identification to show that you have an account at this bank. Like a check or deposit slip."

"They would have my account number on them, wouldn't they? So I wouldn't have to be over here at Customer Service in the first place."

"It's for your own protection."

"I just want to break this five. I should have gone to a drive-in grocery."

"See Miss Frisbee at Window Three."

I trudge across the lobby to Window Three. There are four ahead of me. By the time I get up to the counter Miss Frisbee has put up a "Next Window Please" sign. I am eighth at the next window. My time finally comes. "Would you please either break this five-dollar bill, tell me my account number, or close my account?" I say testily.

The clerk gives me a blank look. "Sir? This is the Life Savers Club window. Five dollars isn't enough to join."

"Huh?"

"A minimum deposit of $500 is required, plus regular deposits. But you get this," she says, pulling out a magazine. "It's our monthly *Life Line*, listing all the events in sports and entertainment, profiles of exciting personalities, and recipes. This month it's chicken cacciatore."

"Never played it."

"That's the recipe. Plus you get a Life Savers' T-shirt, jogging shorts, and a set of Life Savers' swizzle sticks."

"No, thanks."

"And our special Dog Fight Discounts to shows and restaurants."

"Can you break this five?"

"I don't have any money at this window. Try Mr. Miser in the corner."

I dutifully wait at Mr. Miser's desk until he gets off the phone. "Can you break a five?" I ask.

"Five what? Drachmas? Shekels? Pesos?"

"No, dollars."

"This is the International Banking Section. We don't have any local currencies. Try our Take Five." He picks up the phone again after the first ring. "Hello, Raul? *Cómo se llama?*"

I had seen the Take Five sign out front and return there. It is a large machine with a TV camera pointing down at the users who are punching buttons. "Save Time, Save Effort—Bank Automatically!" the sign announces. I am 12th in line. Shortly after lunch I have worked my way to the front. This is my first time to use the machine so I have to go slowly. A screen lights up: "Punch in name." I do. The screen dims, then relights: "Punch in code word."

"What's that?" I punch back.

"You have been issued a code word," the screen reads. "Punch it in."

"But I don't know what it is," I punch.

"It's 'carbon dioxide,' " the screen reads.

"That's two words," I say but know better than to argue, so I punch it in. "Please instruct," the screen reads. I scan the list of buttons but none reads "Change." The only thing I can think to do is place my five-dollar bill in the slot, and the machine immediately takes it in. "Thanks," the screen reads. It dims, then lights up again: "Next."

"Wait a minute!" I holler.

"Move on, buddy," says the guy behind me.

"But this machine took my money!"

"What's the problem here?" asks a bank guard, appearing at my elbow.

"I want my money back!" I shout as the guard hustles me down the steps and out on the curb. "All I was trying to do was break a five."

"This is a full-service bank, buster," the guard says, "not a drive-in grocery."

Guilt-Edged

The route hasn't been worked out yet, but the conclusion is guaranteed: Vietnam, China, and Russia will end up blaming us for that border war, and we'll go along with their finding. For without a doubt, we are the most guilt-ridden people in the history of civilization.

I come to this terribly heavy conclusion after much hand-wringing, wailing, and self-flagellation. But it is undeniably true: humiliation and head-sagging have become our nature. More than that, we love it, we wallow in it. For we are Americans in the late 20th century, and are guilty as charged. We have done an awful thing.

What thing?

You name it.

If a government is overthrown, it is our fault. If a government is not overthrown, that, too, is our crime. We give arms to an ally, we are bad. We refuse to sell arms to an enemy and that's wrong. Our ships are on alert, and we are saber-rattling to intimidate small nations. Our ships lie at anchor, we are a paper tiger, all talk, no action.

The Bee Gees come from Britain to America and make millions; that's OK. But a lone American wishes to act in a BBC television show — 25 percent backed by U.S. dollars — and it's strike time in London, as the Brits honorably defend their island against the Yankee invaders.

The shah stays in, and irate Iranians march in America. The shah goes out, and irate Iranians take over the U.S. embassy in Tehran. The Nationalist Chinese, a people we alone have bankrolled and defended for a quarter of a century, egg our diplomats. The Mexican president publicly browbeats the U.S. president in ways that — had it been the other way around — would have touched off demonstrations from the Rio Grande to the Straits of Magellan.

Yes, we are guilty as charged, and we stand in the dock. Five U.S. ambassadors have been murdered in the past few years, and we do nothing. (Can you imagine if they had been five *Soviet* ambassadors?)

But why? Why does the world turn against us and point an accusing finger, or — just as often — a rifle? That's a good question, and after some genuine repentance, I have come upon the answer, unworthy despot though I might be. It is quite simply this: We, being the leaders of the Western world, hate ourselves. So others follow.

Yes, indeed, Americans lead all others in being anti-American, and no people before us has ever taken such glee in self-hatred. Look at our movie heroes. They aren't heroes at all, they are antiheroes, from Cool Hand Luke to Billy Jack. Look at the biggest American television audience in the history of the medium: *Roots*, awash in national guilt. We enjoyed prime-time persecution so much we're doing it all over again.

Journalists, preachers, and authors make a fortune catering to our masochism. We are the people we love to hate. As an entire society, we turn on our society, and since everyone is antiestablishment, I'm not sure where that leaves the establishment. If everyone is an Out, who's an In? To paraphrase Pogo, we have created the enemy, and it is us.

The world has forgotten about — or never cared to know about — the French in Indochina, the Cubans in Ethiopia, the British in Malaya, the Russians in Czechoslovakia, the Israelis in Jordan, the Rhodesians in Zambia, the Zambians in Rhodesia, the Mexicans in Chicago, and the Arabs in our pockets, but the word "Vietnam" will be synonymous with Yankee aggression for generations to come.

After all, we are the trend-setters, so there's no reason to get upset. On the other hand, I am upset. I am upset that we gave them the idea, that we are so grief-stricken with ourselves that we have set the cadence for the entire world to greet our every action with suspicion, our every good deed with alarm.

Our Peace Corps members are accused of being CIA spooks; our CARE packages are searched for guns. And every tinhorn dictator, in his 32nd inaugural address, can wrench out a surefire round of applause by criticizing Yankee imperialism. Then he immediately flies to Washington to line up another loan.

All right. The rest of you can continue running around feeling guilty. I'm not saying for a second that we're lily-pure, but I have made it my new resolution to stop blaming myself for earthquakes in Sumatra, pestilence in Iceland, and border wars in Asia. I plead not guilty. And with grounds, your honor.

No nation in history has given so much of its gold and blood to others. We taxed ourselves to underwrite nations that would not tax themselves. We drafted our young men to defend nations that would not draft their own. We have laid it on the line for 40 years, when no one else would.

Let's not kid our self-immolating selves. If there were no U.S., a goodly chunk of the world would get down on its knees and pray for one.

This is not chauvinism, nor isolationism. It is self-realization. But we must be fair: we must not blame others for this problem, for we have brought it on. We have told ourselves how bad we are so long and so loud that the neighbors can't help but overhear. And after a while, they begin to believe it, too.

But I've had it. And the next time some sackcloth psychologist carefully explains to me how I killed Kennedy, the next time some exchange student who hasn't seen a classroom in five years castigates me for setting up his nation's oil industry — I'm going to punch him in the nose.

Can You Top This for Openers?

Instructions for Opening a Can

Congratulations. You are the proud owner of a can. Your new purchase should give you long hours of pleasure if you take care of it.

Opening instructions: Hold can in left hand, with ring on top side (see Fig. 1). With right hand, grasp ring (see Fig. 2). Pull ring up (see Fig. 3) and out. Ring and pull-top should come up and off. If not, please return can with carton and instructions to seller. Replacement will be at the convenience of dealer. (Void in Oregon.)

U.S. Army Instructions: Can Assault and Securement
1) Hold container in left hand.
2) Your other left, dummy.
3) Grab ring (Individual, Model 23-8) with right hand.
4) Wait until enemy is within 15 feet (three yards, or almost three meters).
5) Rip ring off.
6) Throw can.
7) Duck.
8) If ineffective, use sharpened part of pull-tab.
9) List next of kin on back of form.

OSHA Instructions

WARNING: *Cans can explode!* This very can might blow up at any moment! Death and destruction might follow, wiping out most of your city, so take care to follow these important instructions. First, don heavy work gloves, federally inspected safety goggles, and umpire's chest protector.

Carefully take can to a safe place — OSHA recommends Salt Flats, Utah — being sure not to shake, dent, or puncture. Keep at 55 degrees at all times. Using a three (3) inch thick steel plate with two (2) five (5) inch round (O) holes, put arms through holes and grasp can.

Very carefully pull tab. At the slightest sign of fizzing or spewing, run like a bandit, then see your nearest lawyer.

San Antonio News-Express-Light Exclusive:

KID CUTS HAND ON CAN!
"IT HURTS, MOMMY"

An 11-year-old San Antonio child, defying his mother's instructions to "Leave that can alone," attempted to open a possibly lethal can of soft drink Tuesday and cut his hand. Blood gushed, oh, my Lord, it's too terrible to relate.

(For details and color photographs, see pages 45–49.)

Memo to Brotherhood
Gravel Truck Drivers and Beetle Stompers:

Get a can, see? Grab that sucker in your left hand, stick your finger in the ring, and yank that mother like a stick shift on a Peterbilt, good buddy. The BGTD&BS urges all members to keep a clean truck cab, so throw that tab out the window. Same with the can when you're through. See you on down the road on the flip-flop, and that's a big 10-4.

Instructions to All Freedom Fighters of the 13th of March
Peace Movement & Bomb Squad
How to Handle Can

First, make sure can is not Coke. Coke is sold in Israel. Hold can in right hand — if not yet cut off — and pull tab with left. Empty contents on ground which our brothers fought for and which the international Zionists are trying to steal. Refill can with gasoline. Stick wick in top. Wait for Israeli tank. If tank fails to come, blame America. If it does come, blame America. If you can't even find a can of Pepsi, blame America.

Joint U.S. Congressional Resolution

WHEREAS, it is the intention of this august body to conserve the funds of the republic and at the same time maintain the decorum of said august body, members are urged to refrain from ordering Lafitte Rothschild '73 at their desks, and;

WHEREAS, it is considered important at this time of national hardship and high unemployment;

BE IT RESOLVED, that members of Congress shall start drinking from cans rather than Waterford crystal goblets.

BE IT ALSO RESOLVED, that each member shall be authorized to hire one (1) additional staff member to handle said matter, and an annual appropriation of $34,000 is authorized each member to cover expenses of said staffer plus an additional $3,000 for said cans.

Staffer is hereby authorized to hold can in right hand while a second staffer (see Tab-Pull Supplement Bill) grabs tab and . . .

Israeli Army Instructions for Can (Individual Model 23-8)

1) Make sure can is not Pepsi. Pepsi is sold in nations which support the PLO.

2) Grab can in left hand, put finger through ring with right.

3) Pull.

4) If ring refuses to come off, return to nearest U.S. Marine outpost and demand a refund.

5) Watch out for shepherds drinking Pepsi.

Press Release

Office of U.S. Representative Charles Wilson:

My fellow good ol' boys from the Big Thicket, I would like to clear up some erroneous press reports of late. I was at a party, see, and this fellow comes up and asks if I want some Coke. I took the can in my right hand and he puts a spoon in my left. Well, shucks, I never drank Coke with a spoon, but I didn't want to embarrass him, so . . .

Exit, Please

THE DEN—"Quiet, everyone," I say over the voices. "I have called this meeting because the place is getting too crowded, and some of you are going to have to leave."

There is an immediate rumble of angry voices. "Quiet! Quiet!" I say. "I'm very sorry, but that's the way it is. Any volunteers?"

"It is not bad to die," says Lieutenant Henry. "It is good. Death is good. But life is better."

"I'd step forward in an instant," says Files-on-Parade, "but they're 'anging Danny Deever in the morning."

"Look, I don't like this any more than you all do," I say. "But my office is overflowing."

"Read the best books first, or you may not have a chance to read them all," says Thoreau. He is always saying that sort of thing. Gets annoying.

"Life being very short, and the quiet hours of it few, we ought to waste none of them in reading valueless books," John Ruskin adds.

"When you call me that, smile," says the Virginian.

"We could be sold to the fascists," says Pilar.

"It is not good," says Robert Jordan. "But life is good."

"Life is good," agrees Pablo, wiping wine off his chin, "but life without death is like . . ."

"A day without sunshine," Joey Adams interrupts.

"Would you all shut up?" I plead.

"Men fear death, as children fear to go into the dark," says Francis Bacon. "And, as that natural fear is increased with tales, so is the other."

"Aye, but to die and go we know not where, to lie in cold obstruction and to rot," says Shakespeare gloomily. He can always put a damper on the conversation.

"Look, no one is dying," I say. "You are all immortal, so quit being so melodramatic. It's just that some of you have to go somewhere else. That's an order."

"A properly trained elephant can understand up to 30 commands," say David Wallechinsky and Irving Wallace in unison.

"What's that got to do with anything?" I say.

"Don't worry about us," say Norman Mailer and Jimmy Breslin. "We're leaving right now."

"This is a stiff bunch," Breslin adds, throwing some half-filled bottles in a suitcase. "They don't like hard-drinking, self-important voices of the little man around here." He leaves.

"Now get this, kid," says Spillane, snuffing out the last of a pack of Luckies. "Maybe I catch hell and get kicked out of business, but if *you* pull the trigger, *you* sit in the hot seat. I'm calling the plays in this game, kid."

"And I'm a better man than he is," adds Gunga Din.

"What you need is a purge," offers Park Chung-hee. "In my country, freedom of the press and publication was asserted, thus encouraging confusion. The government promoted a self-purge of corrupt journalists."

"Do any of you know anyone not here who might volunteer to leave?"

"I know, mas're, but I can't tell anything," whines Uncle Tom. "I can die!"

"Death is good," says Pablo, finishing up his wine.

"But death with honor is better," adds Lieutenant Henry.

"I plead not guilty," speaks up a voice from the back. It's Galileo. "Any idiot knows that the earth revolves around the sun. And Torquemada can kiss my ring."

I'm losing control of this discussion. Maybe I should try to explain a little more. "You all have been good companions over the years, but my problem is that I can't resist buying good books, even bad ones. I've got too many."

"Never trust a man with a vast array of books," says Anonymous. "It simply shows he has no taste."

"A big book is a big nuisance," adds Callimachus.

"Yeah," says de Maupassant. "So get Mencken to move out."

Mencken peers over his glasses at de Maupassant. "I can't pretend that I have covered the whole field in the present volume," he says dryly, "for that field has become very large in area."

"I've got you all stacked up all over the place," I plead. "De Gaulle and Hitler side by side. Ayn Rand living next to John Kenneth Galbraith."

"There goes the neighborhood," sniffs Galbraith.

"And you, Benchley, Benet, Churchill, and Vandiver, all crowded in together. Wouldn't you like a little more room?"

Churchill puffs on his cigar and says nothing. He looks bored with the whole spectacle.

Finally Oliver Goldsmith pipes up: "The first time I read an excellent book, it is to me just as if I had gained a new friend. When I read over a book I have perused before, it resembles the meeting with an old one."

"Hear! Hear!" says Churchill, finally getting interested.

"You all aren't making this any easier for me," I say testily. "I'm doing this as much for you as for me."

Snickers fill the room.

I sigh. No one is leaving. I can tell I'm licked. "OK. You can just stay here, all piled up, covering every square inch of space. But don't come crying to me when you get buried in an avalanche."

"Life is good," says Robert Jordan. "Better than death with dishonor."

"Don't say anything," sighs the countess. "Just hold me."

Digit Fugit

MY SON'S BEDROOM — "What time do you want to get up in the morning?" I ask, not planning to do anything about it myself at that ungodly hour, but willing to pass the word along.

My youngest son pauses for a moment. "At 7:12," he says. Then he rolls over and goes to sleep.

He is not joking. No, he's quite serious. Seven-twelve it is. Not 7:10 or 7:15, but 7:12. There are two reasons for such exact instructions. One, I am told, is that mornings around here are run on a split-second timetable rivaling a lunar landing. But the second and most important reason is that my children, like most, have been raised in the digital decade.

The clocks they see, the ones they use, are all digital. In classrooms, the clocks are usually digital. The signs children see around town are digital. Blinking lights from a bank sign, alternatively telling them the time and temperature in digital fashion. When was the last time you saw a public clock with *hands* telling you the time? Only atop the City Hall, where lighted clock faces are on all four sides, giving you a selection of times tailored to meet your own needs.

Go into any jewelry store (or, more likely, the watch case at the drugstore) and compare the number of watches with hands and those with ever-changing numbers. I don't know if anyone has checked, but I'd wager digital clocks have been the best-selling type for several years.

In the *Post* city room, because of deadlines, we all keep one eye on the typewriter and the other on the clock. What kind of clock? Well, that depends. If I want to know what time it is in Dublin, Fairbanks, or Moscow, I check the bank of round-faces on a far wall. But if I want to know how many minutes till deadline in Houston, Texas, I check one of several digital clocks. This probably means that Dublin, Fairbanks, and Moscow still use the old-fashioned kind of clock and thus are behind the times, so to speak.

Children used to be taught how to tell time. You remember your teacher's big hand–little hand lecture. Today it's just another lost art, like reading and manners. To be sure, digital clocks are great for very young children, who are not yet old enough to read hands, but when these little children become big children, they remain unable to read a clock.

Digital clocks are not anything new. I recall very well that my father had one on his desk at his office decades ago. But for some reason, digital clocks lagged behind the competition. Only in these recent computer chip times have they become popular. Now such timepieces are everywhere. They are built into cars, radios, TV sets, kitchen ovens, video recorders. Look, Ma, no hands.

I'm not so sure just why this old idea has become so popular. Maybe it's because we are getting lazy and don't even want to contemplate what it means when Mickey's big hand points up and his little hand points to the left. Maybe it's just a fad. In a sweep of nostalgia—not to mention energy savings—maybe we'll return to the sundial. If we do, I guarantee within weeks the Japanese will be marketing a digital sundial.

As digital clocks are advancing, those with hands are retreating from our culture. Someday they will occupy a spot in the Smithsonian along with ice trays, fountain pens, and Connally buttons. Little children will tug at their mothers' rolled-up Levi's to ask, "What's that? That round thing with the two arrows?"

This change is also altering our very language. For instance, my son's get-me-up-at-7:12 speech. I would have said, "A little after 7." Or maybe "7:15." But people don't talk that way anymore, because digital clocks are exact. They do not show the proximity of now to then and soon. Only one time is shown: right now. Right now is all we have to go on. So we say it's 12:54 or 9:06. It used to be half past six. Now it's 6:31.

No more could we write songs about it's a quarter till three, there's no one in the place, except you and me. So set 'em up, Joe. Today it would be it's 2:46, at which time Joe would set 'em up at the risk of being raided by the liquor control agents, each pointing to his own digital watch.

Yes, we are honing down our time. The sloppiest people, the most hang-loose individuals, now tell you with the utmost precision that the phone rang at 11:19. No doubt it will get to the point that in a court of law, if a witness says the robber entered his store a short time before midnight, a mistrial will be declared within :01 or :02 minutes.

Beach Bum

THE BEACH — There is something very lonely and private about the beach in winter. It is not the despairing, depressing kind of loneliness that creeps in and surrounds you, but rather the quiet and contented feeling.

The beach this winter has been particularly cold and wet, just like the rest of the nation. Only the wind that howls constantly along the sand seems to accentuate the numbing temperature. No, I take that back. It doesn't *seem* to make it colder, it *does* make it colder. It's the old wind chill factor, turning 45 degrees into zero. But it is one of the hardships one must accept along the beach in winter. It is what keeps the rest of the world away, leaving you all alone out here.

The whole Bolivar Peninsula is virtually empty. No sun-bronzed gods mucking about the grocery stores looking for sun-bronzed goddesses. No VW vans with surfboards lashed to them like so many dead deer on a Hill Country jeep. No dune buggies loping along the beaches, sending small children scattering for safety. And no plastic-ringed six-pack holders blowing among the shells.

They are not here, those summer soldiers and sunshine paraphernalia. They are back home doing whatever it is they do during the winter. For it is too cold and windy out here to attract the faint-hearted. It is up to us, we hearty few, to hold down the beach during the off season, and make sure that the tide goes in and out on schedule.

The wind blows along, rather than into, the beach, sweeping from east to west, so that when you walk along the sand you have to decide whether you wish to have the wind in your face — and thus freezing you solid — the first half or the second half of your walk. I am of the first-half school, so I begin my beach walks into the wind. Out here the wind is all you hear. It totally drowns out all other noises except the surf, but no matter, for there is really nothing else you want to hear. It is like standing in the shower. The outside world has been turned off briefly, allowing you a few minutes of silence.

And shell hunting. Shell hunting and beachcombing are the national pastimes of the true beach bum. Needless to say, the best season for shell hunting is right now, for there are no others out here to rob the beach of what is rightfully yours. There is no need to rise at first light to comb the night's leavings. Midafternoon is fine, for even now there are no footprints in the sand. No Man Friday has come this way and when you look behind, only your own footprints have messed up the carpet.

There are a few fishermen down at Rollover Pass. Manfully they drop their bait into the water, but the fish have flown south for the winter. They are not biting.

Up and down the highway, most of the various business establishments have one message for the outside world: "Closed." They are shut down for the winter, so shopping is generally confined to beer and newspapers.

The vehicular lifeline to the peninsula is the Bolivar Ferry, which still sports its Bicentennial suit. The wait for the ferry is usually not very long in winter, but sometimes the cars are backed up all the way past the lighthouse. Today the line begins back here, and right in front of me is a Chevy pickup truck, license plate HJ 7281. The owner rolls down the window long enough to toss a cigarette wrapper out the window. A few minutes later he tosses a beer can into the roadside ditch. Just before the string of vehicles pulls forward, he throws a paper cup out the window and into the ditch. HJ 7281, you are a real creep.

At night, there is a moon so full and orange it looks like a Gulf Oil sign. It comes up in the southeast, rising just above the water and causing the flat ocean to reflect the lunar light. Then the moon continues rising, turning smaller and more yellow until it is overhead. The waves roll in and the whitecaps catch the moon, reflecting as though there were a string of white lights being washed ashore. I've never seen anything like it. Really eerie.

For those who are either uncommonly brave or at least suicidal, walking the beach at night is an experience all its own. Again the wind sweeps down the sand, only colder than ever. Out on the ocean are the lights of ships waiting to move into Galveston Bay. And there are the offshore oil rigs. They are newcomers to this part of the beach, being run up and torn down, high on their stilts, lighted up like Christmas trees by night. If the weather is cold and windy on land, one can guess what life is like out there on those rigs tonight. Whatever the drillers are being paid, it's not enough.

Still, for all the winter hardships, walking the beach at night has its rewards. The water surging up the sand, then hauling back for another stab. The eternal struggle of man against the elements as I try to light a cigar in the wind. The pleasant lack of billboards and ringing telephones and barking dogs and crying children. The total lack of other people. From the beach, all the cabins are lined up against the sky, dark and lifeless. All shut down and locked up.

All but one. It stands out from the others, alit and lively. From the beach I can see the fire in the fireplace. And by the fire is a bottle of brandy. And a book. So it is that I go back to the warm, snug cabin, yet no closer than before to answering the question I have been wrestling with as I walk along the beach. There has got to be an answer to it somewhere, but it eludes me. Maybe I shall come back here tomorrow and wander among these sands, seeking true wisdom, but I really doubt I will ever know why creeps in pickup trucks throw beer cans out windows.

Just Watching 'Em Delivering the Goods

THE FRONT YARD — It is midday in midweek. My neighborhood is like most around Houston at this time, practically empty except for the burglars. The children have all left for school. The husbands are off at work. The wives are playing tennis or shopping or holding down their own jobs or whatever it is that wives do in the middle of the day.

There is absolutely no sign of life here in Running Rats Acres except for one constant: the repair truck, the delivery van, the brightly colored vehicles telling us that carpets are being cleaned, walls painted, refrigerators repaired, drains unstopped, lamps uncrated. Our society cannot function without an armada of vehicles spread throughout the neighborhoods, keeping our homes functioning.

If you doubt this, drive around your block some weekday counting the trucks and vans parked in front of homes, backing out driveways, pulled over to the curb while the driver tries to figure out where he is. You will soon note that if it moves in your neighborhood between 9 and 5, it has a two-way radio on the dashboard and a Key Map in the glove compartment. What's more, the side of a van can tell you more about your neighbors than looking in their checkbooks, Bibles, or medicine cabinets.

Since it is my style to work at home as much as possible, I have become somewhat of an expert at van viewing. From half a block away I can tell whether a floor is being waxed, a shower pan is leaking, or a television picture is rolling. Indeed, I have neatly categorized the entire situation. For instance, this time of year we see the spring fleet of trucks. They come to fix the air conditioner, fertilize the yard, get things going for the summer. In the fall, we have the heater repairmen, the firewood deliverers, the garage door installers. And throughout the year I can spot the painters. Right now they are putting on outdoor paint. In the dead of winter they only work indoors, and if your house is peeling on the outside, tough.

But most important, you can tell so much about your neighbors' finances by the trucks parked out front. In our area we have a painting contractor who turned down work on the ceiling of the Sistine Chapel because he doesn't do touch-up jobs. I once hired him to paint the garage, but when he finished he tried to sign it. He's now too expensive for me, but I do spot his truck occasionally; thus it's easy to see which of my neighbors is making a killing these days.

Other telltale signs of good times are the trucks denoting tennis court rolling crews, a fur delivery from Neiman's, and the installers' vans from the Perrier Fire Extinguishing System. Conversely, dead giveaways that things are not going too well are pest control vans with tail gunners and those from floor rental companies. Another clue is when the Goodwill truck pulls up and the driver makes a delivery.

This same observance is shown around town in a broader version: the nicer the neighborhood, the more trucks are parked outside during the workday simply because those with money hire people without it to do all the things that those without it have to do for themselves. Drive around River Oaks, for example, and you'll spot one, two, or three pickups and vans parked in the driveway during the day. Drive around my neighborhood and you'll see the same thing — at night.

In the fear that my blockmates have noticed that we rarely have any kind of repair or delivery truck parked in our driveway, I have decided to rectify this situation by buying a shell of a van and parking it on the street in front of my house. Then I shall continually change the sign on the side. One day, for example, neighbors will look out to see a delivery from Jamail's. The next day, Tiffany's. And so on. When I've got them impressed, I shall move on to the Ajax Light Bulb Changing Company, the U.S. Department of the Treasury Bulk Package Delivery Service, and the Servants' Quarters Pool Cleaners, Inc. My neighbors might have a Crown Plumbing Company truck out front. I'll have one from the Crown Polishing Company.

The more observant on my street might notice that, all the time, the van remains up on wooden blocks, which could create a problem. That will be solved when they see a collection van from Classical Tires of Texas, Inc., followed the next day by the A. J. Foyt Wooden Block Company. We hope someday to be a three-repair-truck family.

Bolivar Blues

BOLIVAR PENINSULA — I have sneakily waited until the morning after to leave the peninsula for Galveston. There is a policy to my procrastination: most of the tourists and beach bums will have left yesterday, only to discover that they must wait here at the ferry landing for hours, languishing in the hot sun while their tongues thicken and mirages form in Zam's parking lot.

Poor devils, and so close to the oasis. Yes, it's too bad about them, but today is different. The crowds are gone and thus I may speed quickly to the ferry dock, thence to depart on the POSH side for the island. But if today is better, why am I sitting here in this lengthy line on Highway 87, far removed from the ferry dock? I'll tell you why. It's because all the tourists and beach bums on the peninsula decided to avoid the crowds and waited until this morning to leave.

So the place looks like Danang. Cars, trucks, tanks, refugees, lined up and waiting for the last boat. I stop my engine and get out for a look. I can't even see the ferry, as I am backed up behind the Bolivar lighthouse, which is two days' drive from the ferry slip.

Wait. Wait. The sun is beating down, and I lost my pith helmet in that nasty little ambush back a ways. The woman in the station wagon in front of me is sitting there, calm and cool, mainly because she has her windows rolled up, her air conditioning on, and her engine running. I walk up to her car and tap gently on the window.

She rolls it down. "I'm sorry I didn't hear you," she says. "But I had my window rolled up and my air conditioning on."

I explain the necessity of turning off her engine to keep her car from overheating, which she does, just in time for the car in front of her to pull forward. She shoots me a glance similar to the one John Connally gave Jake Jacobsen, restarts her engine, and pulls up.

More waiting. The sun is beating down, and not a beer around. The big sport for the waiters is to count the number of cars rolling off the ferry, then figure out where you are in line and thus how many ferry boats will be needed to get your car across the wide waters. I figure it to be about 36 cars, but it isn't that easy. For instance, here comes a new load off the boat.

Count the cars, one, two, three. But then here comes one pulling a boat. That would have to count as two. Then a big camper, then a trailer truck, which would have to count as three unless they park Fiats underneath it. Two motorcyclists. What are they worth in the overall count? As I said, it can get difficult.

Now I am within seeing distance of the ferry dock and here comes the ferry, the good ship *Cone Johnson*. The last ship from Danang. Maybe I can sneak ahead if I tell them my suitcases contain gold to bankroll the continuing struggle of free men against the godless communists. And that my sister married a gunnery sergeant from Omaha.

We creep forward, the *Cone Johnson* suddenly reluctant to swallow the same amount it regurgitated only moments before. A fellow in a white hat signals the gate to go down, leaving us on the beachhead. Is that incoming mail? How long can we hold out against such overwhelming odds?

The crowd is growing restless. How is it that the USS *Johnson* took them and not us? Certainly there was room for a few good men. Our rear guard is crumbling. We shall soon fall to the hordes. How many are ahead of me? I count 34. That's too close. One of the 34 is a truck marked Cajun Chef, from some backwater in Louisiana. Cajun Chef is worth three cars. That makes me 35 or 36. But that camper up there—it's a long one.

More waiting. The sun is beating down, and the drums, always the drums. Where is our salvation? Suddenly black smoke puffs up from around the bend, and here comes, eh? The *Cone Johnson*. No wonder the line is so long—they've only got one ferryboat running. Cars come off the ramp, smiling confidently that they have made a trip we have yet to take. Twenty-one, 26, 30, campers, cars, trucks, they come off. I count 35 this time. If I am 36, then all is lost, as the major has just ordered us to burn our files and bury our dog tags.

My line begins to move forward, slowly, oh, so slowly. The *Cone Johnson*'s appetite is nil. A dozen cars go up the ramp and seem to fill the entire ship. The Cajun Chef wallows on board, brimming with hot sauce and awash with jambalaya. Letting those foreigners on first while we who fought with you from the DMZ to the Mekong are left behind.

As each car rolls on, the driver beams confidence. I'm all right, Jack. So long, suckers. They are safe and care not a whit for we who also served. Just look at them parking their cars and rushing back to the fantail to gaze at the crowded, smoking beaches they left. So long, suckers, indeed. Wait till the war crimes trials.

The line inches forward, then stops. Three cars are in front. A blue Buick goes aboard confidently. Then a Cadillac from Alabama. One car. The white-hatted crewmen look around for a space, find one, and the lady goes on, windows up, air conditioning blowing. The crewmen at the ramp look at me. I look at them. They size up the deck space. My sister. The sergeant from Omaha. I got to get to the land of the free so I can write my memoirs and make lots of money.

They finally motion me to the very last place on the ferry and I leap aboard. So long, suckers.

Resistance Dead

PARIS—The Fort of Mont Valerien stands atop a hill of the same name, defending the western approaches to Paris. The hill used to be called Mont Calvaire and was the goal of religious pilgrims. Hermits lived here, maintaining vineyards and gardens and making silk stockings, of all things. There was a guest house at the hermitage that was visited by Thomas Jefferson several times when he was minister to France between 1784 and 1789.

Napoleon thought the hill was a good place to build a home for the orphans of his Legion of Honor, and confiscated the hill in 1811. But during a later visit he decided Mont Valerien would serve better as the site of a fort to guard this side of the city. Those plans were scrubbed by Waterloo, and the place returned to its role as a religious shrine. In 1840, the French Army built the fort and still uses it as the headquarters for the Signal Corps.

All of this does not make Mont Valerien particularly interesting. Any number of hills in Europe can claim more important roles. What makes this place chillingly different occurred a century after the fort was built. In 1940, the Gestapo made Fort Valerien its headquarters. During the German occupation, a total of 4,500 political prisoners and members of the French Resistance were lined up against this south wall and shot.

The execution site was inside the fort and is open to the public only on special occasions. Open or not, I have no strong desire to see it. But here on the outside, along this same wall, the French have established a most unusual monument to the victims.

Looming over everything, far back from the road, is the wall itself, a long, dark, ugly wall, maybe 25 feet high and a football field long. Along the stone structure are 16 metal sculptures portraying various elements of the Resistance in an abstract way: saboteurs, radio operators, assassins, prisoners.

Here in the middle is a huge Cross of Lorraine, symbol of the Free French. In front of the cross is a flame, and around the flame are flowers. On one side of the cross, cut into the wall, is the year the war began, 1939. On the other side of the cross is the year of Liberation, 1945. And carved into the cross itself are the words of General Charles de Gaulle, broadcast from London on June 18, 1940, after the fall of France: "Whatever happens, the flame of resistance will never die."

He was right. The flame of resistance didn't die. But a good number of French did — soldiers and sailors, no longer in uniform but still fighting. Men, women, young people. Intellectuals, politicians, communists, union leaders, business executives. Protestants, Roman Catholics, Jews. Rounded up and brought here to Fort

Valerien in the backs of vans in the dead of night to be questioned. The lucky ones were lined up against this wall and shot.

At the base of the cross are two steel doors. Locked tight. There is a little guard's house far down at the end of the wall, out of sight, and in the house is a tiny old man who has the key to the doors. He comes out, key in hand, shuffling down to the thick steel doors. He unlocks one and lets me in. It is pitch black inside. Then he turns on the lights. Anyone who is not moved to tears by this cannot be moved at all.

Small spotlights from the ceiling shine down on 16 wooden coffins, each covered by the French tricolor. They are arranged in a semicircle, behind a small railing. The boxes are of rich, dark reddish wood, peaked at the top. They stand on beams maybe two feet above the ground. Each one is exactly the same. There is no name, no rank, no date.

"The coffins themselves are empty," says the little old man through an interpreter. "The bodies are buried beneath them, down in the concrete. They came from all over. Some were shot here at Fort Valerien. Others died in concentration camps. Some were in the military, but most were civilians—two were young Jewish girls executed by the Nazis."

The families—if there were any left—donated the remains to this shrine after the war, but only the families and the War Department know exactly who is buried where. "You see," a French citizen explains, "over the centuries we have had so many wars, revolutions, religious upheavals. And every time there is one, our cemeteries and shrines are looted, damaged, and defaced. This way, no one knows the exact burial spot of any of the victims here, and they are all safer for it. We want this to stand forever."

Behind me, back toward the entrance, is a metal sculpture of a flame reaching upward, three to four feet high. "Beneath that," the old man says, gesturing toward the metal flame, "are ashes gathered from all the extermination camp crematoriums. Some members of the Resistance left no bodies to be buried."

Wandering around this small crypt, with its darkness broken only by the spotlights stabbing down on the flags, makes me feel very old and very tired. I wonder if it affects others the same way? I also wonder if there are people selling Mercedes-Benzes in Frankfurt who caused this.

"You will notice that there are 16 coffins, but there is still room for one more," I am told. "That's because we still have one last person to bury here—the 17th Resistance fighter. You see, these people were awarded the Order of the Liberation. In all, 1,053 such awards were handed out by France. Most were French, but the honorees included Churchill, Eisenhower, and the King of Morocco.

"Obviously, no Order of the Liberation medals have been awarded in years. Today there are only 400 living holders of the award. The very last one to die will be buried here. He or she will be the 17th — and last."

Publisher Has Novel Approach to Selling a Turkey of a Book

THE OFFICE—"Great, just great," said the publisher.

"Thanks," I said modestly.

"A best seller for sure," said the publisher.

"Really?"

"Absolutely. I've been in this business for 43 years, and I can spot a winner a mile away. Then there is the Book-of-the-Month Club. A certainty. And movie rights."

"TV series?"

"Naturally. Not to mention a sequel."

"Fantastic."

"Of course, it does need a little polishing. Just minor stuff."

"No problem. I aim to sell."

"The title, for example. *Circumstantial Evidence Pointing to the Possibility that Figs Cause Deviated Behavior in the Mexican Turkey.*"

"What's the matter with it?"

"A little cumbersome to get on the marquee."

"Marquee?"

"The Broadway version."

"Oh, sure."

"How about *Fig Leaves Below the Border?*"

"I don't think so."

"Yeah. Maybe not," he agreed.

"I've got it. *Turkey!*"

The publisher frowned. "Let's forget about Broadway for a moment and stick with the book itself. We need something a little more catchy, to bring in the spy buffs."

"What do spies have to do with Mexican turkeys?"

"Nothing. But they have everything to do with selling books. And all the best-selling spy books have to sound the same. We call it *The Cashier Connection.*"

The publisher picked up his phone. "Hello, Titles? Whatcha got today? Eh? OK. Not bad. Right." He scribbled some notes and hung up.

"We've got *The Delta Factor, The Capricorn Convention, The Apple Affair,* and *The Luck of the Irish.*"

"They don't fit."

"Sure they do. Just put the part about the code in chapter 2. Drop the Yale study and make sure the history of figs in chapter 5 brings in the Yalta Conference being bugged by the Germans."

"Germans?"

"Of course. We've got to have at least some mention of the Nazis."

"I don't get it."

The publisher sighed. "Because of the cover. You can't give away a book these days without a swastika on the cover."

He picked up his phone again. "Hello, Covers? Send up what you got." A moment later there was a rap on the door and a secretary brought in a stack of covers, which the publisher spread out on his desk.

"OK, we got the swastika with the cross, the swastika linked to the Star of David, wrapped around the caduceus, emerging from a meatloaf, and as a background to the skyline of Omaha. Which one you want?"

"None of 'em are even close," I said.

"If you can cut out the part about the behavior of the Mexican turkey . . ."

"No."

"Do they have turkeys in Germany?"

"I don't know. Maybe."

The publisher nodded, thumbing through some more covers. "Good. And I know they've got breasts."

"Turkeys?"

"Germans. Ah, here it is. An Iron Cross on a heaving bosom."

I looked them over. "Frankly, the circumstantial evidence that figs caused deviated behavior in Mexican turkeys really doesn't have much to do with Iron Crosses and heaving bosoms."

"So drop the bit about connecting figs with turkeys. You said yourself it was circumstantial."

"But what do I put in its place?"

The publisher reached for the phone. "Hello, Plots?"

He looks at the list. "We've got the Winston Churchill diet book: blood, toil, sweat, and tears followed by lobster Newburg and chocolate mousse, washed down with a Dom Perignon."

"Anything in a Mexican turkey?"

"Here's one: a crusty Latin American dictator moves to a small town in Vermont and opens a ski resort for lepers."

"You sure you didn't ring up TV Pilots instead of Plots?"

The publisher scanned some more papers. "OK, we've got a researcher who comes up with this stupid study about figs and turkeys and tries to write a book about it. Nah, it would never sell."

"All right! That does it!" I shout. "You have taken my idea and twisted it beyond recognition. You have cut out all my research and put in some stupid junk just to hype sales. You don't care about me or my work or eight years of poking through every turkey lot south of Brownsville. So I tell you what I'm going to do. I'm going to take you down to the main intersection in town and stuff this manuscript in your big fat mouth and set it on fire! You hear that?"

The publisher frowned and reached for the phone. "You'd do that to me?"

"Better believe it, buster!"

"Hello, Publicity?"

Go Texan

A Texan I know, Terry O'Rourke, currently works at the White House. Last month his wife was about to have a baby, so he obtained the necessary equipment:

> The State of Texas — To all whom these presents shall come: GREETINGS: know ye that the contents of the package affixed hereto are authentic grains of Texas soil, such grains having been obtained from the ground of the State Capitol Building located in the City of Austin this 20th day of December, 1979.
>
> In testimony whereof, I hereby proclaim that upon the birth of Baby O'Rourke such soil shall be placed under the

child's feet, thereby entitling him to all rights, privileges and honors of a "BORN TEXAN."

Mark White, Attorney General of Texas.

It turned out that the "him" was Kathryn O'Rourke, five pounds, 13 ounces, but she was a born Texan, and that's what counts. Now, I doubt if this sort of thing is done in other places, but it is done enough by Texpatriates that the state has it down to an orderly procedure.

I mention this because today is Go Texan Day. It's a good time to take stock of our homeland, inherited or acquired. And it is also a good time for newcomers to discover just what sort of club they've joined. This brings us to our first point: for all our problems and perils, we must be doing something right because others can't get here fast enough. We now number more than 13 million. We've passed two-thirds of the nations of the earth in both people and area.

Texas, were it to be a republic again, would be the world's fifth most productive nation. We lead the nation in everything from ranches to cabbage. While much of the world is energy short, we produce more than we can use. Texas uses only 60 percent of the gas that it produces. In '78, natural gas production here was 6.5 trillion cubic feet. We used only 4.2 trillion. We produced 1.073 billion barrels of oil. We used only about 207 million barrels. We don't use much heating oil and I couldn't find diesel usage.

Texas has more Latin Americans than Nicaragua or Costa Rica. More blacks than Gambia or Gabon. We have almost four times as many cars as the Soviet Union. We could put France in Texas and still have more than enough room for Louisiana. This is an unusual place.

How do you explain all of this to newcomers? You don't have to, for we were all newcomers once. The defenders at the Alamo gathered from 20 states and six countries. Eleven were from Texas and 22 just appeared—to this day no one knows where they came from. At San Jacinto, the Texas Army hailed from 24 states and 11 countries. The only native Texians in the army couldn't speak English. Others in other places did what they could to help. Mobs in Philadelphia burned Santa Anna in effigy. New York held benefit performances of *The Tragedy of Venice Preserved* to raise money for the embattled Republic. Two thousand New Yorkers jammed Tammany Hall to pledge their loyalty to Texas. The only artillery we had at San Jacinto were the Twin Sisters, a gift from the people of Cincinnati. We are not alone.

But we are different. We love action and violence. We despise government and governors, laws and lawmakers. By careful design, we have a weak government, simply because we feel that no one else knows exactly where we itch. On the other hand, we are—as a group—easily controllable. Texas does not realize its power. We have often sent to Washington a group of limp-wristed dilettantes who have failed to reflect our strength. We are feeding and fueling much of America and are being treated as not much more than a milk cow, an easily managed colony in the outback.

But it was not always this way. Tomorrow, for instance, is an anniversary. On February 23, 1861, Texas seceded from the Union. Tomorrow also marks the beginning of the siege of the Alamo. "It is the key to Texas," Travis wrote to the Texas government. The siege lasted 13 days, a bit longer than the Houston Live Stock Show and Rodeo. So, amidst the fun and beer, the parades and trail drives, this is a good time to recall what happened and why. It is not only a gringo party—the last defender to slip into the Alamo was Gregorio Esparza, who brought his family. He was one of the few Texans who knew how to fire a cannon, and was bayoneted in his place. One of the three American survivors was a black man named Joe. This is a good time to recall all of that, or to coin a phrase, it is a proper time to remember the Alamo, for the very simple reason that if it had not happened, you'd be back in Toledo shoveling slush.

New arrivals to Texas might find Go Texan a bit too much, grown men in cowboy outfits riding horses down the streets in the fourth-largest city in America. A New Yorker who had lived here for about three years told me that the trail drive was "high camp—funniest thing I ever saw in my life." Perhaps it is. Perhaps Texas is high camp. But we've got a good thing going, and I don't recall anyone being forced to join us. On the other hand, if you like it here, stick around. We've got plenty of room and a lot of work to do. So don't feel left out. Join in.

To get into the spirit of things, you might like to know that 144 years ago a group of our predecessors left a drunken party in downtown San Antonio and gathered at the Alamo, not so that we can ride down Main Street on horseback, not so that children in Washington, D.C., can be born Texan, and not so that others can make their jealous little gibes about us. Rather they did it because they were tired of being pushed around. They had a new idea and this seemed like a good place to try it out. If you have similar ideas, then you've found your home.

Stay Away

After a few years of lying low, Richard Nixon is making his first, tentative feelers into the outside world.

In recent weeks he's been to New York City twice. He's signed another million-dollar book contract, and has given a few sidewalk interviews. Once again he is being addressed as Mr. President. He plans trips to foreign lands. He grants interviews at his home in which he gives his advice on the economy, inflation, the state of the government.

It is clear that, step by step, Richard Nixon is carefully orchestrating himself out of his political purgatory and back into the mainstream of American life, where he has spent most of his adulthood. Perhaps, if things go well, he will return someday to the Republican National Convention where tearful crowds will give him a standing ovation and Nixon will deliver one of his give-'em-hell speeches, castigating his enemies.

Well, they may give him a standing ovation. They may call him Mr. President, and they may cling to his every word of advice on matters both foreign and domestic. But not me. You can—in the immortal words of Samuel Goldwyn—include me out. I don't like Richard Nixon. I don't need Richard Nixon. And, Lord knows, I don't want Richard Nixon.

It is a personal matter. For although we never met, he lied to me. He misled me. He cheated me. He abused the power I entrusted to him. He hurt me.

Let us not forget that this is a man who cheated on his income tax and now has to pay up. His vice presidential papers were backdated. His accountant and his papers' appraiser went before the judge. But Nixon did not. He said he knew nothing about it. You try that.

This is a man who used his elected position to line his pockets, reward his friends, and punish his enemies in ways the meanest political hack never contemplated. He tried to muzzle the press.

He plotted to revoke the TV license owned by the *Washington Post*. Two *Newsday* reporters had their IRS records dragged out after writing less than flattering stories about Bebe Rebozo.

This is a man who preached mother, flag, and apple pie while—in the taped secrecy of the Oval Office—he cursed, schemed, and backstabbed. He was a corrupter, devising ways to make otherwise honest men break the law. He brought down to the gutter with him the FBI, the CIA, the IRS, the Justice Department. He ruined countless lives. When he got into trouble, he willingly threw his aides into the sea to keep his own lifeboat from swamping. A man who touted loyalty as the greatest of assets showed none when it counted.

He lied. He went before the cameras and came into my home and told me lies. Vast numbers, so many that I can't count them. He trotted out volumes of tape transcripts and told me they were the truth, when he knew they weren't. And his only reason for lying was to cover up other lies.

He used my tax money to trim trees, build walls, and landscape his homes. He got the Secret Service to put down under "security" such items as ice makers and drapes.

This is a man who brought my country down to its lowest ebb in self-esteem, and at a time when it could not afford the trip. This is the worst part of all, for he was a thief, not so much for the dollars he took, but for a theft unparalleled in our history: he stole our self-confidence. He robbed an entire nation of its faith in itself.

Now, let us remember what happened. We had gone through the civil rights riots and a series of assassinations. Then we were torn by Vietnam. There were, quite literally, riots in the streets. This had happened to others, but never in our lifetime had it happened to us, and it scared us. We were faced with the chilling possibility that we were no better—and maybe worse—than a second-rate banana republic. Maybe America was not so special, after all. Doubts began to seep in, but we kept telling ourselves that while we had our problems, we were still internally sound. Strong. Honest.

Then one man, Richard Nixon, robbed us of that last remaining faith. The greatest office in the land, the one held up to every schoolchild as an example of the rewards of hard work and honesty, was shown to be no more than a platform for deceit, a power base for paranoia. At a time when we desperately needed to get back on our feet, he cut our legs out from under us.

A nation's strength is rather like the value of stock: it's worth whatever anyone thinks it's worth. All of a sudden the rest of the world didn't think U.S. stock was worth much. Oh, our factories still produced, our armies still marched, our farmers still fed, but our faith, our energies, and, most important, our self-confidence plummeted. We haven't brought it up yet.

Richard Nixon hurt me, he hurt my family, he hurt my country in a way no foreign enemy could. It was an inside job. When the thief was caught, he denied it then and he denies it today, but only for a price. Maybe a million or so.

He is not in jail due to a little help from his friend, who promptly lost the presidency because of it. Today, Nixon lives far better than most Americans, and I'm paying for it.

Now he wants to make a comeback. Perhaps he will, because there is a mood in the land that "he's been punished enough." Well, as far as I'm concerned, Nixon can just stay away, because he's punished me enough, too.

Houston Turned Right at the Fork

CYPRESS CREEK — This is near the spot in northwest Harris County where Cypress Creek is joined by Little Cypress Creek. The trickle of water is about 20 feet across at its widest point, and a foot or two deep. Looking south, you can see power lines, fences, and rooftops where rows of new homes sit on streets such as Ravensway, Twin Sisters, and Texas Army Trail. The neighborhood stables are called Saracen Park.

Turning the other way and looking north along the creek banks, you see no sign of civilization, just green trees, tall grass, and spring flowers. Not much has changed along here since — so the story goes — the Texas Army camped on the way to San Jacinto. At the time, of course, the soldiers didn't know where they were headed, but they knew where they had been — they had been fleeing Santa Anna for several weeks and hundreds of miles. They had come from everywhere to fight but had seen only rearguard skirmishes. They were surly, hungry, ill-clothed, and frustrated. They were also terribly outnumbered, and the countryside was alive with Mexican scouts and dragoons.

Some of General Sam Houston's most trusted officers began to mutter plans of mutiny. With the arrival of the Twin Sisters, Mosely Baker, one of Houston's officers, stormed: "You said you didn't attack the Mexicans on the Colorado because you didn't have any artillery. Now you got two brand-spanking-new cannons and yet you didn't stand and fight on the Brazos. Are you going to Harrisburg or not?" The general didn't answer.

Houston received a letter from President David Burnet: "The enemy is laughing you to scorn. You must retreat no more. The country expects you to fight. The salvation of the country depends on your doing so." Burnet was right about the ridicule. Houston soon came upon a black on a mule who had a message from Santa Anna himself: "Mr. Houston, I know you're up there hiding in the bush. As soon as I catch the other land thieves [the Texas government], I'm coming up to smoke you out."

Support from the civilian side also was somewhat lacking. A few days earlier, while passing through what is now Hempstead, the army attracted hundreds of frightened civilians caught up in the Runaway Scrape who demanded the army protect them until they got safely back to the USA. They were not just afraid of the Mexican Army. Rumor had it that the Indians along the Trinity River, the Coushattas, were on the warpath. Quite the contrary was true; the Coushattas had promised Houston aid and had agreed to send 90 warriors to help the Texians. When the troops camped on the land of a well-to-do settler named Donahoe, not far from here, they began cutting trees for firewood. Donahoe demanded that Houston stop his men. The general agreed, ordering that under no circumstances should any Texas soldier cut another Donahoe tree for firewood — couldn't they see that his fine rail fence was all the wood they needed?

The creek itself must have been running heavy and hard, for it had been raining in this part of Texas for weeks. The few roads were mud trails. Buffalo Bayou was 300 feet across. The rain made it difficult on both armies. Santa Anna, an opium addict, was terrified of water and at every stream crossing had to fortify his courage with a fresh fix. But he kept marching, for he had heard that the "other land thieves" had fled to Harrisburg. That was his final destination. Soon Houston heard the same.

Although Houston had established a medical corps a few days earlier, medicine was in short supply. I have been told that some Texas soldiers died on the march and are buried nearby, but I can't find any confirmation. Besides organizing his medical corps, Houston had set up the 2nd Regiment under Sidney Sherman, perhaps the best-dressed soldier in the army, with his blue jacket trimmed in lace and bright silver sword. Sherman had come to Texas with some volunteers from Kentucky who were described thusly: "The company from Kentucky was composed of the most reckless, drunken and lawless men in the army." Considering the makeup of the Texas Army, that is quite a claim.

When Sherman took over the 2nd Regiment, his Kentuckians were left in the 1st Regiment under Edward "Ned" Burleson, a career Indian fighter who had been elected regimental commander by his men. Mirabeau Lamar was here. A young private in the infantry, he obtained a horse and joined the cavalry, finishing up at San Jacinto as the commanding colonel. He would become president of Texas. Also on hand was Thomas Jefferson Rusk, the one man in camp Houston could trust. Rusk eventually became commander of the Texas Army and a U.S. senator and was seriously mentioned as a candidate for the U.S. presidency. He fought at San Jacinto, he fought Indians, he fought the Mexicans again, surviving all only to commit suicide.

Black clouds rolled over this part of Texas when the army broke camp here, making progress slow and life miserable. Houston, in his soaked and muddy leather jacket, spied upon by his own president, ridiculed, the target of coups and plots, silently moved his troops along. The soldiers went that way beside the creek bank, heading east again for a few miles until there was a fork in the road. The left road went to the U.S. and safety. The right road went south to Harrisburg and the plains of San Jacinto. The frightened civilians took the east road. The army went right.

A Family Curse

It appeared to be a neat enough business deal. Some of the boys at the Kaiser Steel Corporation had a little strip mining company up in Canada—Kaiser Resources, Ltd.

The chairman of the Canada company and vice chairman of the steel firm is one Jack L. Ashby, obviously a relative of mine. Well, it seems that Cousin Jack and two other officials sold some of their stock in the Canadian company a few days after a board meeting was told that (1) there would be some cost overruns and (2) profits would not be quite as high as projected.

Now this sort of thing is frowned on by the SEC, but up in Canada the law is not so sticky. So it appeared that at long last an Ashby had finally recaptured the family fortune. Hooray! But wait, what's this? With the spotlight on the deal, a three-man committee from Kaiser Resources "recommended" that the insiders return to the company all profits from their quickie sale. Predictably, the insiders did just that.

Poor Cousin Jack, he had tried mightily, but he should have known that there was no way. He had fallen victim to the Ashby family curse — money. Throughout history, Ashbys have lied and stolen and cheated to lay on a hefty amount of coin, only to see it slip between their fingers at the last moment. The only Ashby to die rich was a great-grandfather who inadvertently collected the bounty on himself shortly before the lynching.

Legend has it that the curse was placed upon the family in the 12th century when Sir Ashby de la Zouch, a Knight of the Octagonal Table (even then we never made the really big time) pulled a thorn from the paw of a dragon. "O brave knight," sayeth the dragon, "in reality I am a fairy princess. Because you have been so noble, I will grant you and your family any wish of your desire. Name it."

Sir Ashby, needless to say, gave it serious thought. A split level in Tanglewood? Helga R. Hughes' unlisted bank account? The cable TV franchise for Conroe? A lifetime subscription to Miss Oklahoma? Finally he said: "I wish never to have to worry about money."

"I'll go you one better," sayeth the dragon. "From this day forward you and yours will never have any money to worry about."

Sir Ashby, who wasn't too bright, thanked the dragon effusively, made some dreary joke about "the paws that refresh," and raced back to the castle to tell the other knights about his good fortune. They promptly traded him to Montreal for a first-round draft choice.

Whether there is any truth in the story or not — and I personally doubt the part about Montreal — the tradition has held true. For instance, Castle Ashby in Leicestershire had one wall in every four blown up by Cromwell after we took the wrong side in the civil war. We always took the wrong side. Some believed it was by natural instinct, but actually it was the family curse that guided us.

Thus when Captain Thomas Ashby, a Captain of Foot, arrived in Virginia, the British Foreign Office should have known it was only a matter of time before it lost all the colonies. His son, Colonel Daniel Ashby (1759–1834), fought nobly in the Revolution, although later on he had a sticky time at regimental reunions explaining his red coat.

After Fort Sumter, we went all out for the Confederacy, naturally. We bought bonds, invested heavily in cotton futures, and laid claim to Philadelphia. Many of my ancestors marched off in gray uniforms, although most did an about-face at the first sound of battle. General Turner Ashby, our great hope for cashing in on veterans' benefits, unfortunately bought the farm in '62 at the battle of Cross Keys.

Meanwhile, on the business side, we scored heavily, batting .1000 with Aaron Burr, the Mier Expedition, and the Donner Party. The family plantation, which by then was being rented out as a tannery, jumped with greedy joy when word arrived that we had gained exclusive hide-and-pelt rights from the 7th Cavalry in their triumphant push to the Little Big Horn.

After Uncle Americus, the family practical joker, short-sheeted a Klan rally, it was decided that the survivors should emigrate to Texas, where Cousin Lafayette was making a fortune as a salesman. A true liberal, he would hawk his wares without regard to race or color. At the time, he was running carbines to the Apaches. Unfortunately, the Texas Rangers took a dim view of it—he was breaking the blue laws—and cut short a most promising career. The family curse had once more held true.

Still, you must give us credit for trying. While others might have given in to the fates, we pushed onward in our pursuit of happiness, driven by a desire to succeed, a will to win, and a dread of starvation. Turning our collective backs on the then-current craze—oil—we cornered the Stanley Steamer franchise for Texas. Later, we pulled off the same coup with dirigibles. You can't keep a good man down.

In the Business Hall of Fame there should be a monument to J. P. Ashby, who landed a multimillion-dollar contract to sell scrap iron to the Mitsubishi Aircraft Corporation. He announced it on December 6 of '41, as I recall. A court of inquiry failed to appreciate his business ingenuity.

Thus, as one can see, word of Cousin Jack's brief flirtation with wealth came as no surprise. He, too, fell victim to the family curse. But now, finally, I think I have broken the chain, having just bought a controlling interest in the Sharpstown State Bank.

I don't care what the SEC says, Joe Novotny shall rise again!

So stick in there, Cousin Jack. Anyone can be Nouveau Riche, but it takes real talent to be Old Poor.

The Best or Worst of Times?

In our day-to-day lives we tend to spend all our time struggling with the problems at hand. We have to. In order to eat, function, live, pay the electric bill. So it is that rarely do we have a chance to sit back and figure out where we stand in the grand scheme of things. Or, to put it another way, it is hard to gaze at the forest when a tree is falling on you.

But we need to in order to get everything in perspective. To sort out what is really important and what is transitory. Or to consider what historians will say and write about us. What will they say was important in our lives? What 200th, 300th, 500th anniversary will someone be marking in 200, 300 or 500 years from now?

If you really wish to be honest, perhaps nothing is going on. Why should there be? There are vast chunks of history you never studied because nothing of import took place then. Oh, the people living at that time figured it was rather important, perhaps very important.

"Yep, they'll be talking about how we took that castle for centuries to come, Sir Bubba."

"Indeed. Oh, the ballads they will sing. The names they must remember."

Alas, taking a castle became a common pursuit. There are few castles that weren't taken, and over the years no one remembers who did it and why. Wars comprising hundreds of battles have been forgotten, along with the people involved. Indeed, whole civilizations today don't gain a hint of recognition. So why should we be doing anything really worth remembering? Let's face it, the competition is pretty tough. What have we done for us lately?

The moon walk pops to mind. John Kennedy's assassination. Pearl Harbor. There are other developments in our time that we think are important because they are important to us: heart transplants, the Korean jetliner, Gerald Ford, Twiggy, and Miss Piggy. All have been news in our life. How will they bear up? Maybe they won't.

Or, on the other hand, maybe we are selling ourselves, and our sliver of time, short. Perhaps there is something happening today that we don't fully comprehend, much less appreciate. Maybe we are living through the golden age of something. No one realizes they are in a golden age. Things will always be better up ahead.

Conversely, it could be that we are in the midst of a decline. Running around in the only life you have ever known, it is hard to compare how it used to be, much less know how it is going to be. We can only wonder if any Roman, wandering through the Forum, said, "This week is the high-water mark of the Roman Empire." I sincerely doubt that anyone said at Trenton or San Jacinto or during the first black sit-in in Birmingham, "Hey, this is history. I mean, after this, nothing will be the same." What cowboy or Indian realized the West was finally won? Few spot the era for what it is.

To be sure, Columbus caused a bit of a dither, mainly because of the prospect of God and gold—praising the first, pocketing the second. And several of the Founding Fathers noted in letters and journals that they were in on big doings. But reporters covering the Gettysburg Address hardly gave it a mention. The first television program, with Herbert Hoover staring, was virtually ignored.

I guess that the best way to handle this question is to find the 20 most brilliant, far-seeing people on earth and ask them if they know what is going on. This could be the Atomic Age, the Century of Terrible Television, a time studied in the classrooms of 2323 as the Second Elizabethan Age. Or known to historians as The Pits. Yes, find the 20 greatest minds and ask them.

But that puts me right back in the same predicament, because the minds and talents we consider great today may not make the historical cut. Franklin, Churchill, Edison, and Marie Curie were recognized in their lifetimes. But Vincent Van Gogh died unrecognized. So did Paul Gauguin. John Keats died in his 20s, some said from scathing criticism of his work. Scott Joplin died in Manhattan State Hospital, his music little known outside Harlem. Jesus, Socrates, and Sir Walter Raleigh were executed. Which minds to include in the sagacious score?

It could be that we are in historical doldrums, a forgettable age sandwiched in between the end of colonialism and the beginning of rampant vivisection. Or it could be the start—or end—of something big. Maybe this year marks the start of the decline of Christianity, the end of American power, the peak of jogging, the rise of Paraguay. Right before our eyes.

Yet, human nature and morbid curiosity being what they are, really, 99 percent of the history we remember is when times were bad, when people and nations did terrible things to one another. It is like the front page of this or any newspaper: planes that land safely never make the headlines. Maybe that is us. A safe flight.

Student Hoteliers at UH
Have Room for Much Learning

The Conrad Hilton Foundation has announced it will give $21.3 million to the University of Houston's College of Hotel and Restaurant Mangement. It is a fine and much-needed gift, since there is vast room for improvement in that industry. With these additional funds, perhaps the U of H will offer:

Laundry Service 304 — Students are taken on a field trip to a hotel laundry room, where, through interpreters, they learn how the staff makes sure absolutely no guest gets back his own laundry. Students also learn how "Same-Day Service" means that if you turn in your laundry on a Tuesday, you will most assuredly get it back on a Tuesday, although not the same Tuesday.

Knock-and-Open 222 — A fine talent first developed in major European hotels and now brought to this country. Students are taught how to put the key in the lock, open the door, and barge in while, at the same time, knocking and saying, "Maid." The less time between inserting the key and entering the room, the better the grade. For the final exam, students must seek out only rooms with "Do Not Disturb" signs on the door.

What Reservations? 566 — This art form, finely tuned in both Mexico City and Honolulu, requires hours in front of a mirror as students learn how to look squarely at a bedraggled traveler holding a reservation confirmation notice and say apologetically, "But we have no such record. You might try the Y."

Bags in the Lobby Lab — A must for any hotel handling group tours. No matter when the bus leaves, students must make sure everyone's bags are in the lobby by 6 a.m.

Key Workshop — A two-hour lab every week in which students are required to come up with the largest, most ridiculous attachments for hotel room keys. Bowling balls are a sure A.

Room Service 474 — Under the guidance of the professor, students are taught how to handle the overnight room service breakfast order for departing guests. At 2 a.m., students roam the halls, removing the breakfast orders from doorknobs. No matter which time is requested, students learn how to hold up the breakfast until just as the guest is leaving his room to catch a morning flight.

Gideon's Guide — Through hands-on training, students are taught how to carry a guest's luggage down to the lobby and, on the way, judge by the weight just how many ashtrays, sheets, and picture frames are in each bag.

Sign Design 566 — Class is shown a typical hotel room and is given one hour to make sure that absolutely every single square inch of surface space is covered by little cardboard signs announcing bar service, room service, dining rooms available, and the next time you are in Acapulco be sure to stay at our Amigo Arms.

TV Tuning — Professor explains how to take a perfectly good TV set and so turn the dials that the picture is forever fuzzy. For the final exam, students are taught how to say, "We'll have someone come up and fix it immediately," in 32 languages.

No-Tel Motel 121 — Since many graduates will begin their careers working as night clerks in sleazy hot-pillow motels, it is important for them to learn how to call every guest "Mr. Jones," how to get paid in cash at check-in time, and how to get paid more if you recognize the guest. An additional fee may be requested if you discover that Mrs. Jones, waiting in the car, is your wife.

The Ed McMahon Reaction Lab — Students are taught how to laugh uproariously each time they are told:

"The towels in this hotel are so fluffy I could hardly close my suitcase."

"My room is so small I had to go out in the hall to change my mind."

"My room is so small, when I put the key in the lock, I broke a window."

"The fire alarms here are so sensitive, they went off when room service brought me smoked salmon."

"A reservation? What do I look like, Geronimo?"

Religion 312 — In this class, students are taught the story of the patron saint of desk clerks, Saint Formica, who said, "There's no room in the inn, but we have a cancellation in the stables and a rollaway manger." Saint Formica was martyred because he refused to put the curtain inside the tub before taking a shower.

After students have finished these courses, they will be graduated *summa cum ruma*, given a sash inscribed, "Sanitized for Your Protection," and sent out into the world to announce, "You might try the Y."

An Old, Tattered Flag

CHAPULTEPEC CASTLE—They troop through these halls of Montezuma by the hundreds of thousands, about half of them *norteamericano* tourists. Some notice the flag, most don't.

They have already come up the Reforma, perhaps the most beautiful boulevard in the world, and through Chapultepec Park 57 meters below, which is rivaled only by Princes Street Gardens in Edinburgh for cleanliness.

Now the visitors are wandering among the rifles and religion, busts and belt buckles, depicting a proud nation's violent past.

They have gazed at the oil portraits of Hernán Cortez, the Count of Gálvez, Don Miguel Hidalgo y Costilla, and Agustín de Iturbide. Then they walk down the high hallway that once heard the music of Maximilian and muskets of Marines.

For Chapultepec is—in effect—Mexico, and whoever controlled the Hill of the Grasshopper controlled Mexico: Montezuma II, Cortez, the viceroys of Spain, the Hapsburgs of Austria, the presidents of Mexico, invading troops from the north.

And now it is the almighty tourists who, surrounded by guides and guidons, move past the dirty gray flag to gaze at a sign: *Régimen de Santa Anna 1833–1847.*

"And here is Santa Anna," says a guide, pronouncing the name sahn-*tahn*-ya. "He was president of Mexico 11 times."

"So that's him," says a tourist. "He must have been a busy man."

"He's nice-looking," says a woman.

Indeed, the general is rather handsome in oil—dashing sideburns, red and blue uniform, collar up to his chin, gold epaulets.

The crowd moves on toward a mounted statement by Congressman Abraham Lincoln doubting President Polk's account of who started the Mexican-American War.

The flag is ignored, and certainly it is no eyecatcher. It hangs limply on a wooden staff, one of eight in a tall glass case that also holds two officers' uniforms, boots, a drum, and a sword.

Four of the eight flags are Mexican, the other four came from north of the Rio—a Stars and Stripes with an indeterminable number of stars, each with six points; a Texas flag with small moth holes in the Lone Star; and a white flag with a large star in the middle and the word "Invincibles" underneath.

All flew over lost causes and lost battles. All were captured.

Then there is the dirty gray flag with the blue lettering and the eagle in the middle, rather difficult to see as it hangs there.

First Company of
TEXAN
Volunteers
from New-Orleans

The eagle holds a banner reading: "God & Country."

"Here is General Sahn-*tahn*-ya," says the guide. "He had the dubious distinction of having lost one-third of Mexico." The crowd moves on.

The general looks across the hall, ignoring the flag and preferring to gaze at Lincoln. But Antonio López de Santa Anna knows the flag quite well.

The silken banner was white and clean and sported a neat fringe when a pretty girl first presented it to the New-Orleans Greys as they crossed the Sabine River and entered Texas back in 1836. The Greys, a boisterous group of volunteers, were headed for a mission outside San Antonio.

The flag popped up again at dawn on March 6 as Santa Anna's troops began their final assault against the Alamo. It was the only banner flying that morning, although at least two others had been taken into the mission by its defenders.

The sign of it atop the Texans' barracks had so infuriated three color sergeants of the Jiménez battalion fighting in the plaza below that one by one they attempted to climb to the roof to rip it down. Each was killed for his efforts.

Finally, Lieutenant José María Torres of the Zapadores battalion made it to the roof, pulled down the flag, and, with the aid of Lieutenant Damasco Martínez, ran up the Mexican standard.

Rifle fire killed Martínez, then Torres, but the banner of the New-Orleans Greys had fallen.

By 6:30 a.m. the battle was over, and Santa Anna dictated a message to the government in Mexico City aimed at explaining his losses and bolstering his claim that the United States had aided and abetted the rebels.

He put the Texan dead at more than 600. "We have lost about 70 killed and 300 wounded, among who are 25 officers."

The general went on to hail it as "a glorious triumph" although one member of his staff noted: "Another such victory will ruin us."

Still, there was the flag: "The bearer takes with him one of the flags of the enemy's battalions, captured today. The inspection of it will show plainly the true intention of the treacherous colonists, and of their abettors, who came from the ports of the United States of the North," Santa Anna wrote. Then, apparently after looking once more at the rumpled pennant, he added: "God and Liberty."

The flag, with Santa Anna's note still attached, wound up in a drawer in Chapultepec Castle, where, over the next 98 years, it slowly rotted away wrapped in brown paper.

In 1934 the Greys' standard was discovered but stayed in the drawer until about four years ago, when Walter Lord began looking for it as part of his research in writing *A Time to Stand*. The flag was rediscovered and it was decided to display it, so the tedious task of putting it back together began.

Now it stands on a brass-tipped pole in a high glass case and no one seems to pay it much attention, much less be ready to die over it.

Pot Cash-Flow

THE DEN — "The reason I have called this family meeting is that we need to discuss the budget," I say.

"What's a budget?" asks the wife.

"That is part of the problem right there," I say. "A budget is a financial plan whereby Daddy puts a lot of money into a pot from which everyone else pulls it out. Only the problem is that I am not putting it in as fast as you all are taking it out."

"Well, why are you just standing there? Get busy," says the firstborn.

"No, you don't understand," I say. "My plan is not for me to put more in, but for the family to take less out."

"That's ridiculous," says the second-born.

"It may be, but the truth of the matter is that I am going to have to forfeit on my bonds. We have these bills coming due and there is not enough cash flow to handle the overall outgo, nor is there any sign of a pickup in the income."

"What's that mean, Daddy?"

"We're broke."

"I've got some potatoes in the oven," says the wife, getting up to leave.

"My bike is in the driveway," says the second-born.

"I left the bath water on," says the last-born.

"Wait! I have not yet dismissed this meeting. Now, the bath water brings up a point. Our utility bills have got to be cut down."

"Good idea," says the second-born. "From now I'll never drive my bike over 55 miles an hour."

"Don't get wise. We've got to turn off our lights. Our electric bill last month was more money than you all have in your piggy banks," I say.

"I've got $36.75 in mine."

"$52.13 for me."

"An even $47 in mine."

"Where did you all get that money?"

"We balance our budgets," explains the second-born.

"Good. You can lend me your money, because otherwise this family will default and that might well set off a chain reaction throughout the neighborhood."

"Why should we lend you our money?" asks the firstborn.

"I just told you. If this family defaults on its financial obligations, it might well start a chain reaction," I say again, a bit louder this time.

"I do not see that is our responsibility, since you have so mismanaged your own financial affairs," says the second-born.

"Would the French abandon Paris?" I ask. "Would the Russians give up Moscow? Would Liz give up Richard?"

"What's that got to do with the electric bill?" the wife asks.

"I do not think I am getting through to you all," I sigh. "Let me explain. First, I need an immediate wad of money to pay some bills that are coming due. We've spent the money and now we need it."

"Why did you spend money you didn't have?" asks the firstborn. "That's stupid."

"You should watch how you spend your money more closely," says the second-born.

"If you get yourself into such trouble, then you'll just have to get yourself out," says the last-born. "It might be a lesson to you."

"I've got some potatoes in the oven," says the wife.

"Sit down!" I storm.

"If you can't discuss your problems sensibly and calmly, Daddy, let's just forget the whole thing," says the firstborn.

"Quit shouting while I'm shouting!" I shout. "Now, let's think positively. Does anyone have a suggestion as to how we can get out of this mess?"

"What do you mean, 'we,' paleface?" asks the last-born.

"You messed up your room, so you can clean it up, to coin a family phrase," giggles the second-born.

"I will overlook those remarks in the interest of crime prevention," I say testily. "Now let's get down to the nitty-gritty. Like this bill here. Thirteen-twenty-five for cigars."

"You're the only one in the family who smokes cigars, dear," says the wife.

"OK, OK. Then how about this one: $21 for a bottle of Scotch and a case of beer."

"Daddy?"

"Never mind. That's a bad example. Aha! This one. No more slacks and sportcoat, we've got to . . . uh . . . Here's one that is a definite waste: $32.12 for a meal at l'Spoon Greasioux. From now on we eat at home. No more restaurants."

"Daddy?"

"What?"

"That's the football bet you lost, remember? The meal you bet on the Texas-OU game."

"Daddy," says the second-born, "you've really got to stop this wasteful spending. You are exhausting all your monetary resources operating on a fixed income with constantly expanding expenses. Unless, of course, you subscribe to the Keynesian theory of economics."

"Somehow I feel I am losing control of this meeting," I say. "Let's get back on the track. Now, this bill."

"What's that noise? Like dripping water," says the firstborn.

"My bath!" shouts the last-born, racing upstairs.

"Call the plumber," says the firstborn.

"Do you smell smoke?" asks the second-born.

"My potatoes!" shouts the wife, racing off to the kitchen.

Shortly thereafter, while the plumber was repairing the bathroom, we left for the restaurant. On the way out the drive I ran over a bike and that night the French abandoned Paris.

It Was Funny

Oliver Wendell Holmes was an amateur photographer. When he presented a picture to a friend, he wrote on the back of it, "Taken by O. W. Holmes & Sun."
— *Little Masterpieces of American Wit and Humor* (1903).

> Accidentally locked in a tomb,
> A gravedigger sat in the glomb;
> When hunger arose
> He devoured his clothes,
> Till nothing was left to consomb.
> — Lieuen Adkins, *The Texas Ranger*, 1960.

Either, or both, or more probably neither of these two examples will hit you as very funny. Yet, at one time, they were both considered such great knee-slappers as to be put in print and sold to a waiting public, which — no doubt — promptly slapped many a knee.

Humor is the most fragile and private form of communication. No other effort seeking response has such little chance of success. Since the first caveman caused the second to giggle uproariously at the sight of his being chased across the tundra by a bison, people have tried to make other people laugh, and have rarely scored.

In the Athens city festivals, beginning in 486 B.C., comedy was part of the competition. The Romans honed it to a science. William Gilbert (of "and Sullivan" fame) wrote decades ago:

> The world has joked incessantly for over fifty centuries,
> And every joke that's possible has long ago been made.

Comedy today is not exactly in its Golden Age. The funnymen of my childhood are either dead or play to select groups on the Las Vegas strip. And no one has really come along to replace Groucho Marx, Danny Kaye, Red Skelton, Jack Benny, or Noel Coward (a mixed bag, to be sure). The canned junk that television devours in unprecedented proportions has some really funny lines, but they come and go so quickly, and are surrounded by such repetitious pap, that you have to pay a fearful price to find them.

Humor pops up in strange places. Not long ago I was flying to California and plugged in one of those headsets to hear the music. Among the many bands on the tape was a comedy track — carefully selected skits by everyone from Albert Brooks to Foster Brooks.

Even Dean Martin and Frank Sinatra. And it was very, very funny. I felt kind of foolish, sitting there laughing all by myself, but it was good stuff.

What makes anyone laugh? If you can find out, you'll make a mint. I don't laugh at what you laugh at. Sometimes I don't even laugh at something that hit me as hilarious a short time earlier.

Animal House, which is sweeping college campuses these days (and, as one might expect, will become a TV series) was terribly funny in parts, in a tasteless sort of way, and downright dull in others. *Monty Python's Flying Circus* is the best thing on television, but even it strikes out abysmally on occasion.

I found *Silver Streak* to be funny, yet a carbon copy called *Foul Play* left me so-so. Woody Allen is a humorous fellow, but *Sleeper* was a real nothing. I guess it's all up to my particular mood at a particular time. Don Rickles can leave me either rolling on the floor or wishing he would simply leave me. It's not Rickles' fault. He's doing the same thing, but I am not always an appreciative audience.

The absolute kiss of death, to me at least, is for someone to recommend a film, play or book as hilarious. It never is. Maybe I lead myself to expect too much.

What makes you laugh? Pratfalls? Pies in the face? A well-turned bon mot, dryly delivered? There are not too many comedians who are universally accepted.

Puns are another example of the selectivity of humor. They appear in this space every now and again, although it's getting harder to find new ones. People keep sending in the same puns time and again. In any event, some readers write in that they love them. Others complain.

Both are in good company. James Boswell said that a good pun may be admitted among the smaller excellencies of lively conversation. Shakespeare used them quite a bit. Charles Lamb, however, wrote sourly: "A pun is a pistol let off at the ear; not a feather to tickle the intellect."

Some jokes or events, for no particular reason to anyone else, will cause one to collapse in laughter. I have a friend, Dave Crossley, who once read me this line: "Mark Twain hated braggarts. One day he met a braggart. Twain kicked him in the crotch and ran home."

I laughed. He laughed. We both laughed until we shook. We rolled and squealed until we could roll and squeal no more. Now, reading that line will not cause the same reaction with you. But to this very day, it causes me to laugh.

PFC Bill Deal and I were defending a California hilltop one evening, discussing whether our gunny sergeant was shell-shocked. We decided he was definitely crackers. Suddenly a shot rang out from somewhere and this blurred vision whipped past us. It was the gunny, yelling, "Incoming!" as he frantically dug under a log.

We screamed with evil laughter for at least half an hour. It got so bad that the gunny sergeant finally peered over the log to see what was so funny.

You had to be there.

Bubbly Tips

EPERNAY, FRANCE — Do you have a bottle of champagne handy? Good, because today you and I are going to learn the proper way to serve it, so that the headwaiter won't sniff his condescending sniff, your friends won't giggle at your usual ineptitude, and your date will look at you with new appreciation. From now on we will be men and women of the world, ready to hold our own with the snobbiest wine snob.

For openers, for it to be truly champagne, by French law it has to come from this area, the Champagne region of France. New York and California sparkling white wines call themselves champagne, but the locals here are purists. If it's not from Champagne, they say, it's not champagne.

What size bottle? They used to go up to a Nabuchodonosor, at least that's how it's spelled here. It is a huge bottle equivalent to 20 regular bottles. Champagne company officials assure me that this size is no longer sold, and no wonder. The largest now available is this one, the Salamanazar, equal to 11 bottles. For the sake of safety and sobriety, I suggest you buy just the regular-size bottle.

All right, now we have a bottle of champagne. By the time we get it, the champagne has been aged as long as it's going to age, so there is no point in keeping it around in hopes that it will improve. It will never taste better than it does today. But let us say that you want to keep your bottle for some special occasion later. No problem, it will last another four or five years without any damage if you put it in a cool, dark place, on its side. This keeps the cork wet and firm, preventing air from entering. Thus if you have any champagne around the house, put it under your bed, on the side.

Let us now deal with drinking it, which is why they make champagne in the first place. Champagne must be chilled, but not frozen. So don't put it in your freezer for a quick drop in temperature. You'll ruin it. No, you must get a running start, and gently bring the temperature down. Do this by putting your bottle in the warmest part of the refrigerator a day or so before you want to drink it. I suggest the vegetable drawer.

Now comes the big night. Take the bottle from the refrigerator at least an hour before it is to be served and put it in a container half full of ice and water. Yes, water. The ice water does better than ice alone because it comes into contact with a larger surface area of the bottle. You want the container only half full; don't submerge the whole bottle.

The champagne should be between 40 and 48 degrees. Just how you determine that, I have no idea. But the point is that you don't want to get it too cold. A lot of people think that the colder the champagne the better. Wrong. Chilled, but not too cold, is the key.

Now comes the hardest part of all: uncorking it. Take the bottle out of the bucket (or sink or plastic bag or whatever you're using, it makes no difference), and be careful. At this point, you are armed and dangerous. Aim the cork away from you and everyone else, holding the bottle at a 45-degree angle, and undo the wire muzzle holding in the cork.

Do not open a warm bottle of champagne with the idea of pouring it over ice. First, the cork won't pop, it will explode outward. Second, most of the champagne will pour onto the floor.

Now you have the wire gizmo off. Hold the bottle in one hand and the cork in the other—still pointing it away from you. *Turn the bottle while holding the cork still.* Turn and pull, slowly. No matter how dramatic it might sound, you don't want a loud "Bang." You want to let the built-up gases out slowly, or at least as slowly as you can. My own experience is that it goes Bang.

Remembering that this bottle has been lying in a moldy cellar for a few years, take a napkin and wipe off the top, else you may get a free dose of penicillin. Pour about a quarter of an inch of champagne into each glass, then go back and fill them to about two-thirds. I have no idea why, but it's what the champagne people say to do, and I'm not going to argue about it.

Ideally, you will drink it all, but if you have some left, take the cork and trim it down with a small knife, recork the bottle, and the bubbles will stay in for a few hours. One fellow here says it will stay this way for a couple of days, but mine never has.

Some people don't like the little bubbles and use a swizzle stick to beat them out of the champagne. That sounds kind of dumb. If you want white wine, buy white wine. It's usually cheaper, anyway.

One thing more. Except aboard the Concorde, where they serve all the drinks in water glasses because the other kind fall over, the champagne connoisseurs serve their products in tulip- or egg-shaped glasses. They never use those saucer-shaped champagne glasses most people use. The saucer-shaped glasses give the champagne too much surface area and I guess it gets flatter quicker.

One final suggestion: around here they never wrap the bottles in white napkins, since — they say — it only hides the label of a fine product. Considering the kind of champagne I can afford, I usually use the napkin.

All right, there you have it. Let no man argue, for this is The Truth, straight from the companies that have made champagne since it was invented, right here, by Dom Perignon late in the 17th century. On the other hand, there is a higher law among those who truly appreciate good drink: do it your way, because you're the only person in the world who knows what you like.

Look Upsom Sillin Ames Ina Fone Book

You heard of the marriage counselors Baul & Cheyne? Or the radio disc jockeys Kroc & Krol? How about the *Post*'s foreign correspondents, Unno, Doss, and Trez? Those, from Mary Marshall of Brookshire, are only some of the entries we have in our latest all-out effort to win downtown Texarkana, Contez Times.

As you may recall, the idea was to use the most recent Houston residential telephone book and come up with surnames of our neighbors that would go together to make the proper company name for various enterprises. Such as Justice, Hanger & Dethrow for criminal court judges (Cindy Thomas). She also came up with the perfect gastroenterology clinic: Gobble, Earp, Ulch, and Gass.

To get the proper perspective on the names, I find it far easier to say them out loud, because some are sly to the point of obscurity. Such as Goldie Knobler's wedding consultants, Hare, Komsa, Dee, Bried. Or William F. Stephens' Gang of Four Pentagon Planners: Bombard, Newcomb, Killam, Goode. How about the perfect accounting firm? Bottom, Line, Red, Inkley (David Haines).

Some excellent entries we have, containing scores of names, and I am not about to look up every one of them in the phone book to testify to their authenticity. I mean, I'm no recruiting sergeant for the Children's Crusade, but I trust you. Well, at least in this instance. Here are a few more of the best:

Cotton, Picker, Fromm, Dixie

—Manuel Henry

Our congressional delegation: Robb, Steele, Ravich & Pillegge

—Michael Coignard

Mayor Whitmire's clothiers: Takei, Tieh & Suits
The PUC consultants: Yoo, Ben, Hada

—Byron Thornton

The audit staff for the IRS: Medel, Pester, Lefes, Allon

—Jean LeBlanc

Members of the Washington press corps: Hadda, Upper, Keister, Sly, News, Leaks

—Doris Oswald

The public relations firm that dropped the Ed Biles account: Adger, Chance & Bluett

—Jack James

The current owners of downtown Texarkana, Strode and Donna Manley, after having won the last dumb contest we ran, get an honorable mention for some really fine entries this time:

Phone answering service: Etie, Fone, Hom

IRS refund clerks: Fore, Evers, Andah, Day

Sex change clinic: Mankin, Bee, Come, Lady

Beer distributors: Thies, Budzisz, Fore, You

Operators of a running club: Onyia, Marks, Getts, Setogawa

Ah, yes, some fine efforts. Like the Rockets' high scorers, Slamen, Duncan, and Hoop (Walter V. Yokie). And Terry Thomas' team of pediatricians: Sicley, Babes, Heald, Here. Thomas also gives us the Oilers' offensive coaching staff, Luckie, Won, Timme, Ayear. And the four top officers of NOW: Im, Better, Than, Allman.

Some, such as Priscilla Proffitt Lane, used their own names: the CPA firm of Proffitt, Lass, Dollar & Sinz.

Paul Ache III notes that if he got together with a brother's friend, they could form the dental partnership of Dr. Ache and Dr. Payne.

Jan Grape came up with two others to form the cereal company of Grape, Nutt, Flake. That was only one of several good entries from Grape, like the gambling casino operators Ace, King, Queen, Straight & Flusche. And, good for second runner-up, the espionage agents:

Richmond, Poorman, Begerman, Theiss,
Doctor, Lawyer, Merchant, Cheef.
Tinker, Taylor, Solcher, Spies.

Cynthia Hoverson has a great polling organization, Askin, Yore, O, Binion.

Tim McGaughran was on a roll, giving us: The Oriental modeling agency Srey, Ferros, Like, Dates? The Mothers Against Perfumed Pollen: Hachicho, Kirchoff, Whew, and Dripps. And, of course, the apprehended gang of burglars: Collyer, Doga, Offman, Plesums & Quick.

Robert Land tells about the worldwide shipping company By, Land, Sea & Air. The racetrack oddsmakers Win, Place & Show. Not to mention the draft counselors Go, Tu, Canada & Hide. But he wins second place for two of the best:

The auto dealership Dee, Lore, Eon & Coke.

The producers of low-budget horror movies King, Kong, Meats, The, Wolfman & Lassey.

If for any reason the winner cannot, or will not, take downtown Texarkana off my hands, Land has to assume ownership. A close run at the championship was made by Shirley J. McKee of League City, not only for her entry (the game shows hosts Watt, Woo, Joo, Doo?) but also for her explanation for entering: Wasnor Wasser

Little Gull Ho Livin League Citti. She Saw Lynn Ashby Askin Forrister Look Upsom Sillin Ames Ina Fone Book. Hear Dayer.

The winner, however, is Don Ingraham, who entered the advertising agency of Hook, Line & Sinker. The auctioneers Locke, Stock & Barrell. And the worst of all, the cattle company of Bury, Mee, Nott, Onda, Lone, Pray, Rhee.

Bit of History

This is Texas Independence Day.

If you are a new Texan, you might well wonder just why an entire state is celebrating. It does pose a question.

Other worthy states do not drop everything to mark their independence days, mainly because most other states don't *have* them. So the question is not easy to explain — no easier than if a newly minted American asked why you take off on July 4. A simple "That's when we proclaimed our independence" raises more questions than it answers.

The facts themselves are pretty easy to understand: March 2, 1836, was the date on which 59 delegates signed their names to a piece of paper that would be Exhibit A if the charge were treason. They gathered at Washington-on-the-Brazos, a town that boasted two hotels, 50 houses, and 100 people. Meeting in a windowless, doorless building in 33-degree temperature, most of the delegates — chosen in local elections all over Texas — met one another for the first time.

They were a mixed lot. José Francisco Ruíz, a former officer in the Army of Mexico, had fought several of them in the Fredonian Rebellion. Thomas Jefferson Rusk came to Texas trying to collect a debt, and found himself in the role of Acting Patriot. Michel Menard was a French Canadian trapper and honorary chief of the Shawnee Indians. They were mostly young: of the 59 signers, 40 were under 40. The youngest was 24-year-old Junius William Mottley, who would die at San Jacinto.

Most of them had no business being there. In the midst of the convention, Elijah Stapp of Victoria County learned that his home and all his possessions had been burned or stolen by Santa Anna's troops. The delegate from Refugio, Sam Houston, had an army to organize. Ben Goodrich's brother, John, age 24, was in the Alamo.

Jesse Grimes' 18-year-old son was there, too. They would never see them again.

A printer, several doctors, lawyers, a sheriff, a druggist, a schoolteacher. Some were scantily educated, yet one was a graduate of Yale. The best schooled of the lot were the Mexican Americans. Of the 59 signers, only two — Ruíz and J. Antonio Navarro — were from what is now Texas. The rest had moved here from someplace else. Only 10 of the 59 had been in Texas more than six years.

Which brings us to those of you who are new to Texas. You've come down a well-beaten track, and in increasing numbers. The population of Texas has grown 16.2 percent since the 1970 census. There are now more Texans than there are Belgians, Bolivians, or Bulgarians, Swedes, Swiss, or Syrians. We have in Texas more Latin Americans than some Latin American nations; more blacks than some black African countries. Of the 150 or so nations in the world, Texas would rank 48th in population.

Yes, we are growing. Tomorrow there will be more people in the Astrodome than there were people in Texas when those 59 men signed our Declaration of Independence.

So you can see that there is nothing new to being a newcomer to Texas. But then as now, it takes a little getting used to, because, let's face it, things can be different here.

Such as driving 80 in a 20. And calling yourself a Democrat, then voting the straight Republican ticket. Keeping your community free of liquor and gambling, then flying to New Orleans to get drunk and play the horses. Demanding fewer governmental controls, then paying a lobbyist $100,000 to make sure strict licensing is enforced so you won't have too many competitors. Screaming for law 'n' order, then selling old oil as new oil. Writing hot letters to the editor demanding lower taxes, less welfare, and 100 percent crop subsidy.

And, certainly, one of the quaintest rites of the natives is celebrating Texas Independence Day. As I noted at the top, this is a hard one to explain.

The declaration itself sounds somewhat like the U.S. Declaration of Independence, beginning with: "When a government has ceased to protect the lives, liberty and property of the people from whom the legitimate powers are derived . . ." It goes on to tick off the problems, and states that all efforts to talk over the matters have only ended up with Texians — as we were called back then — being tossed into Mexican jails. They wind up by saying, in effect, no more Mr. Nice Guy. This means war.

Actually, there was already war, and in this way, the Texas declaration differed from the U.S. version. The enemy was not across the seas, but coming up the road. The battle of the Alamo was in its ninth day, the Runaway Scrape was beginning, the delegates themselves had to hurry things up a bit—because if they stayed in Washington-on-the-Brazos much longer, Santa Anna would arrive to veto their day's work, and them along with it.

Times were tense. Texas was a battleground. Many of our towns were in flames, or about to be. Farms and ranches were destroyed and looted. The women and children were fleeing; the fathers and sons were getting killed. Now the bad news: one of five copies of the Texas declaration was sent to Washington, D.C., for safekeeping. It took 60 years to get it back. I think maybe that should have been a warning.

Anyway, that's what happened on Texas Independence Day, and that's why we celebrate it. Newcomers might find this whole thing rather quaint, provincial, even silly.

Don't feel alone. So did Santa Anna.

The Art of Merging

The most important aspect of driving on Houston freeways during rush hours is the art of merging. It can be dangerous, frightening, expensive, illegal, and annoying. On the other hand, if done properly, it can be thrilling, frightening, and illegal.

To get the art of merging down correctly, let us separate the drill into two distinct categories, the offensive team and the defensive team. Individually, the *merger* and the *mergee*. The merger is the motorist outside the freeway, beyond the pale, who is trying to get into the moving traffic. He or she is the new kid on the block, attempting to join the gang and swagger on down the street. But it is not that easy.

For the merger is the late arrival, and must go to the end of the line. Of course, there is no end to the line of traffic on a Houston freeway during rush hours. It goes on forever. So it is that the merger must somehow break in.

The city, or someone with more dollars than sense, has put up traffic lights next to the on ramps to assist the merger in his pursuit of a slight space in the line. These lights are obeyed by those who drive 55 and by cars whose engines die at that particular spot. And by no others.

Where there are no lights, there are yield signs. Yield signs are not obeyed by anyone whatsoever.

All right, that takes care of the mergers, those upstarts who wish to poke their bumpers into other people's line of trot. We now move on to the mergees, those already stacked up on the freeway, patiently awaiting the time when the dead 18-wheeler in Montgomery County will be towed over to the side so that traffic on the West Loop might move on. The mergees have been moving along as a body, a giant amoeba slithering across a glass slide under a microscope.

Up and down the miles, over hill and dale, this group of strangers has become a band of brothers, the sole survivors in an armored column. A spirit of kinship and camaraderie has grown up. Some even swap information over CBs, good buddy.

Then, suddenly, a new face appears, and like a young buck who must prove his machismo before being allowed to join the herd, he snorts and paws the earth as a show of courage. Others have been fighting since the Kirby Street entrance to get here, and now this new fellow wishes to slip right in. Well, he can just go back to the Kirby Street entrance and get on like everyone else.

Thus it is that we have these two mutually antagonistic groups: the mergers and the mergees. Now that they are suitably identified, let's move on to the proper role of each.

If you are in the inside or middle lanes of the freeway, then you are a simple bystander, for all the action is on the outside lane. If you are on the outside lane, I suggest you move over, since it is always the slowest lane of traffic.

But assuming you are stuck there, you are a mergee, and as such, you will see cars coming up from your right side trying to get in. As a rule, I allow one car in at each entry ramp. This is not easy to do, for once you slow down and motion for one vehicle to take its place in line in front of you, often a second car will try to slip in, too. *Do not let it!* This will mess up the entire operation. One entry ramp, one vehicle let in. It's the law.

Ah, but which vehicle do you let in? I mean, you are slowly passing by a line of cars on your right, all stopped dead, all awaiting a chance to jump in. How do you select the proper stranger? I suggest you allow in any of these:

- Pretty girls.
- Ammonia trucks that have a running start.
- The 1st Armored Division on maneuvers.
- Any vehicle with dented fenders and a roll bar.

Once that vehicle is in line, tailgate it immediately or the flood is on.

Now we come to the unwritten rule of mergedom. Under no circumstances do you allow in a car that comes on the freeway from the entry ramp and whizzes down the shoulder for several hundred yards, passing all the motorists lined up in the right-hand lane.

No, sir. All the other mergers back there at the entry ramp are patiently awaiting a chance to join the flow of traffic. And so can these line bargers. Thus when you hear thunder on the right and see rocks and dirt showering around you as some car comes flying down the shoulder seeking a chance to cut in, just swerve slightly to the right. With any luck, the line crasher will have to avoid you, and should spin into the mud and stay there until a thoughtful wrecker comes by.

Now, what are the duties when you are poised on the entry ramp, waiting to get in line? First, you should be patient. Second, you should not be *too* patient. What you do is slowly creep up alongside a car to the left, one that is already in line. Then you look plaintively, sending out an unspoken plea to join the club. When you receive the proper nod or hand wave, you quickly slip in and then wave your right hand in a thank-you.

If, however, the fellow does not allow you to slip in the line, you may use any other well-known gesture of the open road.

Traffic merging during rush hours is a little-understood but highly important operation. Done properly, it speeds up the flow of vehicles and allows me to get home before sunrise.

Done improperly, i.e., not allowing my little yellow VW Beetle in front of you, it may be hazardous to your health. My nose gunner is a crack shot.

Sir? Ma'am?

I rise today to propose that we launch a search for some things that used to be commonly found around here. They were once a part of our life and manner and conversation. But they have gone.

They are the addresses of "ma'am" and "sir." They have disap-
peared. Or at least they rank with the whooping crane and the Indian leopard as an endangered species. For people do not say
"ma'am" and "sir" any longer.

They are titles, once belonging to the landed gentry and ladies
of the manor. But they gradually came to mean respect, which may
well be the reason they are no longer used, because no one respects
anyone or anything anymore.

Ma'am is a contraction of madam, but not the kind of madam
like in brothel. Madam like in "lady." Webster notes that it follows
"yes." That is ridiculous on its face, at least it was in my family
when I was growing up. It could be followed by "no" or "please"
or simply stand alone.

"Lynn," my mother would say, as the opening to a question or
order.

"Ma'am?" I would reply. A "What?" or "Yeah?" or "Huh?" would
lead to most unpleasant consequences.

Ma'am was the word I used for any woman of adult age. My
mother, my grandmother, my teachers. A total stranger. It could
be "yes, ma'am" or "no, ma'am" or "I'm gonna rape you, ma'am,"
but it was always there. Sir was used for adult males. If I'd said
anything but sir to my father, I wouldn't be here to tell you. Those
terms were used without social distinction. I would say sir to a porter
or a cab driver. The idea of weighing another's social standing was
not the point.

But such titles aren't used much anymore. Indeed, when I use them
today the recipient of my respect often corrects me. This, I have
determined, is partially because in Houston we have a lot of people from places where they did not use such titles. They did not
say them, and those who did were subservient. Thus when they
are addressed as sir or ma'am, they feel uncomfortable. They don't
like it, or they think I am putting them on. Well, there is no point
in taking them aside and explaining, because (1) I don't have time,
and (2) if they do not know how to receive respect gracefully, they
don't deserve it.

The problem is certainly one of communications, because ma'am
and sir are not used either as a put-on or as a self-putdown. Just
respect. I do not call elders ma'am or sir because I am their lackey.
Conversely, persons who call me sir and my wife ma'am are not
mine. Yet somehow this idea of groveling servitude has caught hold
and vast numbers feel that using these titles somehow demeans them.

The problem is most acute among my children and their creepy little friends. Just as I say "yes, ma'am" to my mother — and shall forever — I require similar respect from my own flock. They try, but they are pretty bad about it, and in all fairness, I can see why. None of their peers do it, so my own children simply are not in the atmosphere of respectful titles. I try to be patient and overlook their occasional slippage. I have found that a quick cuff to the cheek is a good reminder.

The last holdout for good manners is, quite probably, the military. I had no problem in boot camp making sure the first word out of my mouth was sir. It had been that way all my life. But there were others who practically gagged on the word. Once again, a neat cuff to the cheek reminded them. There is something to be said for fatherly discipline.

Perhaps we are living in the twilight of ma'am and sir. Perhaps they will join "methinks" and "hey, nonny-nonny" and "23-skidoo." But if they do, we shall all be the poorer for it. We shall lose a bit of class, all of us, both those who say sir or ma'am and those who are.

The problem, as I noted, is that we have somehow equated titles of respect with groveling serfdom, running against the grain of American independence, so that good manners have become bad news. Yet I say bring back sir. Bring back ma'am. And those who deserve to be so addressed. For my children feel put upon, going through life using anachronisms of address and constantly pointing out that no one else has to say such silly things. But I do, and shall continue to do so, as a term of respect. And those few who dare to call me sir are not my servants but my colleagues in class.

Houston Times/Enquirer/Eyewitness Post

The *Houston Post* is for sale. No telling how long it has been in the works, but, ace reporter that I am, the news came to me via an hourly radio report. OK, we know who the sellers are, but who are the buyers? Who will be the new landlord around here? Whoever it is, I guarantee you two things:

(1) The new publisher will vow that nothing will change.

(2) It will.

There is nothing particularly wrong with that. Since the very first newspaper appeared on this earth, it has carried the imprint of its publisher. As A. J. Liebling said, "Freedom of the press is limited to those who own one." Still, it will be interesting to see how *The Post* is changed. For instance, if it is bought by:

The New York Times

WIFE DISPATCHES
ONSLAUGHT OF
RODENTIA

PITCHFORK, Texas — A trio of small rodents from the genus *Mus* have succumbed to the manifestations of a carving instrument, official sources here disclosed today.

A farmer's wife, Mrs. Sara Lee Cupcake of Pitchfork, Southampton, and East Clabber, citing *Marbury* vs. *Madison* (see related story, "Madison: The Man and the Square Garden," page 34) performed unexpected surgery (see background story: "Surgery in Pitchfork, 1879–1983") on the mice.

"They all came after me," sources close to the source allegedly said. "So I cut off their tails with a carving knife."

At the United Nations, a consensus among Third World delegates was that American farmers should share most, if not all, of what they have with the emerging nations. A Soviet source, however, dismissed the incident as "another imperialist display of naked aggression against smaller forms of life."

Wall Street (see Business News: "Carving Knife Industry Girds for Run") reacted predictably . . .

Marvin Zindler

An *appalling* situation has been discovered by Eyewitness Post — a farm kitchen *overrun* by filthy, disease-carrying rodents. Now wouldn't you think that a farm kitchen would be country-clean? But no, these vile animals were found scurrying around places where folks *eat*! Fortunately, the farmer's wife — when attacked by a mob of mice — had the foresight to cut off their tails with a carving knife.

Thus a mouse infestation — with their little droppings in your ice cream, filthy mouse hairs in the sugar, mouse sweat in the salt —

was caught in the nick of time. Have you ever seen such a sight in your life? *Mar*-vin *Zin*-dler, Eyewitness Post.

The ACLU

A new low was reached in man's inhumanity to mice when three cuddly little creatures, handicapped by a total lack of sight, were set upon and maimed by a knife-wielding WASP. She *cut off their tails* just to see how they run! Suits were quickly filed in federal district court where Judge William Wayne Justice granted the mice $3.4 million in punitive damages, ordered a forced sale of the farm, and placed himself in charge of all agricultural matters for Texas "until there is strict protection of civil rats."

Variety

WIFE KNIFES MOUSE HOUSE
GRAY MATTER DE-TAILED

PITCHFORK, Texas—Sexy sticks chanteuse Sara Lee Cupcake was boffo in Tin Pan Alley this past ayem in a replay of *Psycho*. The Mouse Bros., fresh from a gig in Frisco, came center stage with their evergreen routine, *Let's All Run*, which was greeted with squeals from the audience.

Sara Lee, terpsichorean *par excellence*, brought down the house with her knife act.

Kennedy & Cohen are handling book and serial rights. ABC is piloting a sitcom based on the adventure. Ed (*Lou Grant*) Asner is cast as the tough farmer with a heart of gold, Dolly Parton as his wife. Nebraska backgrounds to be shot in Malibu. Working title: *The Farmer Takes a Knife*.

Silhouette Romances

LOVE'S LUSTY LINOLEUM

Sara Lee clutched the dagger to her heaving bosom. Where was her husband, Chad? It had been so long since he had been around when she really, *really* needed him.

Suddenly, she was aware of a form in the doorway. It was Shawn, the field hand, standing there shirtless, his sweaty body heaving in anticipation.

"See how they run," Sara Lee whispered.

"They look blind," said Shawn.

The Houston Chronicle

MAYOR BLAMED
FOR FARM MASSACRE

PITCHFORK—A farmer's wife was attacked by three blind mice Wednesday and was forced to defend herself with a carving knife.

Experts in pest control say it was probably due to a cutback in civic services because of bumbling in the Whitmire administration. "You can chalk this debacle up right alongside everything else," said a City Council member who asked not to be identified. "El Salvador, potholes, Joe Sambito's arm, and Laredo's unemployment rate. We'd never had all of this if Jack Heard had won."

Meantime, Chief Lee Brown would neither confirm nor deny reports that knife-wielding housewives are a direct result of a total breakdown in law enforcement under a chief brought in from the outside.

The National Enquirer

MAD RODENTS
TERRORIZE FARM!

PITCHFORK, Texas—A helpless farm wife was viciously attacked by a horde of possibly rabid giant rats, probably from a UFO, spreading death and destruction throughout the countryside and very probably contaminating the *very food you eat!*

"I grabbed a carving knife when they came after me," sobbed the farmer's wife in an exclusive interview. "It was horrible. Just horrible!"

If you've never seen such a sight in your life check our exclusive color photos: pages 23–45.

Dodger's Downfall

Now that attention is once again fixed on the draft dodgers, war resisters, and the like, another—and more painful—point is popping up: a goodly chunk of our young men were avoiding the inconveniences of land mines through perfectly legal means.

There were all kinds of loopholes in the draft, and if you had the right daddy—the same daddy who was over at the country club bar, fuming about the draft dodgers—you could escape Vietnam.

There were occupational deferments, which many of my friends took. There were college deferments, which protected others. Then there was the National Guard—a politically protected pigeonhole for prodigals of the powerful. (Eat your heart out, Spiro.)

Yes, those were the days, when every young man who wanted to be an old man was looking for a place to hide. One of them was a friend of mine named Joe. He was the son of a university dean, and a brilliant fellow. At the time—the mid-'60s—he wore faded blue jeans and old T-shirts and had a beard. He was called a hippie. Today he would be called a university dean.

Anyway, we both lived in New York City at the time. I had an apartment and Joe had a park bench. Each to his own. He was writing, doing odd jobs to supplement his income, and generally having a fine time of it. Then one day a devastated Joe was deposited on my doorstep.

"Good grief, Joe," I said in wonderment, terror, and/or astonishment. "What happened? You hurt? Sick? Dead?"

"Worse," moaned Joe, fumbling in his back pocket for a piece of paper. "I've been drafted."

Stunned silence.

Obviously, for the first time in history, the Pentagon had made a mistake. If ever there was a free spirit, a lover of poetry and truth and cheap wine, a friend to mankind, it was Joe. By the same token, if ever there would be a rotten soldier, a undisciplined, left-footed, tardy, slovenly, well-meaning but disastrously inept trooper in the U.S. Army, it was Joe.

If the Pentagon really wanted to put Joe's talents to maximum use to end the war, it would parachute him into downtown Hanoi with a case of Gallo Burgundy. By nightfall he would have flowers growing in the foxholes.

"I dunno what to do," Joe moaned.

We had a mutual friend who escaped the draft by convincing the Army he was gay. When the doctor said, "Cough," he kissed him. I mentioned it to Joe. He shook his head. "I am the most overt heterosexual I know. I could never get away with it."

We thought for a while, bouncing ideas around. Both of us were trying to do the Department of Defense a great favor by keeping Joe out of uniform. Nothing jelled. Finally, reluctantly, Joe came up with his solution: "I'll tell 'em I'm crazy," he said, his eyes blinking and glazing. He could put on a great act.

A few weeks later, when it came time for Joe to report for his physical, he spent the night with us so he could take a shower before reporting. Even hippies have their pride. Then off he went, ready to convince the doctors that the world was Dean Martin and he was Jerry Lewis.

It was a long day. The hours groaned by as I imagined Joe already struggling under the barbed wire at Benning, lobbing grenades into the jungles west of DaNang, appearing on the cover of *Time* as the Private Slovik of the '60s.

That evening, there was the fateful knock on the door. It was Joe, a beaten, whipped, defeated man. Hello, President Thieu. We got one more volunteer.

"What happened?" I asked slowly, already knowing.

Joe didn't answer immediately but sat down and stared at the carpet. Finally he began: "I went down there ready to convince 'em I was crazy. I had it all worked out, you know. Twitching, blinking, grinning. But then, when I got face to face with the U.S. Army, the officers, the uniforms, the signs on the wall telling me not to write on the wall, the forms and questions, well, I cratered. I just couldn't go through with it. The whole thing would have been un-American. Cowardly. I couldn't do it, so I just buckled down and did right. Answered everything straight."

"Poor Joe," I said quietly, pity flowing all over the place. "Never knew what hit him, Sergeant."

"That's the problem," wailed Joe. "I went through it honestly, and the army said . . ."

"Yes?"

"The army said I was crazy."

Rendezvous With a Friend

THE BEACH—It is sort of like visiting an old friend, coming to the beach in winter. An old friend that has changed a bit over the past year, but not so much as to be unrecognizable.

The sand is still here, and the shells, and the birds flying about. Yet, well, somehow things don't seem to be exactly as they have been in the past. I'm not sure what it is.

Maybe it's what has happened to the sand during my absence. The dunes are not like I remember them, dipping where they used to rise, and rising where they used to dip. The wind and the tides have done subtle sculpting around here.

Maybe it's the changing of the shells, which have been washed in by the tons. New shells are one of the great joys of coming here, coming now. For in the summer the shell collectors are in season, and each day by noon the sands have been peered over and poked through to the extent that any fresh arrival has been quickly gathered before I get here. Ah, but this time of year, shells lie around for days, weeks, months, slowly washed clean with each tide, awaiting my arrival.

Today the beach is adorned with beautiful newcomers all around. Big shells, pink shells, conch shells, sand dollars, and shark's eyes, as the kids call them; I have no idea what the proper shellvian name is. The children are running around with sandy hands, grabbing the earth like they were on an Easter egg hunt.

Mosquitoes. Mosquitoes? Why are they here? Gad. It hits me now. Mosquitos are here because there is no wind. On the beach, no wind means lots of mosquitoes. Yes, the beach is not as it used to be; there is not the familiar nest of nautical noise. It's because of the weather. It's too good.

This is a subtle point, appreciated only by a true winter beach bum, or masochist. For the beach in winter must be just the opposite of the beach in summer to be worthwhile. In the summer, you want cloudless days, no wind, hot sun pouring down, high temperatures. A rainstorm can ruin a vacation.

But in winter, every minus becomes a plus. You want really rotten weather, rain and wind and drizzle and fog. Then you can head out into the elements and really freeze your conch shells off, to make it worth the effort.

But today there is sun, and no wind, and the temperature must be heading toward 60. Thus, the mosquitoes. That's it. The weather is too good to be good.

Here comes a pickup truck. It rumbles down the beach spewing sand. Why do we allow vehicles to pollute what little is left of true Texas? Out! I say. Get thee behind me, General Motors. Streets are for vehicles, beaches are for people. Hearing my order, the truck rumbles on down the beach, exuding urbanity with every thrusting cylinder. The truck is gone and God is back. So is the quietness. Clouds are creeping in, so maybe there is hope.

Another hopeful sign is the lack of litter. It seems to be in short supply around here for once. Not that there isn't still enough to go around. A Coors can, plastic milk cartons, half a grapefruit, a Schlitz beer can, plastic sheets, Pepsi Light. When, oh, when is Texas going to get a bottle bill?

Fairy Liquid Cleaner from Newcastle upon Tyne, England. Passing ships give our beaches a truly international flavor. Miss Breck spray, *Hecho en Mexico*. And here is an empty sack of something called Funyuns, from Frito-Lay. Printed on the side: "Don't be a litter-bug, Keep America Beautiful."

The sun is gone and the wind is picking up. So are my children. They have half the beach shells in their hands and pockets. A fine collection, it is.

A word about the water. I mean, you can hardly have a beach without the water. It is as gray as the sky has become. The waves are really quite high. Moving in every few seconds, higher each time. The tide is coming in.

Seagulls are circling above the waves, looking for fish, but they don't seem to be doing too well. They circle slowly, ready to dive for dinner. The waves are awfully high for gull-diving.

The wind is blowing stronger. I suppose a front is coming through or going away or whatever it is that fronts do. Like the tide, they do it without approval or governmental clearance. The children are getting cold, since the wind has picked up and the temperatures have gone down. The children head back to the house, to the fire and shell contests.

Now there is no one else out here at all. Look in either direction, and there is no sign of life. No shrimpers out in the seas this time of year, not even a passing freighter. It's funny, how very rarely we are all alone. When was the last time you could shout to the heavens and no one could hear? The mosquitoes are gone, too. The wind has blown them away. The seagulls are giving up their search for fish.

The sun has gone down and the cold is definitely picking up. A drop of water. Is it really rain? Yes, I am getting rained upon, just a bit. Now more, fine little drops, being blown around. The heavens are opening up.

I head back to the beach house. The rain is soaking me through. The fog is drifting in and the wind is coming up. It is cold and wet and dreadful. Perfect. I can see the beach house and the fire glowing in the fireplace. Maybe I can make it to safety before God gets me. The beach is still my old friend, with dreadful weather, right on cue.

There is much to be said about the beach in the summer. But few know of the deeper delights of the beach in winter.

Four Play News on Location
Denny Dentures Brings Reporters
Back to Station for Dumb Summation

Ha-ha-ha!
Four Play News
Sex and booze.
Fires and crashes,
Tires with slashes.
Don't touch that dial,
It's time to smile,
With Four Play Neeeews.

And now here is everybody's favorite anchorman, Den-ny Den-tures!

Ha-ha-ha. Thank you, thank you. And welcome to another edition of laughs and blood on KAKL-TV's Four Play News. Our first story of the night is from our own consumer affairs reporter, Connie Cleavage, who has been out at the supermarket.

[Connie on screen.] Right, Denny. Out at this supermarket, I'm reporting on loan sharking. More and more people are falling victim to loan sharks. They charge too much. They cheat you out of your money. As one loan shark told me, "We charge too much and we cheat you out of your money." [Long pause.] This is Connie Cleavage somewhere on aisle 2.

Connie, now that you're back here at the station, I want to ask you something. Why do people dislike loan sharks?

Well, Denny, like I said on that tape, they cheat you out of money.

Thanks, Connie. Speaking of sharks reminds me of deep-sea fishing and the out-of-doors. And speaking of the out-of-doors . . .

Denny, you're still trying to blend everything together, aren't you? I mean, that's really stretching it. Sharks to sports. Come off it.

Connie, our consultants say every story should move right into the next one. Otherwise, you shock the viewer. And speaking of shocks, here are some shocking sports scores from our number one fan, Homer Fields, who has been out at the Astrodome. Homer?

[Homer on screen.] There really isn't much sports today, Denny. But we still have to fill up the same time slot, news or no news. So instead of giving the scores in numerals, we'll spell them out there on the screen, which takes you longer to read. As you can see, it was Houston Rockets one hundred and three to the Washington Bullets' one hundred and twenty-seven. Leading the Rockets with twenty-five points was Calvin Murphy. And that's about all the sports news we have, Denny. As one fan put it, "This has been a slow day." [Pregnant pause.] This is Homer Fields somewhere between first and second.

Now, sitting here beside me in the studio is Homer again. Tell me, Homer, who was the leading scorer in that Rockets game?

It was Murphy, Denny. Weren't you listening to the tape?

Calvin Murphy?

Yeah, Calvin Murphy.

Well, Murphy's Law certainly wasn't helping the Rockets. And speaking of law . . .

Here he goes again. Segueing through the bloody program.

. . . there's no law that says Homer has to be like everyone else. Today I can't help but notice you're dressed up like a giant pepperoni pizza.

Right, Denny. I am protesting the price of pizzas out at the Dome. I'll have a biting — get it? — commentary later on in the program on this slice of life.

Speaking of pizza pie reminds me of pie in the sky. And the weather. Here to tell us all about it is our own sky watcher out investigating the weather in Memorial Park earlier today, Rainer Shine.

[Rainer on screen.] Denny, there is definitely weather out there today. As you can see, it is starting to rain. The temperature is 56 and the wind is from the southeast at 7. As one cloud put it . . .

Thanks, Rainer. Now that you've joined me back here in the studio, I want to know why you're wet.

Denny, didn't you see my bit? It was raining out there.

Meantime, the reign in Spain . . .

Wait a minute, Denny.

Yes, Connie?

Look, I'll put up with your stupid segues, but why is it we all had to go out somewhere else and do those dumb stand-ups, then come back in here and answer your questions?

The consultants said we should.

What do they know? They're all in New York.

They saw *20/20*. You know how Hugh Downs always has the reporter who did the story sitting beside him afterwards, and he asks some questions.

Denny, if there is an important point in the story, I put it in myself. You don't have to ask me.

The consultants say I am supposed to take the role of the viewer. After every story, the viewer has a few questions he'd like to ask the reporter, but he can't. So I do.

Denny, if there's anything the viewer should know, I'll tell him myself. It'll be in my story.

The boss says do it. And that's why I'm over here and you're not. Speaking of knot, the knot-tying down at the courthouse took a new twist today. Here with that story is KAKL's own Denny Dentures.

[Denny on screen.] Thanks, Denny. Down here at the courthouse . . .

My Lord, Rainer, he's even got himself out on location.

. . . not as many people are getting married as before. No one seems to know why, but as one courthouse clerk put it, "Not as many people are getting married, but no one knows why." [Pause.] I'm Denny Dentures for KAKL-TV.

Denny, now that you've rejoined me here . . .

For crying out loud, Denny, you can't interview *yourself.*

Why not? I'm the anchorman.

Denny?

Yes, Homer?

Another thing. Why is it that every single story we do out on location has to end the same way, quoting some unnamed source with some dumb, wrap-up cutesy quote followed by a long pause before signing off?

Speaking of dumb, our consultants . . .

> Four Play News,
> Has to cruise.
> On location,
> Source quotation,
> Back to station.
> For summation.
> On Four Play Neeeews.
> Ha-ha-ha!

A Problem Home

THE FRONT YARD—Welcome, welcome, you delegates to the National Association of Home Builders. It is good of you all to spare a few minutes from your busy schedule.

You have already seen the many other displays put up for your edification—the kitchens with their wondrous gadgetry, the bathrooms with sauna baths. You have marveled at the sliding doors, computerized doorbells, electric paintbrushes, and quick-drying contracts.

So with these marvels of the prefab instant-success age of construction in the back of your mind, we shall now take a quick tour through one last exhibit.

My house.

Some of you have seen such a structure in your early childhood or when you took a wrong turn trying to find your latest housing development. It was built to last until the final house payment or the first rain, whichever came first.

Before going inside, look quickly at the shutters across the front of the house. Notice that three shutters aren't there. That's because they literally fell apart and they don't seem to make them anymore. One company generously offered to tailor me some new ones at $70 each. I plan to solve the problem by simply painting black shutters on the brick. It should work. How many people think Groucho really has a mustache?

You may also notice that the wood around my front door is rotting. A contractor patiently explained this to me: "It happens sometimes."

Step inside, please. It may be hard for all 50,000 of you to jam into my front hall, but try. To your right you see the dining room. Now, please, don't shout. Calm yourselves. Yes, it is supposed to be a living room, I know. Yes, the Koran, the Old Testament, and the Constitution require that a living room be adjacent to the front hall. Every house built since Plymouth Settlement has it that way.

But you see, these days no one uses a formal living room. This used to be ours, but for years friends would walk in the front door and nod as they passed by the living room, commenting, "Yes, indeed, that certainly is a living room." And head immediately for the den. All, that is, except my neighbor Calpakis the Wily Greek, who heads immediately for the liquor.

I could put $10,000 worth of decorations and furniture in the living room and still no one would use it. Living rooms today are about as needed as a dirigible hangar and almost as expensive. So the living room is the dining room.

Ah, yes, you ask what have I done with the old dining room? Step this way. It is my office. It is full of books and smells of cigar smoke and the desk is exactly five paces from the beer in the kitchen refrigerator. There is method in my madness. But please don't tell *House Beautiful* of my un-American alterations or they'll come over and burn my deed restrictions.

The kitchen. It is chock-full with the many electric gadgets that make cooking so enjoyable these days. Three of them work.

And here is the den, or family room, I believe you call it these days. By any name, it is the Thrush Central of any home. Here is the fireplace, the stereo, the TV, all the lifeboats of my happy ship. This used to be a gun rack, but I converted it into a wine cabinet, finding Bacchus more congenial than Mars.

The hall, with the doorbell chimes. The doorbell never worked in this house and it took me two days and $28 to fix it. Actually, today both the front and the back door go bing-bong, but it's a step in the right direction.

Here is my shower. Notice that the tile is new. That's because two fellows with sledgehammers had to come in here and smash it all out to replace my old shower pan, which was leaking throughout this part of the house. The reason my old shower pan leaked was that it wasn't there. An oversight, I'm sure.

Oh, I see that you have noticed those funny little lines down my walls in every room. They look quite a bit like cracks running from ceiling to floor. It may appear that I have the only house in town with varicose veins, but actually you will be relieved to know that they are only cracks. Running from ceiling to floor. It seems that I have a cracked foundation. It also buckles wallpaper, jams doors, and lets rain run in around a front window, thereby ruining the carpet. I do not know why my foundation cracked, but certainly there must be a good reason. Maybe my contractor was born in Managua.

There are other items harder to see in one quick visit. For instance, my shingles are falling apart. However, I take heart in the knowledge that it can be rectified for between $3,000 and $4,000. It is good to know there's a cure for my ills.

Now, you may be asking yourself: "How did he get himself into such a mess? He's a big boy with two eyes." You're right, of course, I should have read the small print under the "For Sale" sign. ("Caveat

Emptor.") Indeed, I did read the sworn statements from noted experts that my air conditioning system was in tiptop shape. I must admit that it worked beautifully well into our first summer and was replaced for only $1,100. I was also given a signed statement swearing that there were absolutely no termites in my house. Unfortunately, someone forgot to read it to the termites.

Finally, you may be asking: "Who would have bought such a house in the first place from such a home builder?" I had the same question and eventually found out. It was built by a home builder for himself.

Hello, Uh, . . .

THE PARTY — "Hi, there," says this nice fellow, extending his hand. "Good to see you again. You remember the wife here? I've been meaning to write you about the situation in Sardinia that . . ."

Not a word this man is saying penetrates my brain, because my mind is not on his words. It is on his name. Or lack of it. Who is this? I have no earthly idea. Never seen him before, I'd swear. But obviously we have met. He mentions, in passing, some conversation we had during the Bronze Age. He goes on about the situation in Sardinia while I am desperately trying to remember who he is, where we've met. Was it in school? Which school? No, during a Saturday morning washer run to Wagner Hardware. Maybe Alaska or Bay City. Did we meet in Sardinia? No, I've never been there.

I've got to remember, and fast, because we are at a party and it is guaranteed that within two minutes some other person is going to walk up and say, "Hi, there. Good to see you again. You remember Gladys." Then he will look at the fellow I'm talking to. Look at him blankly, then at me, waiting for an introduction. And I am supposed to introduce by name four people who are total strangers to me. Plus occupations, background, and recall the times we've met before.

When I stand there silent, shuffling from one foot to the other, they will all glare at me, waiting. I will be in bad trouble. And four people will be mad at me. Later they will drive home, all the while saying bad things about me because I'm such an idiot that I can't even remember their names.

The problem should not be taken by them to be a personal insult. They were not singled out to be forgotten. I just can't remember anyone's name. For a journalist, that's pretty bad. One time a magazine story said that if you can't remember names, it's because — way down deep — you don't want to. It is a subconscious rejection of that person. I'd tell you the name of the person who wrote the story if I could.

Still, it is an attractive theory, but totally false. At least in my case, because I really want to remember other people's names. There is certainly no pleasure in making a fool of yourself and causing people to badmouth you all the way home. I'd like to remember names, if only I could.

Other magazine stories say that you should remember a person's name by association. If his name is Oxblood and at least one of his shoes is the same color, it's easy. But what if his name is Shoes and he's wearing boots? The name remembrance by association is limited, for me, to the obvious: Judge Learned Hand, the Lone Ranger, and Chevy Chase, but only when he's in southern Maryland.

For these reasons, I always appreciate name tags at parties. I know, they make you look goosey. In a name tag, I always feel like a DP getting off the boat at Ellis Island, shuffling along with bags and samovars. But name tags save me a lot of problems. When someone walks up and says, "Hi, good to see you again. You remember the wife. I was going to write you a letter about samovars . . ." I stare straight at his name tag and vigorously tell him how good it is to see him again, Charlie or Egbert or the King of Sardinia. For no matter how much you may dislike to be labeled, any social event extending beyond the immediate family should have name tags.

Some people make it easy by saying, "Hi, good to see you again. I'm Charlie Egbert, King of Sardinia. You remember my wife, Queen Hepatitis." Now that is most appreciated. Then I can break into a wide grin and say how good it is to see them again. I used to do that a lot, say hi and give them my name. But this became counterproductive. I'd receive a startled look that would say, in effect, "I know who you are, you dummy. Don't you know who I am?" So I don't give my name much anymore. Actually, in certain places, it's safer not to.

The real gems in my book are those who, when introducing themselves, say not only who they are but where we met. "Hi, I'm Egbert Samovar. We met at the Garth Bates Forgive and Forget Banquet. The one where they counted the silverware between each course." Those are the best of all.

But this guy here now, who's still talking about Sardinia, has yet to identify himself. Ah, but now he's leaving. "See you around," I say gratefully.

"Yeah," he says, "good to have seen you again, King Egbert."

Recollections of Days When Market Followed His Bidding

THE RADIO—"On Wall Street, stocks were up 3.45 points on a volume of 34 million. Analysts say the market, etc., etc., etc."

I suddenly think of cold sandwiches, gulped down with hot coffee. It has nothing whatsoever to do with losing a fortune on Wall Street and thus winding up in such financial straits. Actually, I was making more money than I had ever made before. But to make it, I had to live on cold sandwiches and hot coffee while I created and destroyed fortunes, sent widows out in the snow, caused once-great power brokers to step lightly from their 23rd-story office windows. Ah, those were the good old days.

The days, specifically, were when I was one of several wage slaves at the *New York Times* on the broadcast desk. The only free-lance job around had already been taken: a fellow writer daily cranked out the *Wall Street Report*, broadcast over the *Times'* radio station, which was right there in the same building.

Each afternoon, Monday through Friday, when the market closed, he would rip the financial reports off the various wires, check with the *Times'* business desk for more information, and—during his supper hour—whip out the script for that day. It paid $75 a week, which, for a journalist, is a king's ransom. Anyway, all the rest of us would cast covetous eyes on this fellow as he made the extra bread. Then, one day, he either quit or got sacked, I can't remember which.

"Ashby," said the editor, "you want to write the *Wall Street Report*?" Silly fellow. It was like asking if I'd mind handling the overflow from Fort Knox.

Having watched my predecessor in this task, I knew generally what to do. Unfortunately, I didn't know how long it took and got my first script to the announcer about two minutes before air time. He was not amused.

In the following days I got it written earlier but learned one major lesson: if you stay at your desk during dinner hour, you can't leave to eat. But I had another four hours of employment ahead of me each evening and had to eat something, so it was that I selected

from the food cart that came pushing by every 6 o'clock. Cold sandwiches and hot coffee every night, Monday through Friday. It got
nauseating.

After a week or two, I had the *Wall Street Report* down to a
snap, until the evening when the managing editor came back to my
desk. He'd just heard the show and wanted to know why a stock
I had mentioned had fluctuated so much. I replied that I didn't know,
which was clearly not what he wanted to hear from the *Times'* financial expert. "Check your sources," he ordered.

I nodded agreeably, and he walked off. Sources? My sources were
AP, UPI, and the *New York Times.* Same as his. In panic I searched
my mind and remembered that one of my new friends in New York,
recently departed from an aircraft carrier, was a trainee with a Wall
Street brokerage firm. He was still at his office, so I rang him up
and asked about the stock in question. He didn't have the slightest
idea either. "Hold on," he said. "Let me check." A few moments later,
he was back at the phone. "Rumors of a merger," he declared
authoritatively. The news was passed along to Olympus. I was
saved.

But it introduced me to the major influence on Wall Street: market
analysts. It is not enough to have something happen in the stock
exchanges, you've got to have a staff of druids to tell you why. So
each afternoon I would call up my private wizard of Wall Street
who—backed by his three weeks' experience—would sagely explain
the free enterprise system. Following an ancient tradition of
economics, he was never identified by name, only as "a Wall Street
observer," or "economic experts" or even "top Wall Street analyst"
(his office was on the 42nd floor).

Between us, we observed, pontificated, gave inside tips. I had
this grand vision that late each afternoon, from the back of a long
black limousine winding its way to Fifth Avenue, would come the
order, "Turn on WQXR, Smedley. I want to find out what to do."

"Sure thing, Mr. Rockefeller," would come the reply. Moments
after my show went off the air, a phone call would be made. "Hello?
No, I'm still on the parkway. Tomorrow morning buy Wumpet In-
dustries. All you can get. Right. Got it straight from 'a top market
insider.' "

No doubt there were whispered conversations at back tables of
the poshest restaurants. "That *Times* fellow hit it right on the nose."

"Great analyst."

"Made two million on his advice about Beaver Bros."

"Just two? You gotta *believe*."

Munching cold sandwiches and sipping hot coffee, over the months I graduated from explaining why it happened to the most difficult of all: forecasting what was going to happen. It was honest, mind you, straight and true. I figured my Wall Street adviser was as good as any. The fact that he didn't know anything whatsoever about the stock market had nothing to do with the soundness of our sagacity. "Lox looks good," he'd say.

"The economic forecast for lox stocks is definitely bullish," I would intone. Lox would soar.

"Rails look good," my ace source, Deep Portfolio, would tell me just before air time.

"Rail stocks are expected to rise sharply, Wall Street experts predict," I'd write.

"Turn on the radio, Jeeves, the *Wall Street Report* is due."

"Yes, Mr. Dillon."

"Hello, Throckmorton. Did you hear? I was thinking the same thing. Buy rails."

The value of a share of stock is in the eye of the beholder, so my Wall Street tipster never failed, because whatever you say about stocks will eventually hold true. It was all based on solid evidence, or at least as good as any others had: "Sources said," which translates to "Somebody thinks so." As I pecked away on my typewriter late each afternoon, empires crumbled, endowments withered, fortunes were made, and Gibralter quivered. When I talked, E. F. Hutton listened. "Buy coal. Sell steel."

"Are you sure?"

"OK, sell coal and buy steel."

No one ever complained. Indeed, the managing editor started dressing better. But today when I hear the Wall Street news on the radio and find that analysts feel, observers predict, and market speculation has it that, I think of cold sandwiches, hot coffee, and two total novices—with not a single share of stock between them, running the American economy.

He's a Victim of His Own Creativity

THE BACK DOOR—"Gad. Gasp. It was terrible out there, I tell you."

I am greeted with absolutely no response.

"The freeway. A fender-bender. Traffic stacked up to the Loop. Gasp. Wheeze. In first gear for 12 miles. A new record. Slight rain. Two more wrecks. I'm the sole survivor."

No one seems to be paying any attention to me. Here I am, struggling home after a terrible day at work, followed by an even more terrible drive home. Slick roads. Trucks bent on my demise. The police department has the week off. Hours, it seemed—inching forward along the loops and freeways to home. Now I am here, hanging on to life by my fingernails, and no one cares.

"Hurry up," says my wife. "We'll be late."

Friends, that is not the way for a husband to be greeted upon his arrival home. It is not proper, not even civilized. True, he should not expect golden trumpets and flowers strewn in his path (although it would be accepted). But to crawl through the door after being utterly dumped upon by boss, customer, fellow motorist, the weather, and three red lights that waited until he approached to go on permanent rouge, is quite enough for one lifetime. Then to be greeted by the warning that he is running late is totally unconstitutional.

"Late? I'm late? How could I be late when it only took me an hour and 20 minutes to make a 15-minute trip? Where's my first martini?"

"No time," says my wife. "We're late. And don't wear that dumb sweater."

"Where am I late to?"

"School."

"School? I was at school last night."

"That was the PTA Night."

"What was the night before last?"

"Homeroom Mothers and Fathers Night."

"Then what's tonight?"

"This is the Parents-Teachers Get-Acquainted Coffee."

"I have been to school every night for the last week," I shout. "*I* don't go to school. My *children* go to school."

"Don't wear that dumb sweater," says one of my sons as he walks by, rubbing gook on his pimples.

"Why was I at school Monday?"

"That was band concert night. You still owe for the band candy."

"And last Thursday?"

"That was the fifth-grade chorus night. You heard me sing," says another offspring, speaking from within the refrigerator, probably between the cheese and the Coke.

I plant my feet squarely on the linoleum. "Look," I say rather testily, "just once I wish I could come home and stay home. No band concert. No Indian Guides. No Dads and Daughters Dinner. No Cub Scouts. Not even one church get-together! I am tired, do you hear me? I am whipped. It's a jungle out there!"

"Let's go, Bwana," says my wife.

"I am not."

"You are not what?"

"I am not moving. You go on. You go to the Mother's-Daughter Dance or the Family Flake-Out or the Togetherness Love-In. I am not moving!"

No one is paying any attention. They are all gathering up their purses and belts and brushes and money and heading for the door.

"I am not moving! Every single night, I come home defeated. Beaten into the mud by society. Cowed by angry clerks. Stomped on by my coworkers. Pistol-whipped by truck drivers who purchased the road I'm on. Intimidated and muzzled and run over. A man's home is his castle, not his hassle. There's a distinct difference."

"You gotta come tonight. Mrs. Frisbee is taking roll."

"Roll? I'm not going to school. I flunked out years ago."

"I will not be able to stand up against peer pressure if you don't come."

"Fathers are not peers. They are kings. I'm going to get a bumper sticker that says, 'Have Your Children Hugged You Today?' Equal rights and all that."

"I'll bet your father went to Parents-Teachers Get-Acquainted Coffees."

"My father did not have to go. Nor did he have to drive down the Katy Freeway on a rainy Friday evening with most of the Western world trying to kill him. And he didn't have to put up with children demanding that he go back out again, and be nice to a woman who's planning to strike on Monday for more of my tax dollars and longer coffee breaks. So there."

"Are you ready, dear?"

Sigh. Apparently I'm not getting my message across. The Sunday when the Raiders were playing the Broncos, I was out flying kites. When *Centennial* was on, I was roller skating with the Sons and Seniors. I thought *Roots* was a hair transplant. "No more Mr. Nice Dad!" I shout.

Silence. Mainly because no one is around. They are all in the car, waiting. Now comes a pat-pat-pat of the horn. I'd better go. Tonight I'm being nominated for High Vice President and Coffee Maker for the Seventh Grade Glee Club.

But I'll show 'em. I'll wear my sweater.

Crabbing

THE BEACH—Once more it's man against beach. Living off the land. Turning my back on computerized civilization. It's time to return to nature. So get the pot boiling, slice up some lemons, add a dash of salt, chill the white wine, for I am staking out my very own crab trap.

Now, staking out a crab trap—or maybe it's crab *pot*, I really don't know and, frankly, don't care, either—is no easy decision. And it's a blow to the ego and an open confession of one's inability to handle the problem on the simplest level.

The simplest level, of course, is to go to the store and buy them, $2 for a dozen, live and kicking (or snapping). But that is not my way. I must meet nature on its own terms, the way my forefathers did.

Purists in the profession say that catching crab by using anything more than a chicken neck on the end of a string is unsportsmanlike conduct, and ranks up there with calling on NORAD to plot duck migration. Normally, I would agree. Indeed, I have paid my dues in this regard. Many an hour I have sat on the dock at Rockport with the Indian Guides, waiting patiently for the gentle tug on the string, a nautical signal that a crab is looking for dinner but will soon be mine instead.

Slowly, ever so slowly, you pull the string out of the water and there—clutching the chicken neck and waving in the breeze—is a beautiful, plump blue crab. Then you quietly get a net, which is on the end of a pole, hold it under the crab, then shake the string so that the crab lets go and falls into the net. It is a tricky matter, since there is always the possibility that the little beggar will let go before the net is under him and thus tumble back home.

Yes, that is the most sportsmanlike way. But it is also the hardest, and it requires that you be out of the water. You have to be up on a dock, or boat, or rock. You can't very well wade out from the beach to waist-deep water and dangle a chicken neck down by your toes. You face two distinct problems: First, your wiggling toes may scare the crabs away. And second, they may not.

Some take a more direct route. They use a round net about 16 inches across. They just tie the chicken neck in the middle of the net and pull it up. But like the simple chicken-neck-cum-string, a round net requires that you be up and out of the water.

And that does me no good here, because I am at the beach where there is no dock. Only the sloping sand out to the crabs. So I am reduced to getting a crab trap. It is a simple contraption: a wire box about two feet square. On each side are holes, allowing the crab to enter, but they have a hard time leaving. They are attracted to the box by bait, which I put inside.

The crab trap costs me $10.50. Two frozen mullet cost me about a half-dollar more.

"You got to tie it down," says the little old trapmaker. A ball of twine is 45 cents. "You got a fishing license?" she asks.

"What did the State of Texas do to the Gulf of Mexico so that I need to reimburse the state?"

A temporary fishing license costs me another $1.25.

"You need a weight to anchor it down out there, or it'll wash ashore," I am told. Throwing caution to the winds, I cavalierly state that I can wrestle my own rock from the wilds, and don't need to buy one.

That brings me here to the beach. I find a slab of concrete, put it in the bottom of the trap. Drop in one mullet, sliced to ribbons so as to attract the crab. Yuk. Tie on the twine, pull the trap out into the ocean, get dunked, lose the trap, find it again, resume my march into the sea.

I am now waist-deep in the big muddy, soaking wet, trying to get this everloving crab trap in place without allowing the sliced-up mullet to attract finny characters before I get out of here. Waves are crashing over me, the cord is getting looped around my ankles, and $2 for a dozen crab is looking like the steal of the century. It is now in place. Chill the white wine.

The next morning: I am now wading back out into the ocean, following the string to my crab trap. Here it is. Lordy, it weighs a ton. Must be full of crab. No, just full of that slab of concrete. There is one lousy crab here.

"It's too rough out there," a local informs me. "Got to wait for calm waters."

I can't wait for calm waters. I'm hungry. In goes the remaining mullet. Out I wade to the horizon, with six-foot waves smashing me to the ocean floor every third step. I set down the trap and struggle back to shore to check the line. Funny, it's not here. In taking the trap out, I must have broken the line. That means my entire crab industry is lost out there in the waves. Back I go, feeling around with my toes. Somewhere nearby is a gutted fish deftly attracting carnivorous crustacea.

Ah, here it is. Retie the cord and wait for daylight. Chill the wine. Get the salad ready. Now it is daylight. Back I go to find my meal. Here is my crab trap, up on the beach. And empty. Clearly a poacher attacked my trap during the night and this morning is having crab omelet. There is nothing lower than a crab rustler. Nothing.

But there is a bright side to everything. Now the sea is calm. This time, I am going to have a crab dinner for sure. Chill the wine. Ah, here they are, and without a doubt, they are delicious. Plump white meat. Yummy claws, cracked smartly with a wooden mallet. French bread, fresh salad. Not bad crabs at all, for two bucks a dozen.

Something Seems to Be Developing in Neighborhood

It all began when I looked out my dining room window one morning to see three workmen hammering little stakes into the ground across the street. Little stakes with ribbons tied to them. Shortly thereafter I heard a knock at the door.

"Hi, guy," said this fellow in a business suit. "I'm Frisbee of International Investments. Want to sell your house?"

"No."

"I'll make you a good offer," he said. "Particularly if you accept Canadian dollars."

"No, thanks," I repeated.

"French francs?"

"Not interested."

"OK, we'll compromise. French Canadian dollars."

"You don't seem to understand," I said. "I don't want to move. I like it here."

"I can see why, being so close to the shopping mall."

"What shopping mall?"

"Oh, nothing. Well, better go. If you change your mind, here's my card." He went out to the curb where a surveying crew was setting up.

Later that day, I noticed three men standing in my driveway looking at some blueprints. An hour later, there was another knock.

"Hi, fellow," said a man holding an attaché case. "I'm Gross of Money-Making Properties. I'd like to make you an offer on your house."

"No, thanks."

"Twice what you paid for it."

"Go away."

"But think how much your taxes will go up because you'll be next to the off ramp."

"Off ramp?"

"You didn't get a letter from the highway department?"

"I don't know what you're talking about, Mr. Gross."

"Just forget I mentioned it," he said, handing me a business card. "If you change your mind."

That night I got a phone call. "This is Quincy Quick of Tex-Cash Realties," a voice said. "We'd like to buy your house."

"Why?"

"Oh, let's just say that Tex-Cash is a good neighbor. We don't want our employees parking in front of your house. That can be so annoying, right?"

"But you're located downtown," I said.

"So are you, or will be shortly. You know how Houston is growing."

"You're moving into my neighborhood?"

"Actually, we're only leasing the 28th floor."

I hung up.

"I'm not interested," I told Sheik Abdul el-Arif, who was standing at my doorway the next morning.

"But I am making you a good offer," he replied.

"Yeah, I know. Why?"

"I like penthouse condominiums."

"But Sheik, this is a one-story house, not a high-rise condominium."

"It's still early in the week," he said, handing me his card.

Later I ran into a neighbor, Cranston. "Sorry to hear you're moving," he said, "but I guess the money is too good to refuse."

"Hey, I'm not moving. I was told you're moving," I said.

"Never," Cranston declared. "I like it here in Oaks Rivers."

"Uh, Cranston. The name of our subdivision is Running Rats Acres. Always has been."

"You didn't hear? The civic club has voted to change the name. Sounds more uptown to be Oaks Rivers."

"That's too pretentious."

"Oh, we had other suggestions. The U.S. Army Corps of Engineers even had one."

"What?"

"Flood Wood."

"Don't like it."

"They cited truth in advertising, so I suggested we change it to Misty Meadows."

"Why change the name at all?"

"Because no one wants to relocate at the Running Rats Industrial Park."

"I'd hardly call my kids' lemonade stand an industrial park."

"Oh, you didn't hear?"

Supper that night was interrupted by a knock at the door. "Wong Fu's the name. Land's the game," said a fellow standing there. "International Conglomerates, Inc."

"Not interested in selling my house," I said.

"Sell? Who's talking selling? We just want mineral rights."

"You're drilling oil wells in Oaks Rivers?"

"Actually, this is the Austin Colony Lease 87."

"You can't drill here, or build condos here, or an industrial park. We've got deed restrictions!" I hollered.

"You've also got 55-mile-an-hour speed limits," he said.

"Then we need zoning."

"You want orderly growth, move to Austin or buy a farm near Brenham," Wong Fu replied, handing me his card.

"How would you know about Austin or Brenham?"

"You don't think people like me really *live* here, do you? Why, you don't even have zoning."

Yesterday Cranston bought a farm near Brenham.

Ancestors' Saga

THE DESK—It is time to pay my Master Card bill. If this is the one from the bank that charges me interest from the time I buy the lawn mower until the time I get my bill, then this—I assure you—

will be the very last such bill I pay. If, on the other hand, it is from the kindly bank that handles my Master Card bill like every other merchant in town, and charges interest only if I am delinquent, then I will continue to live and die by it.

In either case, the lucky devil gets my seal of approval. Lackey, the candle! The match! I let the wick catch fire. It glows, then burns slightly, not the bright blaze of your average wick, but then this is not the average candle. This is one of heavy brown wax. As the wick burns, the wax melts, then I turn the candle on its side and let the wax drip, drop by thick brown drop, onto the paper. It looks very much like melting chocolate. Ah, a dark brown pool of wax. Now, the final touch. I push my ring into the melted mess and this otherwise sterile bit of financial flotsam gets a touch of class.

Yes, like The Phantom in the comic books, who swatted his enemies with his skull ring, leaving them forever marked, this bill for one lawn mower now is branded with ownership. And once more, down through the footnotes of history, the Ashbys march on.

My ring is of gold, and bears the seal of my family. Not quite the scarlet A, but close. And older. In the middle is a shield. It is, with typical family cunning, shield-shaped, with a chevron ermine in the middle. That means simply an inverted V with little Christmas trees on it. This signifies the rank of private first class, the generally lowly rank we have held in military organizations the world over. Granted, there were some exceptions, like Heathcliff the Creep, a draft dodger during the Children's Crusade, who later became commander of a boiling oil brigade. Sir John Ashby (died 1693) was admiral of the *Defiance* and led the British fleet in the battle of Bantry Bay. From that point on, no other members of the family were allowed to handle an oar without supervision.

Actually, we had to come to this country in order to achieve our rightful role of leadership. Thomas Ashby, Captain of Foot in the Virginia militia, was the first over to this side of the ocean. His son was a captain; *his* son was a general. Everything went fine until General Turner Ashby, Confederate Cavalry, dashed gallantly across the field at the battle of Cross Timbers, only to be dropped by one Frederick Trullender of Company E, 1st New Jersey Cavalry. Trullender later gained fame as proprietor of the machine works at Salem, New Jersey. The June 27, 1892, edition of the *Philadelphia Weekly Times* noted that Trullender "died today after a long illness." I can only hope that he strangled on ham hocks and grits.

Also on the family shield are three leopards, two on top, one below. This is in remembrance of Earl Ashbee of the Bogs, who used to hunt leopards on his estate each morning. The fact that there were no leopards in England only added to his enjoyment, since that meant there was no season and no limit. The earl, incidentally, was the sixth Earl of Ashbee. The fifth earl was known as Alfred the Impotent, which raises more questions than it answers.

Then there was George Ashby (1390–1475), a poetical writer who owned an estate called Breakspeares in Middlesex. Uncle George was Clerk of the Signet to Henry VI and Margaret of Anjou. After the Yorkist conquest of Henry VI, George was chained in a prison ship but was allowed to row unsupervised. He later translated *French Manuals of Devotion* into English, but no one read it.

Richard Ashby (1614–1680) was a Jesuit priest who taught philosophy; thus, we do not claim direct descent. That comes through another George Ashby (1724–1808), who was president of St. John's College, Cambridge. He was considered something of a radical in supporting the right of professors to marry. I can only assume by my presence today that he succeeded or changed jobs.

The family crest is topped by the turret of a castle. This represents the family residence, which caused Edgar Ashby the Hopeless (1212 – 1213) to observe, "A man's castle is his home." During the Peasant's Revolt he was boiled in brine, and to this day, members of my family get hives when eating pickles. We kept the castle as part of the crest to remind us that no matter where we live, we can't afford it.

Below the shield is a banner on which is written our motto: "Be Just and Fear Not." The family had originally used "Death Before Dishonor" but had to change it after a conflict during the War of the Roses that came to be known as Ashby's Rout. We then opted for "Humility Has Its Place." One branch of the family used "Ask About My Grandpeasants," but it never caught on. Neither did its successor, "I'd Rather Be Serfing." The final version came about when Henry IV ordered an ancestor of mine, Gordon the Gin, to repel an attack on the kingdom by the Scots. Gordon reputedly replied, "Why me?"

Just before being forced on his horse, Gordon was told by the king, "Be just and fear not." The family thought this would go better on the crest than Gordon's final words: "They look funny in dresses."

A lot of people have family crests, and many have stories behind them. Mine is no different from most, if you'd just be honest enough to explore your real family tree, and not accept the version offered by a maiden aunt who left out the good stuff. Indeed, I'm sure the family of Frederick Trullender of Salem, New Jersey, has tales to tell as they sit at their long tables all day opening envelopes for Master Card.

Movie Memories

A few weeks ago, as I was gazing over the local television movie listings, what should pop up but *Pimpernel Smith.*

That night I flipped on the tube, and sure enough, there was Leslie Howard once more, as the absentminded Oxford don, skillfully out-witting Francis Sullivan, the Nazi general, in pre-war Europe. It all unreeled just as I remembered it from some other late, late show years ago. (I didn't see the film when it came out in '41 as I was only three and Father felt I would not catch all the subtle nuances of the plot.)

"Come back!" shouts Sullivan, waving his pistol at the smoke and fog.

"I'll be back," says Pimpernel Smith evenly. "We'll all be back."

Terrific stuff, but it is only one of several movies that I have seen over the years and remember with special warmth — not because they were hailed and awarded, but because they went by without making much of a murmur, and only I in all the world know how memorable they were.

Like *The Americanization of Emily.* Probably the best film James Garner and Julie Andrews ever made, and today it is all but forgot-ten. Great acting and a beautiful story. Even the theme song was good. I file it alongside *Two Rode Together.* That was a western with James Stewart and Richard Widmark that — on the surface — was just another oater. Strictly formula stuff, except that it had some unforgettable throwaway lines so aptly handled by both. I never really considered Widmark a topflight actor until I saw him suffer-ing under Stewart's well-aimed bon mots.

Speaking of westerns, everybody knows that John Wayne was good in *True Grit*, even got an Oscar for it, as I recall, but what about *The Searchers*? I thought so. You've forgotten it.

Comedy? Danny Kaye in *The Court Jester* is another sleeper. His routine about "the flagon with the dragon holds the brew that is true" is priceless. In another vein entirely, Kaye was great in *Me and the Colonel*—another winner that no one remembers. But I think the hardest I ever laughed in a theater was the first time I saw James Cagney in *One Two Three*. I still remember coming out of a theater on Times Square with tears rolling down my cheeks, and everyone thought I had been to see some kind of tragedy. Even Arlene Francis was funny in *One Two Three*, but today no one remembers. No one else, that is.

Another little gem that slipped by unnoticed was *The Flim Flam Man* with George C. Scott. Scott hammed and mugged and was absolutely fantastic, and it had the best car chase scene in ages. But who today speaks glowingly of *The Flim Flam Man*?

The Wheeler Dealers was lousy in parts but great in others, particularly when J. Ray and Ray Jay began wheeling and dealing over oil.

War movies? *Decision Before Dawn* and *Pork Chop Hill* are the best of the lot, far superior to the biggies like *The Longest Day* and *Tora, Tora, Tora!* that got all the attention. Both *Decision* and *Pork Chop* were made in black and white with relatively low budgets. All they had going for them was talent, and thus were ignored.

And *Tunes of Glory*, about a Scottish regiment getting a new commander. Alec Guinness was superb. Maybe his best film ever.

Alas, Guinness also figures in another category I remember: movies which shall live forever because they were so very, very, bad. Guinness got hooked into something called *Situation Hopeless But Not Serious* that should be shown to aspiring actors as a lesson in movies to leave alone.

But Sir Alec must share honors in this category with Peter Sellers for his role in *The Party*, one of the worst ever put on the silver screen. And don't forget Gregory Peck in *Arabesque*, Robert Stack in *John Paul Jones*, and Yul Brynner in *The Journey*. Clinkers every one, but memorable clinkers because no one else realized how bad they were.

Still, the two most unforgettable movies ever made because they were so very bad are *Parish* with Troy Donahue and *All the Fine Young Cannibals* with Natalie Wood and George Hamilton. I have rather warm feelings for them, actually.

But I would much rather remember the good films that have been ignored by those with less taste. Like *Ivanhoe*. Elizabeth Taylor never looked better, not even in *Father of the Bride*. How about

The World of Henry Orient? Then there was *Rebel Without a Cause.*
Georgy Girl. Calling Northside 777. Ah, they are all asleep, but
some day they'll be back — they'll all be back.

Doña Luz's Story

CHIHUAHUA — Doña Luz Corral de Villa leans her canes and
braces against the wall and collapses heavily into a corner chair.
She looks around the cluttered high-ceilinged room at the gathering crowd of tourists, takes a breath, and begins her litany.

In a firm monotone, she speaks of love and family, blood and
thunder, but mostly of her husband, Doroteo Arango, who ran the
neighborhood meat market. He was known as Pancho Villa.

"I first met him in 1910 . . . when he rode into our little town
to buy supplies for his men. It was the town of San Andrés, to the
west of here. My mother ran a store and he came in to buy supplies. And he saw me."

What Villa saw was a plump young girl of 17 with dark hair and,
oddly enough, blue eyes — a peculiarity of the village. Villa never
drank and rarely smoked, but he was known far and wide as a man
of great machismo — a lover, a daring and dangerous man. It was
also known that Villa had several wives when he first wandered
into San Andrés, but that didn't stop him from coming back.

"It was on November 20, 1910, that Pancho Villa first came to
town. My mother ran a little store and Pancho Villa came in. He
came in to buy supplies," Doña Luz repeats. "He came back several
times more, and six months later we were married."

This particular marriage was registered with both the church and
the state, and Pancho retired from a life of banditry and bloodlet-
ting to run the butcher shop here. But the revolution finally crept
across the desert to Chihuahua, and Villa abandoned his wife and
marched off to war. Before long, Pancho Villa was the most feared
and powerful man in Mexico, riding at the head of his División del
Norte.

At the peak, they were considered the best cavalry unit in the
world, Los Dorados, the Golden Ones.

Doña Luz got lost somewhere in the shuffle. "I lived in San Antonio for a while, on Pecan Street in the house of Colonel Houston.
And I lived in Havana. That was in 1917, '18, '19, and '20. It was

many, many years ago." Villa meantime rode and fought and murdered and married. This house at 3014 Tenth Street in Chihuahua served as his occasional home. Twice it was attacked by federalists; the final time it was badly damaged. Villa rebuilt it with barracks behind to hold 50 bodyguards and a side entrance so his men could ride out to flank the attackers as they came down Tenth Street.

But that, too, was many, many years ago. Today poor families live in the barracks. Doña Luz collects no rent. "They are so poor," she says. "They have nothing." And the courtyard — which once rang with the cries of "Viva Villa!" — this Sunday afternoon echoes with nine small voices being led in "Michael, Row the Boat Ashore." And the side entrance where Los Dorados once rode forth now serves as a playground for two boys with a stickball.

"Pancho Villa was 45 when he was killed," says Doña Luz in her slow, mechanical voice. "I first met him in 1910. I am now . . ." She stops and pulls out a notepad. "I am now 79. I was born on June 7, 1894."

The crowd of tourists says nothing. It is very quiet in the high-ceilinged room. The only noise comes from the courtyard, the whack of a stickball and the song of a Sunday school class. Doña Luz stares at a photograph on the wall. Pancho Villa and his child bride.

Down the hall, near the courtyard, is a bullet-ridden black 1917 Dodge touring car. Villa was driving it that day 50 years ago when he was gunned down in the town of Parral. He was going to see a girlfriend.

But the past half-century has refined and polished the reputation of the neighborhood meat merchant. There is a statue of Villa here in Chihuahua and — finally and reluctantly — they put one up in Mexico City near a newly renamed street, the Avenida del División del Norte. And today Los Dorados spread fear on the diamond as Chihuahua's Class AAA baseball team.

After Villa's death, dozens of women stepped forth to announce they were his wives and thus entitled to his vast fortune. There was no fortune, but the government decided that Villa's only true wife was a plump blue-eyed peasant girl from San Andrés. She had borne him a daughter who died at the age of two. She had raised four of his sons by other women. She had done as she was told. She had kept the faith.

Doña Luz finishes her little speech and the tourists file out, handing her three pesos as they leave. And she sits here alone in this high-ceilinged room, surrounded by pictures of a man she hardly knew, so many, many years ago. Pancho Villa peers down over his shaggy mustache. Leading troops, riding horses, smiling with generals, dripping with machismo.

"He was shot in Parral," Doña Luz says softly. "His brother, came to tell me . . . Pancho Villa's brother came to tell me . . . he was shot in Parral . . ."

Vacations Sure Bring Out Those *Post* Morning Blues

WEST OF INGRAM—It has always been a habit of mine, no matter where I happen to be, to begin the day with coffee and a morning newspaper. I prefer, if possible, my coffee black and my newspaper in English. If I do have the luxury of the English language, then I go a step further and try to get an American morning newspaper. And if Lady Luck is with me all the way, I attempt to get a copy of the *Houston Post.* This allows me to keep up with the antics of Bud Adams, the circus at City Hall, the split-second timing of the MTA, not to mention the latest poop on the zum-zum gang, the snide non sequiturs of Sound-Off, the piercing brilliance found right here, and so on. Starting a day without my morning paper is like ending an evening without a cigar.

In times past, out in the boonies, *Post*s have been found in Austin, Port Arthur, even at the train station in New Orleans on Sundays. But not out here in the Hill Country, for civilization stops at the last red light in Ingram, eight miles to the east. Out here, pilgrim, a man's got to do what he's got to do—cry.

For instance, there is the town of Hunt, where you go when you die if you've been good. In Hunt there is a store, one store, called The Store. This reflects the ingenuity of a town which also has The Dance Hall and The Filling Station. Yet there is trouble in paradise, because it does not have The Newspaper—the *Houston Post.* Indeed, if you ask for the *Post* they'll sell you something in cedar. This problem has hit me before and I have complained to The Management of The Store. Last year he vowed to have *Post*s by the bundles this year. Thus it is this bright morning that I come to The Store to purchase my daily fix. But no *Post*s. Not a one. "Sold out?" I inquire of the clerk.

"Nope," says she. "We don't get *Post*s here. Closest they come is Ingram."

"But I was promised," I say with trembling lips. "I was promised that this year you'd have *Post*s."

"Sorry," says the clerk. "We tried, but the guy won't deliver *Post*s out here. He'll only go as far as Ingram."

Sigh. Those nervous Nellies still won't take the stage west of Ingram. Maybe with a cavalry escort they would, but that does me no good this morning, so I pack up and move out, heading east.

My first stop in Ingram is The News Stand (Ingram, like Hunt, is fraught with originality). "Sorry," says the owner, looking at an empty rack. "All sold out. Got three in, and they're all gone. Have a *San Antonio Express*, instead."

I gaze at the headline: UFO DEVOURS MEXICO. I love San Antonio papers. They constantly expand the realms of realism.

"Believe not."

"How about a *San Antonio News*?" the owner asks, holding out the front page: "GOD TOLD ME TO FLY," MOM, 87, SAYS.

"No, thanks," I say. "I don't want a *San Antonio Express* or a *San Antonio News*. Do you have anything from this world?"

"Here's a *San Antonio Express-News*," he says, pointing to another front page: UFO DEVOURS MEXICAN GOD — " MOM, 87, TOLD ME TO."

He shows me several local papers that are no doubt quite good but fail to cover the latest excuses from the MTA, not to mention the Exxon credit cards handed to Billy Reagan's advisers. I thank the shopkeeper and drive on to my next possibility, the local Stop-N-Steal.

"*Houston Post*?" says the clerk. "Sorry, I sold it."

I try Eddie Sears Grocery, but no luck. "I got the *San Antonio Light*," says the clerk, pointing to CRAZED RAPIST ATTACKS OHIO! and VENICE FLOODED!

"No, thanks," I say. "I want to sleep tonight."

My chances are rapidly dwindling. A last attempt to buy a *Houston Post* fails miserably at the local truck stop. The clerk looks at me with pity. "We get a lot of people coming in here trying to buy *Post*s, particularly during the summer holidays. We don't get many when we get any. You happen to know anyone at the *Post* who could help?"

"Good grief, no," I say loudly. "Do I look like the type to consort with known journalists?"

So I head for my car, wondering how far is Kerrville. Then I'll try Boerne and Comfort and the suburbs of Tarpley. In the meantime, however, I am going through withdrawal cold turkey, getting the shakes. I need my morning newspaper to go with my coffee. It's all I know. Maybe, if all else fails, I'll have to buy a San Antonio paper in a plain brown wrapper, or people in that city will see on their front page: CRAZED NEWSPAPER READER ATTACKS DISTRIBUTOR IN HILL COUNTRY! — "GOD TOLD ME TO."

Filling the Void

And lo, the Void said, "Go out and bring me more nourishment, for I am hungry." And it was true, for the Void had already consumed all that the populace could offer to the god of Current Goodies.

It had tossed into the Void the Beat Poets and the hippies, the antiwar movement and the American Indian. Each one had briefly satiated the Void, but only briefly, for the Void is all-consuming. It takes the hottest thing going and lofts it high into the heady clouds of notoriety, then swallows it whole, the quick flight of fame ending in a hollow, soft nothing. That is what happened to Jane Fonda, Tiny Tim, William Westmoreland, Andy Williams, Patty Hearst, Henry Aaron, and Milton Berle. Each one, in his or her own time, was sent catapulting above the masses, to dwell on Olympus, nibbling ambrosia, to savor the delights of immortality. Then the Void called it home.

Johnny Cash went that way; so did Herb Alpert and the Kingston Trio and Harry Belafonte. The cover of *Time*, the talk shows, chatting with John Lindsay or Ethel Kennedy, playing golf at Burning Tree with Barry Goldwater and George Bush. Lawrence Welk, Hadacol, seat belts, plane hijackers, each had a fling at the edge of the Void, then toppled inward and downward, head over heels, never to emerge again except in nostalgia film clips.

The masses fed the Void oil-rich Texans, oil-rich Arabs, oil-rich Israeli occupation troops, but the Void was not satisfied. It demanded more. President Diem and Madam Nhu went to the top, and then in. So did Castro and Ché, Haldeman and Ehrlichman, Sonny and Cher. Martin and Lewis, Mrs. Robinson and Benjamin, love and marriage, white socks and black loafers, Quemoy and Matsu.

"More," said the Void. In went Joe Namath, James Bond, Jackie O., little girls caught in wells, government agencies spying on private citizens, exorcists, ecology, civil rights marches through

Mississippi, and Nikita Khrushchev. The masses were spellbound as each sacrifice was brought forth to be showered with attention and a spot on *The Hollywood Squares.* How important they were, each one the center of the center ring.

Then the Void gobbled them up, swiftly, silently, and no one noticed, for attention was no longer on the center ring but was now riveted to the next act, which was far more important than the warm-up. Begone, George McGovern. Go away, Cadillac fins. Buzz off, 38th Parallel. You are no longer of interest. Into the Void.

"More," said the Void. The masses looked around. There was not much left at feeding time. Ringo Starr had been breakfast, the decriminalization of marijuana was lunch, and Cyprus was dinner. With Peter, Paul, and Mary for a midnight snack. Each fad had its time, then slipped quietly over the edge.

Where to look? What to bring forth? What small corner of our being had not yet been exploited to satisfy the Void? The talk shows were edgy, the magazine covers were waiting, the feature writers were gnawing at their pencil tips. Gloria Steinem was gone, fed to the Void in '74. Martha Mitchell, oil spills, streakers, astronauts, the Surgeon General's Report on Cigarette Smoking, and tie-dyed T-shirts had long since filled the *NBC Evening Report, Time,* and *New York Magazine.*

The Void was restless, not to mention hungry. Where is it? Bring forth the newest fad. And lo, the masses hurried forth across the land. The flower children were passé, the fighting young priests were old hat, the pig-farmer communes were zero. Where, oh where, was the next meal for the Void?

There was much fright in the land. Much gnashing of teeth and gnightly pleas for help. The high priests burned last month's copy of *Cosmopolitan* and *Playboy,* and scattered the ashes over Dick Cavett. The Void was growing even hungrier. We need one volunteer to move from Out to In.

And so they came. From Cut-and-Shoot and Yazoo and Altus and El Campo, from behind the counters, from behind the plows, from behind the bars. Look! Up in the sky! It's a bird, it's a plane, no, it's the Rednecks! Huzzah!

Riding forth in their pickup trucks with their gun racks and Wallace stickers, with their cans of Bud and their lovable Neanderthal outlook on life, the Rednecks! Discovered at last! The focus of movies and songs, of magazine stories and sociological studies. Politicians hailed them as the True American, Abe Lincoln with a tattoo on the arm and fuzzy dice on the rearview mirror. Radio stations cranked out their gospel and manufacturers enshrined them with Jerry Jeff Walker T-shirts. And everyone made an awfully lot of money off the fortunate Redneck.

Then he, too, went into the Void, and the high priests began their search once more.

Forebearance

You may have noticed a recent newspaper story about names, specifically, that unusual names such as Percival, Horace, and Maurice are unpleasing to the ear and cause the owners sorrow, humiliation, and the heartbreak of psoriasis. But such bread-and-butter names as John, Jim, Ann, and Wendy lead one to riches, success, and the ultimate good.

Bosh, I say. I'd say more than that, but this is a family newspaper, and besides, I don't know anything stronger than bosh. Anyway, bosh. Are we now becoming so look-alike, think-alike, monkey-see, monkey-do, that we have lost all our individuality? Must potential parents check in their creativity when they reach puberty? The world is bosh-deep in Bills and Bobs and Toms and Dons. Where, oh, where are the Cassandras, the Lucindas, the Amandas? At this rate, we shall all end up with the same name, our identities known only to the IRS and the FBI.

Now, to be sure, no parent should stick a name on a poor defenseless baby which shall cause him embarrassment throughout childhood. Somerset Maugham and Ivan the Terrible were no doubt permanently scarred by the thoughtless names given them by the Maughams and the Terribles. We must use common sense and not go off the deep end in this.

Still, there is plenty of maneuvering room between Joe and Juritta, between Ann and Anastasia. In the olden days, most American families had several dozen children, hoping one or two would live past adolescence. Thus it was that the first few names were easy: Bill, Bob, Suzy, and so on. But by the time the parents were down to child number 14 or so, they were into Ambler, Verdie, and Elbridge. At this point, the Bible was always a big help, so our past is dotted with Abraham, Noah, Ruth, and so on.

In my own family, we tend to name one another for those who have gone before us, which leaves a lot to be desired, but a lot to work with, too. In my own case, Lynn—like the poor—has been with us always. I was named after my uncle, who was, in turn, named for his father, my grandfather. It goes back through bunches of Lynns to one Lynn Kesinger (born February 22, 1802). When I discovered this, I was elated as it not only meant I was related to Henry, but it changed my ethnic background as well. (I haven't been doing too well with the one I have.) Further research showed that I was wrong on both counts. That particular Lynn's father was one Solomon Kesinger, a priest in Essen, Germany, who fell in love with a nun, Eve Gruenwert. They fled to America and had 11 children. Solomon was a bad priest but a good Catholic.

Down through the years, my family came up with wondrous names, some of which were abruptly changed when crossing state lines. Among the Ashbys, there were Emagine, Euphemia, Texas, Saphronia, Broley, Washington Breckenridge (can you imagine some three-month-old kid being told by his mother, "Now go to sleep, little Washington Breckenridge"), and Abeneeser. Also we had Zachariah, Lovelace (quit snickering), Appeline, Church, and Abasalom. We have beaucoup Abasalom Ashbys, just why I don't know, but it's better than Nimrod. We had more Nimrods than Abasaloms.

Colonel John Ashby, one of my ancestors, had eight children including my great-grandfather, Charles. Colonel John also had a flair for names, calling his other children, in order:

> Nicholas
> Christopher Columbus
> Lafayette
> Somerville
> Americus
> Mary
> and America Elizabeth

Of the lot, Mary is the only what-you-might-call-usual name. Then again, how many people do you really know who are named Mary? Not many, I'd bet. There aren't as many Marys as people think. It's like having a dog named Fido. If Colonel John was weird when it came to names, Marshall G. Ashby was even more imaginative. His children were Osceola, Sciota, Alpharetta, Othello E., Tullahoma, and Nedawah. Actually, we don't mention Marshall much in the family, and it wasn't because of his name selection. It seems he fought for the Union.

Flair, creativity, imagination — that's what we need these days when it comes to naming names, just as our forefathers had. Where are our Novies, our Ormans, our Zillerans? Now everyone is Tracy, Kimberly, Mark, and Craig. Fine names, to be sure, but do they hold a candle to Parasada? Of course not.

Sometimes, the best-laid plans of names fall apart. One of my brothers is Christopher (being Scottish, another is named Jock), who was named for Christopher Columbus Ashby. He is called Kit, and when he was growing up there was not another soul in his school named Christopher. It was an English name, and thus suspect. So my firstborn is named after my brother, and is also called Kit. But today this is a popular name and there are more Christophers around than Nimrods.

Another son is named Tristan. Thus far that name seems safe enough, but if ever the Tristan tide hits, I am prepared. I shall dig out the family records and choose a new one from the old. Nickles, Ovy, Jeremish, Brodie, Ebenezer Jonathan. Not all are very original. We had one Ashby Ashby.

Gad, here's an Aggie Ashby. Illegitimate, no doubt. Risden, Raleigh, Remus, Obediah, Oatie, Orman, and my grandfather, Ulysses Ottawa Ashby. He was a large man, so there was nothing very funny about his name. He was not humiliated. He didn't even have the heartbreak of psoriasis. Cirrhosis was as close as he could get. Now that I mention it, I think I had an aunt named Cirrhosis.

Swiss Army Learns to Fight
So That It Will Never Have To

THE FIRING LINE — Bang! The familiar noise, the familiar jar of steel into my shoulder, the familiar whine from me. "A little high," says the lieutenant as the sergeant and a row of recruits look on. The bullet was last seen somewhere over the Alps.

This is a Swiss Army base where recruits are following an old Swiss tradition: citizen soldier. Every male at age 20 is drafted. Every male serves. Albert Einstein included. Once past recruit training, he attends refresher courses off and on until he is 50. The constitution of 1874 gives no provisions for conscientious objectors and in 1980 some 350 were taken to court and tried. Most were jailed. There are, however, approximately 100 noncombatants in the army who, for religious reasons, refuse to carry weapons. Any Swiss male who is too handicapped to serve in the military is assigned to the Civil Defense but pays an additional tax on his income. Women are not drafted, and now that Switzerland has passed its own ERA, there is a debate over whether women should also pay the extra tax for not serving.

If these measures seem strong, they are. No one seems to object, though, for joining the army is as old as the nation. No – older. For generations Switzerland was a poor, backwater nation of peasants and the only hope for money came in serving as mercenaries in other nations' armies. Swiss mercenaries were much sought after and fought throughout Europe. Today they still guard the Vatican, but after the debacle at the battle of Marignano in 1515, in which Swiss mercenaries fought on both sides, it was decided to call the boys home. Napoleon's invasion interrupted this nation's peace, but that was the last time a Swiss soldier fired a weapon in anger.

Serving at home has a corollary: no Swiss fights abroad. It is against the law to serve in any other nation's military. (The Vatican's Swiss Guard doesn't count.) Swiss who volunteered in the Spanish Civil War were "punished" upon their return, and the 146 who were killed in that war to this day are condemned by the government. Young Swiss who seek adventure join the French Foreign Legion – I am told you can always find plenty of Swiss there – but one Legion hero who came marching home, a Lieutenant Colonel de Tscharner, was promptly tossed in prison. Nor do Swiss consort with others: during World War II, although this nation was neutral, 17 Swiss were executed by firing squads for treason or attempted sabotage.

Citizens emigrating to other nations who might someday want to return posed a special problem. One of Switzerland's very first treaties after becoming a nation was with the U.S., in which it was agreed young men could be drafted into each other's army without losing citizenship.

Bang! High and to the left. At 11 o'clock high. The lieutenant walks over and adjusts my scope one click. The recruits snicker.

This is an S.I.G. assault rifle, the standard weapon of Swiss infantry – infantry makes up almost half of the army. Every able-bodied male is issued this rifle or a pistol, 24 rounds of ammunition, a pack, and a uniform.

After 17 weeks of basic training, the recruits take the weapons home – no one pays any attention to a young Swiss walking through a train station carrying a semiautomatic rifle slung over his shoulder. At a time when the U.S. is arguing over gun control, the Swiss are issued automatic rifles. They are under orders to keep the weapon in good shape, fire for qualification once a year (and keep firing until qualified), and keep two days' rations ready. Within 48 hours, Switzerland can muster 650,000 troops, or approximately 10 percent of the nation's populace. Each soldier has a duty assignment near his home, an area he has practiced defending for years. This happened at the beginning of World War II and the Swiss like to think this is why Hitler's planned invasion was called off.

When mobilized, Switzerland has 15 armed men per square kilometer, the heaviest concentration in Europe, plus 17 battle tanks and eight fighter planes per 1,000 square kilometers, another mark rarely equaled. All the tunnels, bridges, and highways into Switzerland are mined. The country can be sealed off with a phone call. They call their defensive strategy "the high price of admission."

Pilots flying low over this country daily check maps indicating where the army is firing artillery, where the jets are strafing, because the Swiss Army is always on maneuvers. At any given time, 30,000 men are in training or refresher courses. The standing army itself is only 1,500 instructors and top brass, so Switzerland is either the most or least militarized nation around, depending upon how you look at it. Yet there are problems.

First and foremost, it is not an army but a militia. As the recruits jump over their barricades, instructors laugh and joke with them. Discipline is not what you'd call strict. Officers who get together for annual training speak of it as more of a social engagement than a sharpening of their skills. One lieutenant here is wearing a shabby leather belt that would disgrace a Bataan death marcher. Several recruits sport dark glasses.

"They aren't here long enough to warrant a haircut," a sergeant explains, looking at a bearded, shaggy group of recruits wandering by.

Second, while the Swiss build their own rifles, put together jet fighters under license, and build some of their own tanks, they are greatly dependent upon other nations for weaponry. The Swiss use West German buses, Austrian trucks, and French jets. Their armored personnel carriers are made in the U.S. and sport Swedish guns, and there is the language problem.

"I can direct a tank battalion in either French or German," says an officer. "We put recruits in units of the same language."

"But what happens if, say, a German battalion takes a position next to a French battalion and calls for air support from an Italian-speaking fighter pilot?" I ask. That possibility doesn't seem to bother anyone but me.

They have no general here except during time of war; then—in true Swiss tradition—the Parliament elects one. Well, actually, they do have one right now: General Otto Bornhauser, who formerly was consul general in San Francisco and now is commander of the Swiss Army in Korea.

"It is a peacekeeping force," a defense ministry official explains. "Since we are not in the United Nations, we were asked to be a neutral party. But Bornhauser has to deal with generals on both sides, so for protocol reasons, he has been temporarily promoted to general."

Bornhauser commands 10 men.

The Swiss are trying to upgrade their defenses, although for the first time in years they are now spending more for social welfare than for defense (20.8 percent of the budget compared to 20.2 percent), giving the military 2.2 percent of the GNP. That is not a very big chunk of the GNP, but remember that the Swiss Army is an economical outfit with cheap help.

"We need equipment that is not too sophisticated," a training officer says. "Just simple, good, basic, for part-time soldiers. On the other hand, we are very clever."

(In answer to the question you have all been wanting to ask, yes, the Swiss Army carries the Swiss Army knife.)

Bang! Bull's-eye. I quit while I'm ahead.

It might seem contradictory for a nation to have such a military machine and, at the same time, harbor such a reluctance to use it. Dr. H. R. Kurz, of the Federal Military Department, wrote of the Swiss Army: "Its highest goal is not, paradoxically, to fight a war successfully, but to avoid war. It is not primarily geared toward military involvement, but toward not having to fight. It must be able to shoot in order not to have to shoot."

Ah, That First Car: Chariot of Fire, Love, and Freedom

Do you remember your first car? Of course you do. In later years you may forget your name, rank, and serial number. You may forget your firstborn or your third spouse, but you will never forget your first car.

This is probably more the case with men than with women, for reasons that elude me. But men have always put more stock in cars. Also, in our culture, it is not nearly so important for a young woman to have a decent-looking car as it is for the male of the species. It is the swain who comes by early on a Saturday evening to pick up his date. And the car is most important for that young man. He whips up, looking as elegant and dashing as he possibly can, and presents the best pumpkin possible. While the female has spent a long day getting herself and all that she wears ready, he has been under the hood, over the radiator, making the coach proper for the woman he is desperately trying to impress. Don't knock it — it works. That's why you're here.

I will not bore you with deadly dull reminiscences — I don't care about your growing up, why should you care about mine? — but it was a Ford. A blue '51 Ford, two-door, with an I-block six-cylinder engine that I could take apart and put together during lunch break. Depending upon your age, you were under the hood of a V-8 Chevy, a Buick with the air holes in the fenders, a pickup truck with the loudest muffler in town, or an over-the-hill Corvette that looked great and ran badly. No matter, it was your first car.

Do you remember buying your first car? Absolutely. You had a certain amount of money and plans. Then you went shopping. It was a terrible time. What you wanted, you couldn't afford; and what you could afford, without question, you didn't want. Everyone hopes for a deal. There is no deal. In this life, the first thing you learn is that milk can also come out of a bottle. The second is that there is no such thing as a deal.

Some end up with their parents' discards — a humiliating situation unless your father is Mario Andretti. Some end up with rejects from a demolition derby. Others opt for the shiny exterior and worthless, rusting interior. Some, alas, with mouths salivating, go in far over their heads and live to regret it almost as much as does the repossessing agency.

Do you remember what you did when you finally bought it? That car was squeaky clean and polished by the previous owner the day it became yours. And what was the first thing you did? You polished it some more. You scrubbed and washed. You changed the oil and the air in the tires. You vacuumed the floor and Windexed the windows. That ancient engine purred with a heavy lubrication of love because it was *yours*.

Today, if someone tried to sell you such a collection of trouble, you would gag and laugh. But back then, ah, it was a chariot of fire. It was yours, to prowl and preen, slip down the side streets with the radio humming. On the make, that '37 Studebaker, that '67 Fiat, that '77 Olds. For those newcomers to this game who laugh condescendingly at the thought of warm sentiments for an aging Nash, don't show your ignorance. The front seats dropped back to make a bed. And for those whose first car was brand-new, a gift from your parents, well, you missed a lot, mostly bad, but not all.

That first car meant you were no longer ground-bound, allowed to move only when your parents approved. Freedom! Hot damn! Time to get it on. Time to move. To ooze along the asphalt. Time to see and, most important, to be seen. My first car. With the fuzzy dice or the armadillo decal, the Confederate mudflaps or the *peace* bumper sticker. And, to be sure, the old school sticker. You are hot, and cool. That's hard to be at the same time. But not when you're in that first car.

Do you remember the oil checks? Once a day, maybe twice. Down goes the dipstick. A careful scrutinizing of the oil level. Never mind that the blind bandit who owned it before you drove 20,000 miles on a can of Quaker State and the engine is about to go. The only visible way of feeling the pulse of your new machine is to check the oil. Daily, at least.

Mud? It never dried on your fenders. Dust? It never accumulated on your dash. The ashtray was always empty. Usually it was emptied on the way home for fear that your parents would notice it the next morning. The trunk was swept and the spare was on red alert, ready to come off the bench. That was the only car you ever owned with a regularly washed drive shaft.

Do you remember your first car? A silly question. It's like asking if you remember your first love. Actually, it probably was.

Summer Madness

THE BED — I leave this diary for any soul who might come upon my dehydrated body, lying here in the burning heat, prostrate, thick-tongued, and medium-well. I'm the one with an apple in my mouth.

But let me begin at the beginning:

12 noon Saturday — Young, my next-door neighbor, comes over. He had to cut down a small tree, so he rented a power saw, only they made him pay $12.50 for the whole day. He only wanted it for 30 minutes and is being took. Do I have anything that needs cutting? To make it worth $12.50?

I do, indeed. A mechanized beaver, I cut dead trees, limbs, firewood, two fingers, and an ankle.

12:30 — A big tree, long dead. I need help. Young comes over and lends a hand.

12:31 — Calpakis, the wily Greek, wanders by — beer in hand — and is pressed into action despite his whine about persecuted minorities.

12:45 — The tree falls. I cut up the tree for firewood while feeling as though I am returning to nature. Keep one eye out for Apaches. Must remember to check the beaver traps and the winter supply of jerky.

1:30 — It is hot, the sun is burning down on my pink body. Water. Water. All I have for a cup of cool water. To mix with my Scotch. You just can't drink Scotch straight, not on a hot afternoon.

1:47 — The house is hot, something is wrong. Check the air conditioning, it is pumping away, wind is shooting out from the chutes, and certainly it should. I have a totally new air conditioning system, the old one having died within weeks after I moved in, armed with a written guarantee that the air conditioning was in excellent shape. Three weeks later, the written guarantee and $1,100 got me a new air conditioning system.

2:30 — Call the air conditioning folk who installed the new one and, for a ridiculous fee, check it out every decade. They say since it is a weekend it will be double time for repairman: $18 for him to drive up the driveway, $6 for every 15 minutes thereafter.

2:31 — I am in mortal agony and agree to their ransom. Perhaps I can sell my body to Baylor Medical College.

3:12 — The repairman arrives with his son. I use the term "accomplice," but he fails to see the humor in it.

3:30 — Repairman announces that the compressor is shot. My warranty covers it, but the labor will be $150.15. He has me cold — so to speak. The paint is blistering off the bathroom walls, it is 98 in the refrigerator, and in the cabinet my bottle of Scotch is calling for water.

3:31 — I give in. Maybe Baylor Medical would be interested in my immediate family, too. I'd throw in Calpakis' liver.

3:32 – It's a deal. One problem, it is Saturday and no business is done on Saturday, anywhere, ever. Wait till Monday, first thing Monday a new compressor. He leaves.

3:33 – It is 3:33 on a Saturday afternoon in July in Houston, Texas, when dogs run mad and God looks down upon us all and says, "Ten lousy little rules and you all couldn't even follow them. So you get Saturday afternoons in July in Houston, Texas. Next time you'll listen."

5:20 – I am curled up in the freezer when Calpakis bounces by, this time with a glass of ouzo. I explain my problem. "Don't worry," he says, reaching for the phone. "I got a friend." I could tell Calpakis I am in need of a left-handed kangaroo with a bad rash and a knowledge of the Crimean War and he would tell me not to worry because he has a friend. With a rash.

6:12 – His friend, an air conditioning repairman, arrives.

6:13 – Repairman goes to work on my air conditioning system.

6:18 – Prudhomme from across the street comes over. "What's the trouble?" he asks. I explain that it is 110 degrees in the lampshade. "No problem," says Prudhomme. "Sleep at my place."

6:19 – Young, who earlier in the day helped me cut down half a forest, comes over with Brown. Both are working on Brown's boat and drinking beer, not in that order. "What's the problem?" they ask. I explain. "No problem," says Young. "Come over and sleep in my house – we got an extra room." "Have a beer," says Brown, offering more immediate courage. I accept beer, decline comfortable air conditioned room as this repairman is obviously going to get to the root of the problems, eschewing such idle gossip as the first technician. Compressor, indeed.

6:26 – "It's the compressor," says the repairman. I cry softly.

6:28 – "If you won't move in, then at least use my fan," says Young.

6:29 – "I got a fan that will blow you right out of the room," says Brown.

6:30 – Being greedy, I accept both offers. It is nice to have friends, but it is even nicer to have fans.

7:14 – "No problem," says Calpakis, the ever-wily Greek. "We got plenty of room, stay with us." I figure in the meantime he will rent out my house as a sauna bath and make a small fortune. I decline. "Then have a drink." I accept and rush into his air conditioned comfort.

8:01—I am sitting in Calpakis' den enjoying his Southern hospitality and Southern Comfort.

12 midnight—I am lying here in bed, sweat trickling down my fuzzy cheeks. Death is not far away. The Grim Reaper is near. He is probably a good friend of Calpakis'. Death, where is thy stagnant, stifling sting? Yet it is nice to know that in this cold (so to speak), cruel world, there are still good neighbors, even if you don't have good fences.

Perhaps I should do something for them in turn, something that would brighten and enrich their lives. I asked Calpakis. He suggested that if I really wanted to do something to make everyone happy, I should move.

James' Icy Dowry

LERWICK, THE SHETLAND ISLANDS—They use a deactivated mine as a collection box for shipwrecked mariners, rental houses note when the toilets are indoors, the lone cinema is closed on Tuesday and Friday for bingo, and birdwatching is the big attraction for outsiders, who can ring up the bird warden by dialing 8.

The Shetland Islands are not exactly the hub of the universe, yet what they lack in modern life is easily made up for by their bad weather. This is a damp and windy July afternoon, yet the fellow pushing the white cart reading "Ices—Stop Me and Buy One" is doing heavy business along the pier.

These islands, as far north as Greenland and Siberia, are Britain's most northerly country. Their location along the subarctic trade routes has left them open to numerous invaders since the dawn of civilization. The islands have more prehistoric sites per square mile than any other county in the nation. Christianity came here about A.D. 200 but fell before another invader 600 years later, the Vikings. The Norsemen settled here and used the islands as a stopping-off point on their raids farther south.

Scotland got them in 1469 when King Christian of Denmark couldn't make payment on the dowry of 60,000 florins he promised Scotland's King James III if he would wed the Danish princess, Margaret. King Christian pawned the nearby Orkney islands, as well (for six times more, as the Orkney folk like to remind visiting

Shetlanders), and the Scots never got around to giving any of them back.

Yet even 500 years of British rule has failed to erase the Viking influence. All place names here are Norse and the present dialect spoken by the populace contains many Nordic words. The big event each year is on the last Tuesday of each January, when they celebrate Up-Helly-Aa (roughly: Thank God winter is almost over), in which they burn a wooden Viking ship.

The festival was more or less suspended during World War II, but the war gave the Shetlanders a chance to revive a tradition, albeit in a different direction. It was from here that the "Shetland bus" staged sea raids on occupied Norway. The name came from a Norwegian expression that when things got too hot for an Allied agent, they put him on the Shetland bus. In 206 trips by small fishing boats across a choppy sea, the Shetlanders delivered 192 men and 383 tons of military supplies while picking up 73 agents and 373 refugees. They lost 10 boats and 44 seamen.

Here comes an honest-to-gosh Shetland bus, creeping down Commercial Street — the main drag of the islands — winding in and out the narrow flagstone route. The bus, full of tourists, parks without fear of much competition from other vehicles, although the tight abutment of houses to the street doesn't leave much room. The streets are stone gray. The houses are stone gray, as well. The rock cliffs and sky are also stone gray. From afar the Shetlands look like a fleet of battleships moored at sea, awaiting another invasion.

There are about 17,000 people living on 22 of the 100 islands that make up the Shetland archipelago. Of these, about 7,000 live in Lerwick. Things used to be better: in 1911, the island's population was about 25,000. Today, the marks of departed islanders are left on abandoned houses and farms. Yet after this steady decline, the locals see some sign of an about-face.

This hope springs from the construction of fish processing plants and the hint that there may be oil out there in the North Sea. The government has set up an office to aid young people in getting jobs and thus staying here. The islanders report varying degrees of success.

Near the employment office is the town hall. Having tea and biscuits in the council hall gives a visitor a break from the raw wind and slight drizzle. On the door outside is a plaque from two Norwegian motor torpedo boat squadrons. In here is a stained glass window, apparently given by the city of Hamburg in memory of some of its fishermen lost in the nearby sea.

One is never far from the sea in the Shetlands. Literally no more than three miles, figuratively less than that. Stores advertise "oil-skins—rubber boots—life jackets," while nearby is "James W. Irvine—Ironmonger and Shipchandler."

The docks are crowded with fishing ships, large and small, flying a multitude of national ensigns, for out there in that ridiculously rough, cold sea are some of the world's best fishing grounds, and last year the herring catch was the best in 60 years.

Two thousand years ago, Tacitus the Roman wrote of the Shetland Islands: "Nowhere does the sea hold wider sway, it carries to and fro in its motions a mass of currents, and in its ebb and flow it is not held by the coast, but permeates deep into the land and winds about in the hills, as if in its own domain."

There are, however, some few parts of these islands not directly related to the sea. For instance, knitting is still done here by the women of Shetland, who make those fine sweaters. Yet more and more of them are coming to town to work in factories that make the same sweaters, although with less tender loving care. Shetland ponies are still around—on the island of Fetlar the ponies still carry peat from the hill to the crofting townships—but I have not yet seen a single one.

Here we are out on the rolling hills, brownish with a hint of green covering. Windy and cold, damp and dark. Here on an islet in the Loch of Clickhimin is a Bronze Age fort, standing in stone-gray truculence, a remembrance of things past. And right across from it is an offshore drilling rig, looming huge and ugly like some kind of sea monster. This time the invaders are from the west.

Extra! The Untold Story Behind Big-Time Journalism

JOURNALISM 123—Class, today we have a special treat. Your favorite press critic-at-large and consultant to most American newspapers, Type Hype, is in our class today. For the past few weeks, I have been sending Mr. Hype copies of the *Daily Campus* for his observation. And so, without further ado, here with his critique of your efforts is Mr. Hype.

Thank you, professor. The *Daily Campus*, overall, has some really bright spots and some downers, too. This story here, on the labor union taking over the coal company. The headline reads UNION CONTROLS FIRM. You missed a really good chance there. It should have been UNION GETS THE SHAFT, with a subhead, COMPANY OUT OF SITE, OUT OF MINE. Cute headlines are a great way to get people to read a deadly dull story. I mean, who cares about this particular article? No one. But a cutesy head is a surefire bait.

OK, last week was fine spring weather, but you had only three photographs of dogs catching Frisbees in the park. You are under your quota. Every nice spring day, you get all your photographers out in the park to snap those dog-catches-Frisbee shots. It's a must.

All right, this page here: page one of last Tuesday's paper. It has lots of white space. A picture here, one over there, big headlines. Terrific. People buy the newspaper to read white space. Don't clutter up a pretty page with news. Remember, the more white space, the better. My aim in life is to put out a newspaper with totally blank pages. People like blanks. It makes me wonder how they can even give away the *Wall Street Journal*. All it has is news.

Now, let's turn to the sports pages. Kids, I want you to know this is a beautiful job. Not a single story about a sports event says who won, who lost, or the score. And the leads are fantastic: "Like a giant aardvark attacked by a crazed gila monster . . ." "When he was four years old, Hank Aaron was tossing rocks against a . . ." "In 1238, the Incas retreated through an Andean pass pursued by . . ." And so on for 12 paragraphs. Not a fact about the game in it. Just color. That's great. Make the reader wonder what the story is about, even what sport you're dealing with. Make him work.

A good use of nicknames: Big Earl, Big Apple, Big D, Pinstripes, Little Miss Baby Cakes, 'Stros, and everyone's favorite, the porcine spheroid. Now, on the negative side, you ran a story about the Dallas Cowboys without once using the term "America's Team." Watch that in the future. In sportswriting, above all, cuteness counts.

Next we come to the editorial page. I liked the editorial on God Is Good. Although, frankly, toward the end there, you started taking sides. Remember that editorials are only supposed to raise questions, never supply answers. End every editorial with "It's a serious question that bears further study." Or "If things don't get better, they are sure to get worse." My favorite is "We must watch this situation closely." You've got to be firm.

A few other points I'd like to make. Some of your reporters show absolutely no skill in writing and should certainly do well as editors. Never forget that a good reporter stays a reporter. I also understand that your drama critic can act and your music critic can sing. That will never do. And of course your letters-to-the-editor column really needs some changes. In your replies to readers, if you can't say something snide, don't say anything at all. But be sure to do it anonymously.

We used to call this part of the paper the Women's Section, and it dealt with old rich. Now it's called Trends or something like that and deals with the more meaningful and deeper facets of life, like the new rich. I particularly like the Persecuted Woman page, but I see that you went two days straight without once mentioning alternative lifestyles. Watch that.

Throughout the paper I think you could use fewer names for attribution and more "sources said." Also, in an interview, if you have no idea what the person meant, just put what he said in quotation marks. Then all the readers will think that they are too thick to understand. Put the load on them. Your columnists seem to be sufficiently smug, abrasive, and opinionated. Very good. Above this full page of ads designed to look like hard news, I think the word "Advertisement" is a little too big. You can almost read it.

In closing, I can see that you haven't taken a single note all class period. Most of you are red with anger. You, there, put down that chair. This reaction simply underscores the most important rule of the industry: journalists love to dish out advice but hate to take it. You appear to be headed toward a promising career. Class dismissed.

Corps Birthday

Wednesday is the birthday of the U.S. Marine Corps — a modest group of gentlemen given to intellectual pursuits and philosophical discussions.

They are also fond of rhetorical questions with a Socratic slant, such as: "Gawdamighty, who ever let yew in th' Corps?" This was posed by my gunny sergeant as we swayed atop a lurching LST in the Pacific. At this point let me explain that an LST is a rather flat-bottomed landing ship manned by gleeful sailors who halt their craft out of harm's way, dump the Marines into wooden bathtubs, then haul anchor and race for San Diego. A gunny sergeant is the Marine Corps' answer to Vince Lombardi with a hangover.

The Pacific Ocean is a body of water that laps at the beach of some ridiculous island a stone's throw off the California coast. And I am a dreadfully seasick lance corporal festooned with weaponry, wondering why I am about to assault an undefended beach at 4 a.m. when I'm not mad at anybody, except, of course, for the gunny sergeant, who is supposed to be on my side, anyway.

Actually, I didn't have to join the Marines in the first place, even if it was a family tradition. I could have simply changed my name. Furthermore, I was an enlisted man, the first in my family since some forgotten spear carrier at Runnymede. On one of those other ships was an older brother, an officer, sipping coffee and watching movies while the troops were down there rowing as the drum beat.

We lined up in the dark, a rope net was tossed over the edge, and down we went. Usually at this point in the movies there is a stirring march in the background, but all I could hear was the insane laughter of sailors.

We all got into the boat with the aid of a shoehorn, and it bobbed away toward similar boats going around in a circle. This is part of the script. The landing craft — the kind with the front ramp that drops down so John Wayne can leap out — must bob around in a circle until every man jack in the craft is deathly ill. We did our part, although Private Hernandez was a holdout, explaining that he had somehow passed up our mouth-watering breakfast aboard ship. Lasagne and yams, as I recall.

Some 11 years later the boats lined up like racehorses at the post, the driver kicked open the throttle to an earsplitting blast, and we lumbered toward the shore a scant mile away. It was at this point that I detected something amiss. I was up to my cartridge belt in water. Still, anytime you pack 44 heavy Marines and one craven coward into a boat built for a well-fed elf, you must stand by for trouble.

Fortunately, another craft came by and our driver shouted out a nautical code, something about "Save me, save me!" The seaworthy one pulled alongside and we clambered over — not an easy task when one is carrying a rifle, reams of ammunition, bayonet, helmet, pack crammed with flares and food, two canteens, and six cartons of cigarettes, which can be purchased aboard ship at cut rates.

Ah, safe once more. The new home was empty except for a jeep, which must have belonged to a high-ranking officer — the gas tank was full. As you may have noticed, Marines operate on a shoestring, and a knotted one at that. Why else did we have to turn in used hand grenades for refills?

We puttered merrily toward the beach once again, still no march music to fill the air, only the whine of Private Hernandez, who, alas, had not passed up last night's supper as well. All was in ready, we got back into line, and the gunny sergeant began warming up for his spine-chilling beach yells just in case any cameramen were waiting.

It was at this point that a strange thing occurred. The front ramp dropped off and simply began floating away. To this day I don't know why it happened, but it did. Needless to add, the Pacific Ocean saw its opening and came in. Once more I was afloat. By this time we were close enough to wade ashore, although John Wayne would have been humiliated. I staggered the last few waterlogged yards up the beach and fell behind a rock, totally wiped out. I could not have repulsed an all-out attack by the Junior League. It was probably the first case of a Marine defeat at an undefended beach.

Others, however, were doing their part. Bang-bang, yells and bayonet charges. More banging. Thump-thump, mortars. Something was smelling quite peculiar. My rock. Now rocks, as a rule, do not smell, but this rock turned out to be a dead seal. Just lying there on the beach all these weeks. I joined Private Hernandez in harking back to last night's supper.

Now, cleansed and renewed, I felt it was time to fight. First, I checked my supplies — six cartons of seawatered cigarettes. It was just as well, I didn't smoke cigarettes anyway but just couldn't pass up a good deal on the price. I unhooked them and began lobbing the cartons over the seal. "Take that, you commie rat! And this for Stinky! And this for the kid from Brooklyn!"

I was suddenly aware that some yahoo with an eagle on his collar and a clipboard in his hand was staring at me somewhat incredulously. "Are those cigarettes you're throwing?" he asked in awe. "Yessir," I said. "Throat cancer takes a little longer, but it kills 'em just as dead." He failed to appreciate my ingenuity. Spoilsport. It was probably his jeep wallowing out there in the surf. "You're dead," he said, making a mark on his clipboard.

Thus I gave my all to the cause, another sacrifice to Mars, the god of war. But there are other and better men to fill my unshined, waterlogged boots. They are out there somewhere today, even as you sit here minding your martini. So, happy birthday, Marine Corps. You don't look your age.

What's in a Name?

If you are from Houston, you are a Houstonian. If you are from Fort Worth you're a Fort Worthian. But if you're from Dallas, you're a Dallasite. I suppose you could be a Dallasian, which is harder to say than Houstonite, which sounds like a building material. But what are you if you're from Corpus Christi? Are you a Corpuscle? A Christian? A Corpus delicti?

Titles are tricky. Everybody has got to be from somewhere, but it gets a bit difficult on occasion as to just what title to use. Once in a column from Sydney I referred to the Sydneyians and got several irate letters from Sydneysiders. How about a native of New Orleans? You could be a New Orleander or a New Orleansian ("Cajun" doesn't count). But you probably call yourself a New Orleanian – without the s – or, among friends, just an Orleanian.

Recently a publication called *Informensa* ran a test about what you call people from certain places. If you are from Moscow, you are not a Moscowite, but a Muscovite. And one of my favorites, from Liverpool, the Liverpudlians. Can you imagine the problems they have around the world, with people calling them Liverpoolers? *Informensa* also had Cairene and Madrilenian, I guess from Cairo and Madrid, although I'm not sure.

Actually, I am not even sure what the term is for the names of people based on where they came from. "Toponym" means place name, which is close, but there's probably a better word.

Let's see how good you are on what to call people. What are you called (the real names, folks – let's not get funny) if you are from:

Monaco
Glasgow
New Hampshire
Quebec

Taking them in order, if you hang around the casino and catch a few rays in Monaco, and are a native – of which there are very few—you are a Monegasque. If you are, then you might hang around the casinos, but you can't go in. To prevent the locals from losing all their money, Monaco has a law preventing Monegasques from entering any place where there is gambling. For that reason, you usually have to show your passport at the door.

From Glasgow? You're a Glaswegian. A native of New Hampshire is a New Hampshirite. From Quebec? Well, that is fraught with political overtones, depending whether you are of English or French stock and want to stay in Canada or join Monaco in a power bloc. Thus you can be either a Quebecer or a Québéçois.

The people of Quebec are not the only ones with more than one name for themselves. In Catalonia, the northeastern part of Spain, they are either Catalans or Catalonians. Then there are the Malaysians or the Malays, the Mayas or the Mayans, even the Serbians or the Serbs. None of which explains why the country is the Netherlands; outsiders erroneously call it Holland, and the people call themselves Dutch.

There are the Walloons, but there is no Walloonia. The name means "strangers" in Dutch, a name given the French-speaking Protestants who fled to the Netherlands in 1567. The Tatars can also be called the Tartars (with an extra r) who came from Tatary or Tartary. Originally it was Tartarus, which is Latin for "hell."

If you are from Paris, you are not a Parisite. Well, you could be, but not necessarily. Generally, the people from New Jersey call themselves New Jerseyans, although an acquaintance from southern New Jersey says people there call themselves New Jerseyikes.

Texans are called Texans, but not always. Once we were called Texicans, apparently a spin-off of Mexicans. Later the gringos in what was then the state of Coahuila and Texas began to be called Texians. In many of the letters and newspapers during the Republic of Texas you can find the handle Texian. It was used up through the War Between the States, although gradually Texian was shunted aside in favor of Texan.

Yes, what people call themselves is interesting, and not always predictable. There are no Walers, only Welsh. No Palestine, only Palestinians. No Azteca, no Pygmalia, no Vandalia. But what if you're from Minneapolis?

My favorite name is for the people of the Isle of Man off the British coast. They are Manxmen and Manxwomen. I have no idea why, but at least they can gamble in Monaco.

Cutting Back

THE DEN – "All right, little family. Please take a seat. I have called this meeting because we face an economic calamity."

"Not again," says one of my offspring.

"It is time for serious measures," I say.

"We've heard this before, Daddy. It's too early in the season for reruns."

"Oh, I know we've all given lip service to putting our nose to the grindstone and our shoulder to the wheel while tightening our belts," I continue, "but what has it gotten us?"

"A double hernia?"

"If you wish to ask a question," I say testily, "please hold up your hand. This meeting will be held with decorum."

"Did you have to listen to this jive when you were a child?" one asks.

"No, because even at your age I knew the value of savings, of hard work, of frugality. Also, I had a rich father."

"Why aren't you rich?"

"I flunked out of pre-med."

"Then what are you going to be when you grow up, Daddy?"

"We seem to have wandered from the point of this meeting," I say. "The point is not the income but the outgo. The latter is larger than the former. Now, a family is like a government. It cannot live beyond its means for very long or it will go into debt. There will come an economic judgment day."

"How bad is it?" my wife asks.

"Well, let me explain," I say. "This is a dollar bill. It equals the sum total of this family's weekly expenses. Now this is 81 cents. It equals this family's weekly income."

"Well, don't just stand there, Daddy. Get busy."

"There is no way I can get any busier. What I *can* do is make across-the-board cuts. We must do away with fraud, cheating, inefficiency, and unnecessary regulations."

"Like what?"

"I have figured it all out, but there isn't any quick fix. It took us years to get into this mess and it will take a long time to get out of it."

"Can I go?" asks my daughter.

"Sit down while I explain. Now, if all the chocolate cookies consumed in a single month by certain members of this family were stacked in one pile, it would be taller than the refrigerator."

"And if all the beer cans emptied by you each month were tossed in the garbage cans that had to be hauled out to the street by certain members of this family, those certain members should get paid more for doing it."

"Ah, yes. Allowances. We'll have to cut back on your allowances."

"How can you, Daddy? We don't get allowances."

"Then you've got nothing to worry about. I try to look out for you."

"Thanks."

"Here you see a chart showing the growth of our grocery bill in comparison to my receding hairline."

"I don't get the connection, Daddy."

"Economists have proven there is a definite correlation between the health and happiness of the family breadwinner and his financial state."

"Want to lie down?"

"My general health and happiness will show a marked improvement if we cut down on expenses. For instance, we're going to set the thermostat at 85."

"That will cut down on expenses?"

"That particular money-saving program doesn't start until July. For the present, we'll keep the house at 40."

"I think your general health would improve if you stopped smoking cigars."

"I rarely smoke."

"If all the cigars you smoked last year were lined up end to end they would reach the American Cancer Society."

"We are not yet to the point of cutting out necessities," I explain. "Only the luxuries."

"Like what?"

"Lunch."

"Mother fixes them here," a son says. "We take our lunches."

"Right, and from now on I want you to take them from a classmate. Find somebody little."

"Dear," my wife says, "can't we find other ways to ease the family finances?"

"All right. You see here a one-dollar bill. Here's a five, and a 10. You will find them in cash registers at convenience stores and filling stations around town. Don't come directly home."

"Daddy, if all your ideas for balancing the family budget were placed in a Cuisinart . . ."

"It'd be great."

Snow Business

Frankly, I feel that the entire episode is shocking, absolutely shocking. It once again shows man's inhumanity to man, and no doubt historians centuries hence will look back upon this time in wonderment, asking one another: "How could it have happened?"

The story, itself, is a national shame and is well known to us all, but I shall review the high points: through no great planning, but simply dumb luck, the northern part of these United States has a stranglehold, a total monopoly, on the national supply of ice and snow. Simply a freak of nature, it is, that they are the haves while the South is the have-nots. But there it is. The facts are totally clear and inarguable.

The Norsemen have always been singularly blessed, and in times past have grudgingly shared a bit with us—every now and again they would allow a blue norther to sweep down on Dalhart and smother it with a blizzard. But these were mere gestures. The Yankees kept most of the ice and snow for themselves. Now we in the South are in need. Summer is looming right over the horizon and the thermometer will soon be climbing into the 80s, then the 90s, and 100-degree temperatures cannot be far behind.

Yet in our hour of need, will our own countrymen allow some of their white gold to be piped south? No, indeed. Oh, I know what they are saying, that they hardly have enough for themselves. I have seen the biggies in the ice and snow industry dogsledding to Capitol Hill to lie through their teeth to some congressional committee. "We have so little for ourselves," they say. "We need it for the ski business in Vermont, the winter wonderland developments in the Maine woods. If we start shipping it south, we won't have enough for a decent daiquiri."

Horsefeathers of the meanest sort, I say. I have inside knowledge that there are vast reserves of snow in Wisconsin. My cousin's first wife had a brother who saw fields—yes, fields—of ice in Pennsylvania. They have built up huge reservoirs of sleet in Cleveland but deny their existence. Why? In a word: money. They are waiting for the price to go up, pure and simple. So they backpedal and throw up all these ridiculous reasons why they can't spread the snow around.

To be sure, they can make more on intrastate shipments of freezing air than they can on the interstate market, due to outmoded ICC regulations. For instance, Dayton has vast amounts of ice all over the place, while here in Texas we have to pay up to 75 cents for one lousy bag of the stuff. A block of ice in San Antonio can run up to a dollar, while they have it to melt in Detroit. It's all based on greed, I tell you. When the price goes up, you'll suddenly see all kinds of "newly discovered" sleet.

The president has demanded emergency action from Congress, which should go along, in the name of humanity if in nothing else. He wants Americans to share and share alike in all 50 states, and it's high time, too. That way, Massachusetts, for instance, will no longer be able to sit smugly on its ice while Wichita Falls bakes in 110-degree heat. They will have to send some zero temperatures down here.

The President has also hinted darkly that he wants "accurate" accountings of the nation's snow and ice reserves. It's jolly well time, if you ask me. Do you realize that all the figures on the national snow reserves come from the industry itself? Syracuse claims to have only 135 inches of snow, yet I have seen photographs of drifts stacked much higher than that. We must subpoena records, grill executives. We need accurate information on our dwindling sleet stockpiles, our reservoirs of ice, our snow supplies, and we can no longer depend upon the industry itself to furnish us these figures.

Then there is another point to consider. Now, I am not one to be suspicious by nature, but I have it on good authority (Jack Anderson) that there is a conspiracy within the industry. Dayton, Fargo, International Falls, Boston, and Buffalo, the Big Five, are in silent partnership with OSEC (the Organization of Snow Exporting Countries). And I say that it is not coincidental that a great number of Minnesotans speak Swedish. Indeed, some of them even *look* Swedish.

We need action, and we need it immediately. For we are suffering untold hardships. Do you realize what has happened to the toboggan franchises in Midland? Do you know the heartbreak of life as a sherpa in Shreveport? Construction grinds to a halt in Houston on August afternoons because of the heat. In Dallas, roofing companies have to knock off at noon because of the July temperatures. Our schools are forced to close during the summer months. Our air conditioning bills are such that the poor must choose between food and frost. And all the while, in New Jersey they drive around in their snowmobiles with bumper stickers reading: "Let the Texans Sweat in the Smog."

I have heard their arguments: "We planned ahead. We have conserved our supplies. We have invested heavily in snow chains, rock salt, and mittens. And now when things get tight down south, you come running to us demanding that we share our supply of cold." But I ask you, is this any way to treat a fellow American? I have approached several Yankees about this problem, trying to reason with them, as I speak their language (fluent money). They have listened with attention and understanding, and to a man they have replied thoughtfully: "Let the Texans sweat in the smog."

All right, that's snow biz. I can understand their feelings. But mark my words: they should be nice to us in our hour of need, because some day in the far distant future, *we* may, just may, have something *they* want.

Strike It Rich

Once again I am going to try to make you rich. You keep fighting me on this point, preferring your simple, peasantlike existence in the fields over the life of luxury in the castle. But I don't give up easily. This is a surefire fortune awaiting anyone who can spot trends. It's so simple everyone else will go wandering around saying, "Why didn't I think of that?"

The secret word is "thobe," or "thawb," depending upon your background. It's pronounced to rhyme with "robe," mainly because it is one. A thobe is the long, usually white, flowing robe you see the Arabs wearing. The design is older than pants, older than the Bible. Thobes are the perpetual garb of millions of persons in the Mideast but have never broken into the American fashion world. Until now, for you are going to be the breakee, and pocket a fortune.

Why should anyone ever want to buy a thobe? Simple. Because they are so very practical for Houston's climate that no one will want to be wearing anything else. I have on one now. A thobe is breezy, cool in the summer, loose and comfortable, the perfect thing for watching TV or knocking around the house.

My introduction to the garment was found in the laundry list in my hotel in Dhahran. It looked like any other such list until: "trousers, sweater, tie, overcoat, thobe, . . ." (Which reminds me: The hotel couldn't find one of my good white shirts. The only thing I can think of is that it got mixed up with the laundry of a Saudi businessman who tried it on and discovered that a white shirt would be just the thing to wear for lounging around the house. Even now he's probably figuring out how to introduce white shirts to Saudi society and make a bundle in the process.)

I got my thobe in the souk, or marketplace, in the town of Hofuf, which is out in the Arabian desert. Walking through the little dimly lit warrens of shops, any number of them were selling these thobes. They'd have a few hanging up for display, but the bulk were packaged. Bundles and bundles of thobes. So I decided to get one for each member of my family. This is always a deadly game, because I keep remembering my children the way they were three years before, and inevitably bring home something that is too small.

The size markings in the collar were no help. They read 40, 46, 50, and the like. That could be anything from millimeters to miles to Mecca. They made no sense to me. So it was that I held up thobes alongside every passing Arab child. The parents would smile and wait indulgently as a perplexed father went through the familiar sizing routine. I got one for my wife, too. When we're all in them, we look like either a Christmas pageant or a KKK rally.

After careful study on my part, I have determined thobes have two distinct collars: the high type like on a fencer's jacket with two buttons holding it together in the front, and the regular western shirt collar. Arabs do not wear ties with them, which shows a great intelligence on their part. I was invited to a family dinner in a Saudi home and noticed that the host had on the high-collar type, which he immediately unbuttoned when he got home. His brother-in-law wore the western-style collar. Both types have a front slit with about three buttons down the chest, so you put on a thobe over your head. They have large side pockets and a top pocket on the chest, for cigarettes. (Every Saudi seems to smoke constantly.) And no rear pockets. The tag in mine says "polyester 65%" and "polynosle 35%."

What do they wear under them? That's like asking a Scot what he wears under his kilt. I'm not about to. They all look the same and are a great social leveler. Everyone from cab driver to sheik looks the same. Even pictures of the king show him wearing a plain white thobe.

So here I sit in what is basically a loose shirt that flows to the ground. Mine is a size 56, whatever that is. Saudis are wiry people with shoulders slightly narrower than the shoulders of most Americans, but this one fits fine. Since it's a loose-fitting garment, I wouldn't recommend it for working under the car, mowing the grass, or painting the garage. And until everyone is wearing one, I wouldn't wear a thobe down to the 7-Eleven for a six-pack. But for around the house on a hot day, a cool thobe can't be beat. When I get home in the evening: Zip. I'm out of my working gear and into my thobe. So is much of the family. And so will much of America once you introduce the thobe here. They're easy to wash, and no ironing. And you're always color-coordinated.

To get one for yourself, just hit up one of your friends who goes to Saudi Arabia regularly — Houston is full of them — and ask him to pick up a thobe next trip over. I recommend driving two hours across the desert to Hofuf, finding the souk, going down the main passageway, taking a right and asking for Ahmed, second shop down. But any department store in any city will do.

Ah, but, you say, I am already being bled dry on the price of oil, so why should I pump even more money into the Arabian coffers? I've thought of that. You see, there's one more tag in the back of my thobe, and every other one I could find in the souk. It says, "Made in China." It doesn't say which China, and since Saudi Arabia and South Africa are the last major countries that still keep embassies in Taiwan, it could be either China. Your job is to find out which one and buy direct. I can't do everything for you. Then once you've cornered the thobe market in America, just sit back and count your money. I get my usual 15 percent.

Jogged Hedges

THE WINDOW — There he goes again. Horace. My neighbor. He jogs around the neighborhood every evening about this time, accompanied by a dog that tries desperately to keep up. Horace looks like he's in good shape, and probably is. He is an expert jogger, holding the third-degree black belt in cross-neighborhood hedge jumping.

Horace is almost to the point where he never sweats. Soon I shall see him jogging along in a sport coat and tie, working up to a three-piece suit. Then he'll start carrying an attaché case. And he'll never sweat. Just loping across the front yards and leaping over back fences in his Brooks Bros. suit and alligator attaché.

Every time I look out this window about this time each late afternoon and Horace comes jogging by, I feel a thrust of jealousy. That's because I never learned to jog. Oh, I've tried, all right. I did everything I was supposed to do, but it didn't work.

My first step, figuratively, was to make the actual decision to jog. It was a serious commitment, one I didn't take lightly. There was much to be said against jogging: pulled muscles, wasted time, twisted ankles, attacked hearts. I had to consider the many obstacles to really becoming a champion jogger: the training, the sacrifice, the Mack trucks trying to make me a hood ornament. But none of these negative factors really mattered when weighed against the overwhelming argument *for* jogging: peer pressure.

Once I had declared the moral equivalent of war on immovability, my next step was to prepare myself. I got all the jogging books: *How to Jog, More How to Jog, Jogging Around El Campo* and *Jogging With God.* I subscribed to the *Joggers Weekly.* I watched track meets on TV and listened to track coaches on the call-in talk shows. I drove all over town tracking down theaters showing *The Marathon Man* and *The Loneliness of the Long Distance Runner* and *Run Silent, Run Deep.*

Fully informed as to the nature of jogging, I was now ready for the next part. The equipment: Nike jogging shoes at $43.99 plus Aces Laces, the ties that bind, and the Golden Arches footpad to give me better mileage. Joggin' Toggin's had a special on color-coordinated jogging shorts and shirt. My custom-made warm-up suit ran me — so to speak — another $67. Luminous sweat band, wrist band, small plastic water bottle on a string around my neck, key and coin holder attached to my Aces Laces, and towel came to another $41.90. I put on my equipment, just to admire myself in the mirror, and found that I could hardly move.

The preliminaries were over, I was now ready for the main event. And it was a disaster. Simply put, I never learned to jog. I took jogging lessons, I studied instant replays, I joined jogging clubs. Nothing worked. It required a natural talent, one that eluded me then and eludes me now. Just as some people have a natural ability to sing, dance, make papier-mâché apples, or shrink heads, there are people who have a natural ability to jog. They make it look easy, which is the true sign of any professional.

I'd watch them as they ran by, nimbly skimming over the paths of Memorial Park just as Horace glides over driveways. "Come on," they'd say to me. "It's easy. Don't be afraid." Summoning up my courage, I'd adjust my sweat band, retie my Aces Laces, and set out. It was like the maiden voyage of the *Spruce Goose*. Do you know what it's like to be running along the jogging path and be passed up by a fellow jogger *and* his nurse? The only jogger I passed was coming the other way.

In desperation I bought a season ticket on the jogging lift, feeling that mechanical aids might help. At the top of the path I looked down and froze in fear. It took two burly jogging instructors 10 minutes to pry my fingers from a tree. "You'd better try the beginners' path," one of the instructors advised me. Totally humiliated, I did as I was told, and took to the beginners' path to pant and puff. This time the only person I passed was a jogger whose crutch got caught in a pothole.

So now I just watch as my sole brothers glide by like so many gazelles on grease. My jogging togs hang limply in the closet, constant reminders that taking things in stride can mean different strokes. And every time Horace whizzes by, drip-dried and smiling, he waves, and I wave. Then from behind the window here I say: "Break a leg, Horace."

America Has Run out of Money, Run out of Time

It is there. It is there for the thickest among us to see. It is ever so clear. It is what we are doing to ourselves.

What is happening is not the possession of any political persuasion, not the baggage and garbage of any one group. Both parties shun it from the beginning of the campaign to the end, which is chiefly why were are in what we are in.

A mess. A mess that will get bigger and bigger, despite a few upswings, until it falls down upon us like the house of cards it is. And then everyone will run around saying to everyone else, "Why weren't we warned?" Next, of course, comes the blame-throwing.

But I get ahead of myself. Let us look at things, not as we wish them to be, but as they really are:

As a nation, we are spending more than we are making.

We have borrowed from the past, the present, and now far into the future.

Some, not all, of our labor unions have wrested massive wages for the rank and file that are clearly too much. The auto workers, the steel workers, the camera and television assembly line workers, have brought such unrealistic wages upon themselves that after the short run, they have simply priced themselves out of the market and out of a job.

Management in this country in many cases is dreadful. Braniff, Penn Central, Chrysler, and on and on. Six-figured incompetents running multimillion-dollar companies into bankruptcy while salting away their own pensions. I'm all right, Jack.

Our military is overpaid. No nation on earth takes such good care of its men in uniform as we do. Oh, they love to wallow in self-pity, but stack up our pay against any other nation's. Worst of all, we spend too much on our veterans. I could now be retired from the service and drawing a fine pension. You would be taking care of me until the day I die and then you would pay to bury me. There is no reason for that, for I am in fine shape, and so are so many millions of others who milk the mother breast of the U.S. Treasury, all the while preaching about free enterprise. They are on the dole, and don't let them tell you differently.

No nation in time of war has spent as much on the military as we are in time of peace. We are underarmed? Show me a general who ever said he had too many troops. Show me an admiral with too many ships. The military expenditure is a bottomless pit. It is never enough.

Major General "Red Mike" Edson, holder of the Medal of Honor and two Navy Crosses, leader of the feared and famous Edson's Marine Raiders in WWII, retired from the service in disgust. And wrote: "I am a military man and proud of it. But when we reach the point where the military are directing, rather than supporting, our country's policies, we are far along the road to losing what this country has always stood for."

Our tax structure is a laugh. It is getting so that the richer you are, the less you pay. Washington, D.C., is Loophole City. I doubt there is a line on the U.S. tax form that was thought up by any member of Congress. No, it was prepared by some $250,000-a-year lobbyist-lawyer who packaged and presented it to a congressional committee, probably with some perfectly legal and totally immoral campaign funds. Bingo, it is law. So now you can deduct your apple orchard.

There will always be rich and there will always be poor, but we have decided against that. We wish to make everyone at least middle class. By doing this, we have so saddled the middle class with burdensome taxes that, labels aside, they are as worn and poor as we can make them. The American middle class is supporting this nation, and that tired burro is just about to turn belly-up.

Social Security is not a federal pension program. We are trying to make it that, but it was never intended to be and was never taxed to be. "I can't live on my Social Security check," they say. The unvarnished answer is that they are not supposed to. They never saved a dime, they never invested, never entered into their company's pension program, but at age 65 they say, "OK, America, take care of me." We can't.

Not that we don't want to. Not that we don't want to feed the poor and clothe the naked and build the battleships. We want to, but we can't. The heart is not empty, but the wallet is. We still have our good intentions, our love for humanity and regard for human life, but the rubber band can stretch only so far. Then it snaps. It breaks. Then there is all hell to pay because we have not paid attention. And the truth is that the rubber band is just about to snap. Thus the silly, shallow promises of spineless politicians bent only upon their reelection are going to go unfulfilled.

This is not a placard of "The End is At Hand." I am simply pointing out the obvious. As a nation, we have run out of money and we have run out of time. We have promised too much, or at least we keep electing those who do. We have refused, absolutely refused, to look at the situation as it really is. So, in our very lifetime, the most glorious, most magnificent, most prosperous and beautiful government ever devised by mankind has become bankrupt.

Why? Well, let me give you an example. When you voted for Mark White, you knew way down deep that by pulling that lever your HL&P bill would not go down. His promises were transparently empty. But what the heck, it was worth a try, right? So that is the lever you pulled. He told you what you wanted to hear. They all do, so there's no reason to point to any one candidate. And you bit. So who's to blame?

A leader who tells us the truth and nothing but the truth would not be a leader. A blood, sweat, and tears speech would be drowned out by the promises of a brighter tomorrow. We listen to those who tell us what we want to hear. But the truth is quite another thing: The truth is that we have deliberately deluded ourselves into thinking this circus can go on forever. The truth is that it won't. And every sign is there for anyone who cares to see — our economy is crumbling. Not from war or corruption or class struggle, but from trying to make two plus two equal five.

It would take the kind of gumption we have not seen for a politician to say, "Farmers, if you can't sell it, don't grow it, for we can no longer afford you. Students, if you don't have the money to go to college, the awful truth is, you must get it the old-fashioned way. Israel, we can no longer afford you. Mexico, we can no longer take care of your millions of unemployed who go north, any more than Canada could take care of ours. Germany and Japan, if you want the U.S. military to protect you, then you'll have to pay for it, just as you would make us, were the boot on the other foot."

We wish we could. We have done these things for years and would like very much to keep on doing them. But we can't anymore. Sorry, we just can't. And like it or not, that's the truth.

Harassing the Troops

You may have a husband, son, or neighbor who is not with us this bright Sunday morn. He is in bed, lying there moaning softly and begging for a mercy killing.

His eyes look like a Gulf road map. His face is the tasteful color of AstroTurf. His expression is that of King Faisal caught in a Tel Aviv traffic jam. He is, in two queasy words, hung over. Why? In all probability (don't let it get around) he is a Marine. Yes, a leatherneck, a jarhead. And last night he was celebrating the 198th birthday of his beloved Corps. That's right. He stuffed himself back into his 1944 dress blues and went to the birthday party, where he retold how he won the war single-handedly. While AWOL.

Do not harass the troops. Leave him there. Alone with his memories. For this is the time of the year, every November 10, when former Marines grow misty-eyed recalling those thrilling days of yesteryear that didn't seem at all thrilling at the time. For instance . . . the time that . . . I'll never forget . . .

That's me there. The lowly private, 1st Marine Division. Lowest of the low. I am hunched over trying to keep warm, sane, and in line, all at the same time. I am in a long file of Marines climbing up a mountainside in California. Don't laugh. You will recall that the Viet Cong never, ever, pulled a really big offensive in California. We did our work well.

It is a cold winter night on the mountainside. My job is to follow the person in front of me, who happens to be in a jeep.

In the jeep are the officers. They always ride in jeeps. It says so in the U.S. Constitution. "Officers shall ride in jeeps while privates shall walk behind. Except in the case of land mines." We walk onward, covered with gear like the Frito Bandito after a raid.

But what's this? We are stopping. Our gunny sergeant (referred to as the Missing Link) calls me over. "You stay here," he says.

"What do I do?" I ask.

"Nothing. Just stay here and don't let anybody pass. I mean *nobody*."

"Yessir," I say.

The troops trudge on into the fog, to be swallowed up like the Brigadoon Brigade. "Remember, idiot," comes a familiar voice from the dark, "nobody passes." And they are gone. And I am alone, to guard the road and let *nobody* pass. But who's nobody? The Viet Cong? Apaches? Redcoats? It is very quiet and dark and foggy. The noise is broken only by the purring of a jeep and . . . eh? What jeep? Purring or otherwise? Who is trying to sneak up my road?

"Halt," I say, always quick with the bon mot. "Who goes there?"

The jeep grinds to a halt and several uniformed folk get out. One approaches me. "What's the password?" he asks. I always thought the guard was supposed to ask that, but this is no time to be sticky about protocol, particularly since I don't know the password.

"Halt," I say again, lowering the rifle at them. One fellow approaches me. He looks me up and down, from boot to helmet, and does not appear overly impressed.

"What are you?" he asks.

"The guard," I say. "What are you?"

He sighs a deep, heavy, depressed sigh. "I am the regimental commander. Your leader." For the first time I notice two small silver eagles peering up at me from his collar.

"Says you," I reply. He is not getting up my road, no matter how heavy he lays on the rank. Regimental commander, my aching arches. Obviously a spy, even if he doesn't speak with a British accent. They all get back in the jeep, which cranks up and nudges forward, but I refuse to move, holding my rifle across my chest.

The jeep's horn honks ever so nicely. I stay put. It honks again, more aggressively. I stay. It is not that I am brave, or even law-abiding. It's just that the gunny has strange ways of enforcing his laws, and I do not wish to test his patience.

"Move!" comes the order.

"Halt," I say, since I can't think of anything else.

"Private," comes a steady voice from behind the glaring lights. "Move. Your. Tail. Immediately."

"Halt," I say with less enthusiasm. I could be on thin ice if his accent is real.

"Move asiiiiide!"

"Halt."

The ersatz bird colonel gets out of the jeep and comes forward, looking me squarely in the eye. "This is an order, Private. You will get to the side. Of the road. To the side. *Do you understand?"*

"Halt."

I had never seen a full colonel weep before. He limps back to the jeep, which does a fast U-turn almost costing the government a new pair of boots, and disappears into the gloom.

An hour or so later, the gunny comes down from Olympus. "How's it going?" he asks.

"Fine. Just been obeying your orders. No one's come through."

"Good," he says, and trudges back into the dark.

Several hours later the maneuver was called off. They couldn't find the colonel.

Fry, Fry Again

THE RESTAURANT — The food is mediocre, the service lousy, the prices astronomical. Anyone can do better than this. *I* can do better than this. So I opened a restaurant. It was standard American fare, fried chicken and mashed potatoes and apple pie. No one came.

"Americans can eat American food at home," I was told. "You've got to give them something more exotic. You need a place with a location theme."

But all the good places were taken. Houston has Burmese restaurants and Mexican restaurants and Italian restaurants and
Chinese, Afghan, Scandinavian, and Vietnamese restaurants. All
that was left was Delaware, so I opened the Delaware Deli with
a ticker showing the DuPont stock quotations. I only hired waitresses
named Polly and Esther. No one showed up for my grand opening, and business tapered off from there.

"Houston is sports crazy," I was told. "Open a restaurant with
a sports theme." So I gutted the deli and built the dining room in
the shape of a boxing ring. I called it the Punch Lunch. Customers
sat on stools in the corners while waiters dressed as seconds swabbed
them with wet sponges. The customers threw in their napkins and
went home.

I went to a restaurant consultant who, for $650, advised me to
open a French restaurant. "But there are plenty of them in town,"
I said. "And they're all making a bundle," the consultant replied.
So I took out the boxing ring and turned the place into a French
restaurant. At dawn the next day I was invaded by a German
restaurant. Trying to make the best of the situation, I opened the
only Chinese-German restaurant in Houston. Business was good
for a while, but the customers noted that two hours after eating,
they were hungry for power.

"Mexican food is the key," the consultant told me. "There are
plenty of Mexican food restaurants in Houston, and they're all making a bundle. All you need is a new twist." So I opened a Mexican
restaurant with American citizens working in the kitchen and illegal
aliens as customers. A week later, I was closed down by the Justice
Department for not having bilingual menus.

About then I noticed that restaurants in Houston spend more on
their interior decorators than on their chefs and the busiest were
those with a gimmick. There were several restaurants with railroad
themes, so I tried something different. I opened an eatery with a
bus theme and called it the MTA Cafe. That wasn't a success, either.
The air conditioning didn't work, the food was hours late, and the
customers complained about paying with the exact change.

Without a doubt, things were not working as I had planned.
Everyone else in Houston had opened a restaurant. Where had I
gone wrong? "Movies are all the rage in dining," the consultant told
me, pocketing another $650. "We've already got a Harlow's and a
Zorba the Greek. At one time we had two Godfathers. Use a movie
theme." Now, that was the best advice he'd given me, so I gutted

the MTA Cafe and turned it into a restaurant with a decor and menu based on a hit movie. Unfortunately, I chose *Bridge on the River Kwai.* The only people who liked it were war criminals.

By then I was getting desperate, and my finances were running low, too. After three weeks and four customers, I decided to alter my theme a bit, but still retain the overall military effect. I changed the place into a brig and dressed all the waiters like MPs. It was called Locks and Bugles and lasted a month, with time off for good behavior. As a last, desperate attempt to make a go of my military furnishings, I turned the place into a general's headquarters, put guards by the door, maps on the walls, and called my new place Aide-de-Cramp. The customers called my steaks Patton's Leather, slapped me, and left.

"Like Conrad Hilton said about hotels," the consultant told me for another $650, "the three most important aspects of a restaurant are location, location, and location. Maybe you should move."

So I rented a bankrupt drive-in movie lot and set up all the booths like the back seats of automobiles. Business got so bad I had to show films. I tried a different location by renting out the Houston City Council chambers at night and calling my new establishment The Pot Hole. I dressed up all the staff to look like council members and hired a chef who had great experience as a home builder. Within weeks, the waiters had hired aides and were getting mileage from the kitchen while the chef went on a fact-finding mission to Acapulco. The final blow came when a customer asked if the garbagemen had made their delivery that morning.

"Your problem is that you are trying to appeal to everyone. You've got to specialize," my restaurant consultant told me, stuffing my check in his pocket. I took his advice and went after the Cajuns who work in the oil fields, calling my new place Beau Derrick. I cooked the red beans and rice in 30-weight oil and refused to speak English. Eventually the place went out of business due to a low profit and high tide. After it went broke, I was really depressed. People would stare at me on the street corners. I'd get anonymous phone calls at night. It wasn't easy being the only person in Houston without a restaurant.

Now, however, my problems are solved. My restaurant consultant put me on the right track. "Franchises," he said, holding my mother's wedding ring up to the light. "Franchises are a surefire success." He was right. I'm joining a new string of restaurants that must be doing great, since I see their signs all over town: "For Lease."

Bringing It In

The wine-tasting evening we discussed here yesterday is still echoing in my mind with every slamming door and every honking horn. But it brings to mind another wine-related experience that seems worth mentioning, if for no other reason than as a warning.

This one began at Charles De Gaulle Airport in Paris, where the Ugly American was booking passage back to the States. That's me there, standing in line, patiently waiting my turn. The fellow in front of me is also an American—we can spot one another quicker than you can say "button-down shirt with Dr Pepper stains."

We strike up a conversation and it turns out that we are both going on the same plane, he with his wife and baby. I am pleasant enough but don't get too chummy. One must never get too chummy with total strangers on international flights, else they innocently ask you: "I say, old shoe, but I'm all loaded down, would you take this bag through customs for me?" That and a false bottom will get you 10 to 20. So I keep all strangers at arm's length whilst crossing borders.

OK, I get my ticket and then head straight for the duty-free shop. They have a nice one at De Gaulle, and I poke among the goodies. Yes, here they are: boxes of the forbidden fruit, Havana cigars. I have been assured by airport clerks from Oslo to Tunis that it is perfectly all right to take Cuban cigars home to America, when it is not all right whatsoever. Uncle Sam gets downright surly.

My sole purchases in the duty-free shop are a box of American cigars—which, in truth, are more expensive than back home, but it's the thought that counts—and a bottle of Grand Marnier, which is cheaper in the shop. That's it, all I'm allowed. I pay and depart to browse among the stalls as I await my flight number being called.

Eh? What's this? A wine shop, a veritable cornucopia of French delights: red, white, champagne, ah, mouth-watering just to look, so I look.

"I'll take two bottles of this, and one of these," says a distinctly American voice.

"You sure you can bring them in?" inquires another red-white-and-blue accent.

"Sure. You have to pay duty on them, but it only comes to about a quarter a bottle. Heck. That's still a lot cheaper than New York."

Curious. I didn't know that. Still, the gentleman obviously knows what he is doing, or he wouldn't be buying all that booze. I approach the clerk.

"Is it true that I can bring more than a quart of liquor back to the States?" I say in childlike tones.

"Only one quart of hard liquor," says the clerk. "But all the wine you wish. You have to declare it and pay duty. That's all."

Gee. And to think of all the times I sashayed through customs, declaring only my measly little quart of the hard stuff, while I could be groaning along with banging bottles of cheap wine, at a quarter duty a bottle. They are calling my flight number, so I pick out a rather expensive bottle of something. Dunno what, the label being in a foreign tongue. Still, if it costs this much in France, just think what the Galleria gets for it.

Put it in my flight bag, which sags on my shoulder. Onto the plane where the stew says the bag is too big to fit above and will have to go on the floor between my feet. Thus I sit still for 10 hours, afraid to wiggle a toe for fear of damaging the merchandise. On one of my few trips away, I drop by steerage, where I see the fellow I met in the ticket line, there with his wife and baby. I smile briefly — don't want to get too chummy.

Houston. Off the plane, carefully waiting till all others are off for fear of banging the bottle against the door. To the customs baggage pickup, then to the customs line. Everyone is waiting as the customs officials poke through the Kleenex boxes, looking for submachine guns. There is one fellow in customs uniform wandering around, looking like he knows what's going on.

I approach him. "Sir, where do I declare this bottle of wine so I can pay the 25 cents duty?"

He surveys me with the same look Jack's mother gave him when he returned home with the magic beans. "You a Texas resident?" he asks.

"Yes."

"Then you got two choices; you can give it to someone else to take through the line for you, or you can give it to me and watch while I pour it in the john."

Chalk up another for the world traveler. I don't want him to pour it out and I don't know a single other . . . hee-hee. There's my old buddy from the ticket counter, with wife and child. Certainly he will take the bottle through for me, seeing how I was so friendly. I approach him and deftly ask: "Do you have a bottle of booze to take through the customs line?"

"No," says he. "I'm from Fort Worth."

Some of you might not understand the logic behind this answer, but don't bother me now. This is high international finance. "Here, take it through for me and I'll pick it up right outside those swinging doors, where the federal fuzz won't know."

"Well," he says, rather reluctantly for a good friend, "OK, but in case anyone is watching, here's a penny. I have now bought it from you. Legally it's mine."

"Right," I say, allowing him in the customs line in front of me. He goes through the line with the ease of a phone rate increase and heads for the door, giving me a wink on the way out. I wink back.

Now it's my time, and I honorably declare my purchases, then grab my bags and rush through the swinging doors to call in my bottle of fine French wine.

And the scoundrel is nowhere to be seen. Absolutely vanished.

Do you ever get the idea that life has handed you the Planned Parenthood franchise for the Vatican?